TO BUILD A WALL

American Jews and the Separation

of Church and State

CONSTITUTIONALISM AND DEMOCRACY

KERMIT HALL AND DAVID O'BRIEN, EDITORS

Kevin T. McGuire
*The Supreme Court Bar: Legal Elites
in the Washington Community*

Mark Tushnet, ed.
*The Warren Court in Historical
and Political Perspective*

David N. Mayer
*The Constitutional Thought of
Thomas Jefferson*

F. Thornton Miller
*Juries and Judges versus the Law:
Virginia's Provincial Legal
Perspective, 1783–1828*

Martin Edelman
*Courts, Politics, and
Culture in Israel*

Tony Freyer
*Producers versus Capitalists:
Constitutional Conflict in
Antebellum America*

Amitai Etzioni, ed.
*New Communitarian Thinking:
Persons, Virtues, Institutions, and
Communities*

Gregg Ivers
*To Build a Wall: American Jews and
the Separation of Church and State*

TO BUILD A WALL

American Jews and the

Separation of Church and State

GREGG IVERS

UNIVERSITY PRESS OF VIRGINIA

Charlottesville and London

THE UNIVERSITY PRESS OF VIRGINIA

Copyright © 1995 by the Rectors and Visitors
of the University of Virginia

FIRST PUBLISHED 1995

Library of Congress Cataloging-in-Publication Data
Ivers, Gregg.
    To build a wall : American Jews and the separation of church and
state / Gregg Ivers.
        p.   cm. — (Constitutionalism and democracy)
    Includes bibliographical references and index.
    ISBN 0-8139-1554-6 (cloth)
    1. Jews—United States—Politics and government.   2. Church and
state—United States.   3. American Jewish Congress.   4. American
Jewish Committee.   5. B'nai B'rith.   Anti-defamation League.
    I. Title.   II. Series.
    E184.J5I92   1995
    322'.1'088296—dc20   94-40781
                                                                    CIP

PRINTED IN THE UNITED STATES OF AMERICA

CONTENTS

Acknowledgments   vii

Introduction   1

1 Law, the Courts, and Political Jurisprudence   7

2 The Political Organization of American
    Jewry, 1906–1947   34

3 Challenging the Public Schools:
    The Released-Time Cases   66

4 Separation to the Fore: *Torcaso, Engel, Schempp,*
    and Beyond   100

5 Litigation and the Public Purse: The Parochial
    School Aid Cases   146

6 Defending the Status Quo: Litigation in a
    Changed Environment   189

Conclusion   220

Notes   229
Bibliography   255
Index   265

ACKNOWLEDGMENTS

When I first conceived of this book in the spring of 1988, the Atlanta Braves were on their way to the first of what would be three consecutive last-place finishes. Since then the Braves have won three consecutive division titles and played in two World Series that baseball fans will remember forever. As the Braves have changed, so has this book, which now scarcely resembles the doctoral dissertation it once was. Even the name has changed—although at least the Braves have remained the Braves.

I wish I could thank all the people who have given so generously of their time over the years to help me improve this book. Whatever its remaining and inevitable shortcomings, my friends and colleagues are not among the guilty parties. That burden remains for me.

For whatever positive contribution this book may make to our understanding of law and politics, Karen O'Connor deserves more credit than I could ever hope to convey here. I have looked forward for a long time to writing these acknowledgments, so I could tell her how very much I appreciate everything she has done for me—only now I am almost at a loss for words. When I was a student at Emory, she was a doctoral advisor of limitless intelligence, patience, and compassion. Karen has since remained a great friend and a source of constant encouragement, for which I am forever grateful.

I was also fortunate to work with Tom Walker, Randy Strahan, and Mike Giles, all of them extraordinarily gifted teachers and scholars whose influence can be seen everywhere in my own scholarship and teaching. Although Juan del Aguila, Rick Doner, Alan Abramowitz, and Tom Lancaster did not work directly on this project with me, they all taught me something important about political science—and let it also be said that there could be no better teammates on the softball field. Unlike them, my former classmate Greg Haley is no softball player, despite his best efforts, but he was then and has remained a good friend and an indispensable foundation of support. The assistance and friendship of several exceptionally talented undergraduate students that I had the pleasure to teach at Emory made the initial stages of this project much more enjoyable than they might otherwise have been. Kristen Wigh, Evan Hochberg, Amy Weinhaus, Matthew Stiglitz, Dean Miller, Bryant McFall, Rocco Testani, Amy Sanders, and Jennifer Weiss have all gone on to bigger and better things, but I will never forget their help in those early days.

Since I have joined the faculty at American University, the School of Public Affairs has provided continual financial assistance that enables me to conduct interviews and travel to libraries in lands far beyond the Beltway. Ron Shaiko has been an invaluable colleague during this entire process: I cannot imagine having written this book without the aid of his exacting eye and critical judgment. Nor could I imagine having better research assistants than Jon Parker and Fred Turner, who did everything I asked of them and more.

I also want to thank Bruce Field, Robert Goldschmidt, John Reteneller, Scott Stephenson, and Jim Verhoff. None are academics nor have they any idea what political scientists do, but I could not let this opportunity pass without thanking them for their friendship. I must also again acknowledge the special assistance of my best friend, Scott Diener. Another nonacademic, Scott nonetheless commands an encyclopedic knowledge of the Penski file that proved instrumental in the latter stages of this book. Like any truly good friend, Scott is usually just an irritant; this time he was actually useful. I am also grateful for my conversations with three public interest lawyers, Brent Walker, Steve Green, and Nadine Strossen, who not only made highly intelligent suggestions regarding this manuscript but encouraged me to rethink how political scientists have approached their craft.

The staff at the Syracuse University library has been terrific in arranging for access to and reproduction of Leo Pfeffer's papers. Similarly, no one I came into contact with at the American Jewish Committee, the American Jewish Congress, and the Anti-Defamation League was less than enthusiastic and professional in responding to my requests for interviews, access to file depositories, and other internal data. In the countless conversations I had with staff professionals and attorneys from each organization, I learned more about the relationship between law and politics than I would have guessed possible before I started this book. For that, I will remain forever appreciative.

Robert Alley, Greg Calderia, and David O'Brien all reviewed and commented on the initial version of this manuscript. These are scholars whose work I have admired for several years; to have the benefit of their constructive criticism and encouragement gives me an unfair advantage over other young scholars working in this field. I especially want to thank David for the enthusiasm he has shown this book from the beginning. Richard Holway has been a more compassionate, patient, and precise editor than I deserve, but I am grateful anyway. Pamela MacFarland Holway has been, without question, the finest copy editor with whom I have ever worked. So sharp is her command of style and language that I could not have imagined finishing this book without her.

For years now, my father has been telling me that I married over my head. I will not contest that. I love Janet because she has never questioned the sanity of someone who can sing, however badly, the entire Beatles repertoire, remember exactly where he was the first time he saw Sandy Koufax pitch, and talk for hours—often without benefit of an audience—on the essence of Bill Evans's pianism and Thelonious Monk's matchless brilliance as a composer, but still manages to misplace the checkbook, typically forgets to write down ATM withdrawals, and continually loses the car keys. Without her I could not imagine a life so full of love and happiness. This book is for Janet—finally.

TO BUILD A WALL

American Jews and the Separation

of Church and State

Introduction

Although consensus on the proper constitutional boundaries between religion and the state remains elusive, there has been no shortage of efforts by organized interest groups, whether religious or secular, to influence that relationship through active involvement in Supreme Court church-state litigation. Moreover, the Court has promulgated in clear and convincing terms that religious organizations possess rights equal to those of their secular counterparts to participate in public affairs. In *Walz v. Tax Commission* (1970), its only direct pronouncement on the constitutional status of religion as an organized representative on public policy questions, the Court acknowledged that "adherents of particular faiths and individual citizens have [the] right ... [to] vigorous advocacy of legal and constitutional provisions."[1] Far from engaging in a departure from the intent and text of the First Amendment religion clauses, the Court thus recognized through constitutional adjudication the enumerated right of religious organizations to advocate their views on politics and public affairs in the public square, both to advance the interests of their constituencies and to engage the broader debate within the polity. Since *Walz*, religious organizations have become, in their own right, even more astute and influen-

1

tial forces in the litigation process as it affects the separation of church and state, as well as other concerns pertaining to public law.[2]

Ever since the end of World War II, American Jews and the organizational structures that represent their interests have been at the forefront of organized efforts to influence the church-state jurisprudence of the Supreme Court. Through the sponsorship of test-case litigation, the submission of amicus curiae briefs, intervention as third parties, and extrajudicial efforts to influence constitutional doctrine, Jewish civil rights organizations have had a historic role in the postwar development of American church-state law and policy. In their formative confrontations with state-sponsored religious practices in their new homeland, American Jews recognized that their minority status would require nontraditional routes of collective action if they hoped to abolish what was often the de jure presence of pan-Christian values in American civic culture and public institutions. Indeed, organized Jewish interests were among the first to understand litigation as an effective method of collective action to advance communal interests and to instigate constitutional reform—whether such action challenged religious practices in the public schools or state-mandated programs to assist parochial institutions.[3]

But prior to the end of the war, the major national agencies that now carry out most Jewish public affairs advocacy—the American Jewish Committee (AJCommittee), founded in 1906, the American Jewish Congress (AJCongress), founded in 1918, and the Anti-Defamation League of B'nai B'rith (ADL), founded in 1913—had been relatively impotent forces. Even after arriving in significant numbers in the United States and establishing a strong communal presence, American Jews "simply did not think of themselves as a community of citizens who could or should make heavy demands on their government, who could or should assert themselves in a politically organized fashion to achieve goals of critical importance to them." On public affairs and politics in general, but on church-state issues in particular, the major Jewish organizations thus kept a low profile because of their concern that any concerted action to challenge constitutionally suspect majoritarian religious practices would bring latent anti-Semitism to the surface and raise questions about their loyalty to American values. Instead, American Jewish organizations relied upon the social relations model—namely, on public education and public relations efforts, interfaith negotiations to enlist the support of sympathetic Christian denominations, and compromise with public authorities over what religious values and methods of instruction could and could not be aided through state action—to advance their case in the public arena.[4]

Over time, however, the AJCommittee, the AJCongress, and the ADL realized that education programs and good-faith appeals to the institutional structures associated with majoritarian religious values would not win Jews their rightful place as equals in the scheme of American pluralism. As a result, their almost sole reliance upon community education programs, public relations, and the other techniques associated with the social relations model was gradually replaced with an emphasis on legislation and litigation to rectify inequalities in the law. This strategy, known as the legal reform model, has since guided in substantial part the organized efforts of American Jews to influence public policy. Although at one time the major Jewish organizations contrasted law with education as a force for social change, with law "almost always . . . given an inferior role," that attitude began to wither after World War II.[5] Tumultuous events at home and abroad forced American Jews to recognize that direct action through law and litigation, rather than dependence on indirect appeals to the Christian conscience, was needed to turn the promises contained in the Constitution into a reality.

Evidence of the rapid changes within the corporate structure that represented American Jewry quickly surfaced on two fronts. The first consisted of a sweeping campaign initiated by the AJCongress, soon joined by the AJCommittee and the ADL, to attack the anti-Jewish discrimination practiced by colleges, universities, and professional schools, in rental housing and the real estate market, and in private sector employment. Second, and far more controversial among Jews (for reasons that will be addressed in chapter 2), was the decision of the AJCongress to concentrate its attention on church-state separation issues and to place law and litigation, and by extension the courts, at the center of its systematic efforts to promote policy change in this area.

Litigation as a means to represent organizational interests and to advance communal goals has been long recognized as a potent instrument for minority groups unable to influence the elected branches of government—a phenomenon well documented in the law and political science literature, as I discuss in chapter 1. Frustrated by their previous efforts to effect genuine reform of the nation's well-ingrained empathy for the promotion of pan-Christian values in American public life, the AJCongress, and later the AJCommittee and the ADL, soon found in litigation a much more expeditious route for the redress of their consti- tutional grievances in the area of church-state relations. To be sure, the three organizations approached the activist and confrontational nature of constitutional litigation from different perspectives. Whereas for de- cades black Americans were, as a group, able to rely on the National Association for the Advancement of Colored People (NAACP), formed in the early twentieth century, as the uncontested chief organizational representative of the African American civil rights movement in public law litigation, American Jews comprised a much more heterogenous population. They had accordingly formed several defense agencies to represent their varied interests in law and politics, each of which re- flected the concerns of different segments of American Jewry. Ameri- can Jews, unlike African Americans, thus found themselves in a posi- tion to choose between the AJCongress, which had articulated a "direct legal action" approach, and the AJCommittee and ADL, two powerful organizations in their own right that "espouse[d] less direct educa- tional methods such as good-will propaganda and . . . avoided more direct" tactics for the organizational representation of Jewish interests.[6] Each group eventually recognized, however, that changes in status of American Jewry would not come about merely as a result of pressure on the legislative and executive branches of government, but would require direct appeals to the Constitution as well.

The first concerted effort of the AJCommittee, the AJCongress, and the ADL to influence the constitutional law of church and state at the Supreme Court level through the legal model came in *McCollum v. Board of Education* (1948).[7] In *McCollum*, the Court ruled that an Illinois released-time program that allowed public school facilities to be used for religious instruction during regular hours violated the establish- ment clause of the First Amendment. For the major Jewish groups, the positive outcome in *McCollum* had a dual significance. First, it marked an important initial step in their subsequent drive to redefine the con- stitutional relationship between organized religion and the state. Sec- ond, given the influence that the AJCommittee, the AJCongress, and the ADL believed their amicus curiae brief had in the resolution of the case, *McCollum* also proved that litigation could have a demonstrable and successful impact on the achievement of their organizational ob- jectives (as will be explored further in chapter 3).

Since *McCollum*, the AJCommittee, the AJCongress, and the ADL have been extensively involved in Supreme Court church-state litigation. Through their participation both as direct sponsors and as amici curiae, or friends of the court, these organizations have exerted a considerable influence on the development of the First Amendment church-state law over the past forty-five years. That these major Jewish representative bodies—which several scholars have found to be among the most effective religious lobbies in American politics—relied so much more on judicial decisions than on legislative initiatives to secure their organizational goals indicates, for them, the limitations of majoritarian politics in the church-state arena. The advantage of such a strategy is clear: in one precise judicial stroke, a positive decision can replace the different customs, approaches, and rules of various regions, states, and localities with uniform national constitutional standards. But there is an equally obvious risk. The same channels, which can so conveniently enable an organization to bypass the process of incremental change, can also lead to a negative outcome, namely, the establishing of a precedent than can dash a group's collective hopes as quickly as adopting the strategy once raised them.[8]

Precisely how the AJCommittee, the AJCongress, and the ADL have advanced their organizational goals through litigation in the church-state arena, the evolution of their strategies over time, and the similarities and differences in their approaches to resolving this complex issue are nonetheless questions that have evaded serious scholarly treatment. Granted, scholars have acknowledged the significant role of American Jewish organizations in shaping and defining the use of litigation as a vehicle for constitutional change and their prominence as organizational litigants before the Supreme Court. But there has as yet been no larger effort to describe and explain the collective and individual behavior of the AJCommittee, the AJCongress, and the ADL within the framework of the legal reform model.[9] The purpose of this book is to do just that, while treating the research questions outlined above in the theoretical light of the literature on interest group litigation.

Chapter 1 of this book will describe this literature and then discuss this work's intended contribution to our understanding of how interest groups use the courts. In chapter 2 I examine the historical origins of the AJCommittee, the AJCongress, and the ADL, and their evolution from benevolent ethnic societies to sophisticated political interest groups. I will also explore the roots of the similarities and differences, both then and now, in the ways they have confronted major church-state issues in the modern constitutional era. Chapter 3 describes and explains, within a historical as well as theoretical context, the organizational behavior of each group in the crucial litigation over the issue of released time for religious instruction in the public schools, litigation that spanned a period from the late 1940s until the early 1950s. In chapter 4 I will address similar concerns through the landmark cases, dating from the middle of the 1950s to the early 1960s, that involved both religious oaths for public office and religious doctrine in the public schools. Chapter 5 concentrates on the litigation-based efforts of the major Jewish organizations to tighten the constitutional noose around public funds for parochial schools and related institutions, a goal that dominated church-state litigation from the late 1960s through the early 1980s. Chapter 6 will look at how the major Jewish organizations have adapted to a litigation environment that favors the status quo. This shift in the legal climate was triggered by critical changes in the composition of the federal courts, changes fueled by the resurgence of political conservatism as a force in American politics and, by extension, public law litigation. This new, more complex environment, coupled with internal changes within the AJCommittee, the AJCongress, and the ADL, has produced important changes in their view of litigation as an efficacious instrument capable of advancing organizational goals. The book closes with an assessment of the efforts of these three major American Jewish organizations to effect constitutional reform through litigation and suggests what we can learn from their experience about the behavior of organized interests in constitutional litigation more generally.

1

Law, the Courts, and

Political Jurisprudence

Upon witnessing the almost universal faith that common citizens held in the power of private, voluntary organizations to promote effective participation in their still fledgling democratic institutions, Alexis de Tocqueville wrote that "better use had been made of association in [the United States] than anywhere else in the world." The Americans, according to Tocqueville, applied this powerful instrument of citizen action with unparalleled sophistication and skill, and to an almost endless number of social aims. Nowhere, however, did associational politics have a more powerful effect than when "uniting the energies of divergent minds" toward a common political objective.[1] Having also observed that, for the most part, controversial and divisive political questions eventually turned into judicial ones, Tocqueville would probably not blink an eye at the prominent role that organized interests have played in shaping and defining the use of litigation as a tool of collective action in modern American politics.[2] Nor would Tocqueville express much surprise that the courts have been the principal locus of constitutional and political conflict over the proper relationship between church and state, and that the leading force behind this protracted litigation has been a vast and diverse collection of religious and secular organized interests.[3]

The American constitutional arrangement, whereby power is divided among various spheres of government, offers multiple points of access to organized religious interests seeking to influence our political and legal institutions. As the literature on the representation of organized religion in the political process amply indicates, the strategies and tactics employed by religious organizations bear a striking resemblance to those of their secular counterparts. Organizations representing the diverse, multireligious, multidenominational character of American religious life have brought pressure to bear on Congress and the executive branch in much the same fashion as secular lobbies, and carry with them considerable moral and political clout.[4] Moreover, religious organizations, like their secular counterparts, have not confined their collective resources or strategic advocacy to the elected branches of government. Rather, in a pattern of behavior shared by interest groups more generally, these organizations have viewed litigation as an essential element in effective institutional advocacy. Perhaps not surprisingly, organized religious interests have played their most visible and influential role in the litigation process in cases involving the First Amendment religion clauses.

For decades the scholarly literature informing our contemporary understanding of church-state politics was predicated upon a rigorous, empirical examination of constitutional litigation initiated under the control and direction of organized interests. Students of church-state politics generally viewed the judicial attack mounted by predominantly liberal, separationist organizations on federal and state laws touching upon the establishment and free exercise clauses of the Constitution along the lines of a single model: as a descendent of the political jurisprudence pioneered by the NAACP Legal Defense Fund in the late 1930s. In so doing, scholarship on interest group conflict in the courts over the role of religion in American public life based itself on the research tradition established by Clement Vose in *Caucasians Only*. The outcome of a pioneering set of studies on the role of the NAACP, and to a lesser extent the National Consumer's League (NCL), in constitutional litigation, *Caucasians Only* provided the first extended treatment of how constitutional litigation—far from serving merely as a mechanism for simple conflict resolution—could function as an effective vehicle for social and political change.[5]

In *Caucasians Only,* Vose found that the strategic use of litigation proved an invaluable political weapon for organized interests representing constituencies otherwise at a disadvantage in the elected branches of government. Interest groups that engaged in litigation, whether through direct sponsorship of cases, through third-party intervention, or through participation as amicus curiae, could be successful in forcing compliance from recalcitrant political bodies previously unresponsive to their organizational goals, thereby making political jurisprudence a powerful tool of collective action and constitutional reform. Vose's documentation of the NAACP's brilliant litigation campaign to have state-enforced restrictive real estate covenants declared unconstitutional, which culminated in the Supreme Court's historic 1948 decision in *Shelley v. Kraemer,*[6] demonstrated how organized interests, because they possessed the time, finances, and skill that individual plaintiffs did not, could successfully circumvent the political process in order to achieve social and constitutional reform. In Vose's analysis, disadvantaged constituencies practiced a minoritarian politics that allowed them to reach beyond the limits of the political process by making direct appeals to constitutional principle through litigation. Vose's work left a tremendous imprint on a subsequent generation of legal and political science scholarship on the relationship of organized interests to the litigation process. How organized interests worked to condition the ebb and flow of litigation through the judicial process, utilized amicus curiae briefs to represent their viewpoints in court, and employed extrajudicial strategies to influence constitutional doctrine thus became the dominant methodological approach for scholars interested in the political dynamics of constitutional politics.[7]

American Jews, along with the secular and religious agencies that represent them in politics and public affairs, are no strangers to the practice of minoritarian politics. The organizations that represented Jewish interests were acutely conscious of the minority status of Jews in the American religious and cultural milieu and the limitations that it placed on their power to influence the political process. When it came to the politics of church and state, these groups understood from the start that their best strategy for abolishing state-sponsored religious preferences in the private sphere lay not with hopes of precursory action by the elected branches of government but in pursuing a constitutional mandate issued by the courts. The most powerful and activist of the major Jewish organizations that entered the judicial arena to challenge the extant law of church and state—the AJCommittee, the AJCongress, and the ADL—all viewed the promise of litigation as a forceful instrument for constitutional reform. But for litigation to animate the process of constitutional change, as numerous organized interests active in the church-state debate wanted, the Supreme Court had to signal that it was willing to become the locus of this conflict. In this context, two factors stand out as critical: how the Court assumed jurisdiction over what had once been matters of state and local concern and how this transformation in the Court's role as arbiter of the church-state debate encouraged a litigation environment that soon became dominated by organized interests. Both provide important contextual clues regarding the decision of the AJCommittee, the AJCongress, and the ADL to enter the judicial wars.

The Nationalization of the
Religion Clauses

Modern constitutional doctrine on the no-establishment and free exercise guarantees of the First Amendment—"Congress shall make no law respecting an establishment of religion, or prohibiting the free exercise thereof"—begins with the incorporation of the religion clauses into the due process clause of the Fourteenth Amendment. Prior to the landmark decisions in *Cantwell v. Connecticut* (1940), which made the free exercise clause applicable to the states, and *Everson v. Board of Education* (1947), which held that the establishment clause applied with equal force to state action, the Supreme Court had failed to give either clause a meaningful, much less a definitive, judicial construction.[8] From 1791, when the Bill of Rights was ratified, through to the early twentieth century, the Court had decided just a handful of cases at scattered intervals involving religion-based claims brought under the First and Fourteenth Amendments.[9] In none of these cases, however, did the Court define the substantive content of the establishment or free exercise clauses, other than to say, in 1872, that Congress had no power to legislate on internal church matters or to regulate or criminalize the religious faith of private individuals, and, in 1923, that religious freedom was among the "liberties" protected by the due process clause of the Fourteenth Amendment.[10] Federal court jurisdiction over legal challenges brought against state laws that burdened constitutional rights did not broaden in scope until 1925, when the Court, in *Gitlow v. New York*, ruled that states were prohibited by the due process clause from abridging the freedoms protected by the free speech clause of the First Amendment.[11]

Gitlow initiated a gradual but firm expansion of the Court's jurisdiction over state statutes that raised federal constitutional questions. This landmark procedural and doctrinal evolution in constitutional law, whereby states have been forced to uphold the freedoms guaranteed by the First Amendment, is most often referred to in the legal and political science literature as the "incorporation doctrine." The Court's support of the incorporation doctrine, begun in *Gitlow*, was soon extended to make the other provisions of the First Amendment applicable to state action.[12] It eventually came to include as well most of the criminal due process guarantees of the Bill of Rights, although the Court has never acknowledged in an opinion that the Bill of Rights applies in toto to the states.[13] It has instead relied on Justice Benjamin Cardozo's interpretation of the Fourteenth Amendment as set forth in *Palko v. Connecticut* (1937) for its theoretical justification of the incorporation doctrine. In *Palko*, Justice Cardozo concluded that the due process clause protected those freedoms "implicit in the concept of ordered liberty," which included those "principle[s] of justice so rooted in the traditions and conscience of our people as to be ranked as fundamental."[14] *Palko* thus ratified the Court's decisions handed down over the previous decades that interpreted the due process clause of the Fourteenth Amendment to limit state actions that violated federal constitutional rights. In doing so, the Court laid the foundation for what Richard Cortner has called the judicial enactment of a second Bill of Rights.

In *The Supreme Court and the Second Bill of Rights* (1981), Cortner describes the Court's slow but steady determination to make the federal constitutional guarantees contained in the first eight amendments to the Constitution enforceable upon the states. Cortner recounts the desire among several of the justices to proceed apace on the nationalization process once *Gitlow* was decided and illustrates the frustration within the Court over how best to develop a theoretical justification for using the due process clause to make the Bill of Rights applicable to the states. Part of the Court's frustration over the slowness in moving forward on the incorporation doctrine was due to the reactive nature of constitutional litigation, an institutional characteristic of judicial politics that sets the courts apart from the elected branches of government. Unlike the elected branches, which are by nature and design responsive and accountable to citizen pressure and thus able to launch public policy initiatives of their own, the courts cannot take preemptive measures to reform constitutional doctrine. While they can offer clues through the language of prior decisions, courts must ultimately wait for litigation to come to them.

As Cortner noted, the Court gave ample indication in the cases it decided between *Gitlow* and *Palko* that it wanted to nationalize the Bill of Rights.[15] Not until its seminal 1938 decision in *U.S. v. Carolene Products,* however, did the Court make clear just where it intended to take the direction of its constitutional jurisprudence. In *Carolene Products,* Justice Harlan Fiske Stone, writing for the Court, held that the Fourteenth Amendment "embraced" the "fundamental freedoms" of the Bill of Rights, making them applicable to the states. But even more pivotal was Justice Stone's opinion that legislation that fell within these constitutional boundaries might be considered to have "a narrower scope of operation of the presumption of constitutionality" than claims against economic and property rights. Under the terms of this methodological innovation, economic and property claims were now considered nonfundamental rights that could be regulated if the government was able to demonstrate a rational basis for such action. Justice Stone's opinion in *Carolene Products* provided the intellectual ballast for the Court's post–New Deal constitutional jurisprudence in cases involving civil rights and liberties. But in the short term, the sporadic and episodic nature of constitutional litigation made it more difficult for the Court to develop, much less control, an agenda appropriate to fulfill the objective of nationalizing the Bill of Rights.[16]

The Court's determination to move forward on the incorporation agenda, however, was not lost on those societal and political constituencies who stood to benefit the most from a more expansive interpretation of constitutional rights and liberties. Foremost among the Court's allies in the nationalization process were the growing number of cause-oriented interest groups who believed that their constituencies could only receive the full protection of the Bill of Rights under one condition: if the constitutional restrictions that prevented the federal government from encroaching on individual rights were made applicable to state action. Organized interests whose agendas included broader social and political change, such as the NAACP LDF and the ACLU, were now prepared to commit their resources in full force toward such action. The new sophistication that organized interests brought to the resolution of constitutional litigation led Cortner to comment, in an earlier but nonetheless seminal article, that the major cases responsible for landmark decisions regarding constitutional doctrine did not arrive on the Supreme Court's doorstep like orphans in the night. They were instead the result of concerted and calculated efforts often supported by organized interests. The process whereby the free exercise and establishment clauses of the First Amendment were incorporated into the Fourteenth Amendment not only confirms Cortner's observations on the influence of organized interests but attests to the powerful group dynamics that have long been at the center of constitutional litigation on church-state issues.[17]

The Free Exercise Clause

The contribution of the Jehovah's Witnesses to the modern constitutional development of the Court's free exercise jurisprudence is inverse in proportion to their status in the American religious milieu. Unlike the mainline Protestant denominations, and even Catholics and Jews, the Witnesses do not trace their lineage back to the colonial era, but only to the 1880s.[18] When they emerged along the East coast in small but concentrated numbers during the post–Civil War period, moreover, the Witnesses were often viewed with contempt by established religious denominations. In the communities in which they chose to settle they were frequently ostracized for the militant posture of their vigorous public proselytization and other perceived peculiarities associated with their religious conduct. But not everyone despised the Witnesses—and even some of those who did still respected their right to the free exercise of their religion. Despite their small number, the Witnesses attracted much support and admiration from mainstream civil libertarians, as well as other unpopular religious denominations, for their persistence in fighting what was often government-sanctioned persecution directed at their religious conduct.

David Manwaring has recounted the formidable political and legal obstacles that stood between the Witnesses and their constitutional rights in his meticulously researched classic, *Render unto Caesar: The Flag Salute Controversy* (1962).[19] In his book, Manwaring describes in exacting detail how the Witnesses were subject to frequent state criminal prosecution and flat-out government-condoned private harassment both for their public proselytizing and, as is better known, for their dramatic refusal, on religious grounds, to allow their children to participate in the compulsory ceremony of saluting the flag common in public schools nationwide. The Witnesses consequently decided to pursue the vindication of their constitutional rights in the courts. Albeit on rare occasions, the Witnesses were able to plead their case regarding public proselytization to state and local officials and thus to convince them not to enforce statutes that such activities. They were far less successful, however, in persuading school boards or even individual school principals to exempt their children from the compulsory salute to the flag that customarily began each school day. As Manwaring commented, the Witnesses were, in the classic sense, the epitome of the "discrete and insular" minorities that Justice Stone referred to in his *Carolene Products* footnote: relegated to a position of powerlessness in the political process; subject to purposeful and sustained discrimination; and burdened with legal disabilities.[20]

Scorned for their position on the flag salute laws and ridiculed for their public religious conduct, the Witnesses stood virtually no chance of achieving a favorable outcome in state legislatures or municipal bodies where such repressive statutes were in place and were enforced by local authorities.[21] As their leadership understood, if the Witnesses were to secure the promises set forth in the free exercise clause of the First Amendment, a well-planned and well-financed litigation campaign was the only feasible avenue to pursue. Only through such litigation could they hope to obtain, once and for all, a favorable resolution regarding the constitutionality of laws that punished them and their children for asserting their right to exercise their religious conscience. As Manwaring points out, however, the Witnesses faced a different strategic difficulty than other major organizations such as the ACLU and the NAACP, which for some time had been engaged in landmark constitutional litigation of their own.

The difficulty was this: the Witnesses were dependent upon local criminal prosecution to trigger litigation. Only then could they begin their more comprehensive assault on the noxious state laws that defined the parameters of their constitutional rights, and by extension the rights of all religious individuals, under the free exercise clause. Moreover, as Cortner noted, when hostile government action forced the Witnesses into litigation, they were placed in a reactive, defensive posture, which left them with relatively little discretion over the strategic and tactical choices best suited to their objectives. In contrast, the ACLU, the NAACP, and other organizations active in constitutional litigation were not dependent on criminal prosecution to get their lawsuits off the ground. In their initial venture into the realm of political jurisprudence, both the ACLU and the NAACP focused their respective lines of attack on civil statutes that openly denied to certain classes of individuals their constitutional rights. The comparatively selective approach that these organizations were able to take allowed them to retain more control over how and when to utilize their resources.[22] Cortner attributes the Witnesses' eventual success in *Cantwell v. Connecticut* (1940), which struck down an antiproselytizing law, and *West Virginia v. Barnette* (1943), the second flag salute case, in part to the infusion of their organizational resources into the litigation campaign. He nevertheless concludes that neither outcome bore the distinctive mark of "classic test case tactics."[23]

In retrospect, Cortner's assessment of the Witnesses' involvement in this litigation, particularly in the *Flag Salute Cases*, understates the systematic nature of their sustained campaign to achieve a favorable outcome in the Supreme Court. Granted, the Witnesses were dependent on criminal charges before they could initiate a lawsuit. Once having been placed on the defensive, however, they stood out for their willingness to represent as many defendants from as many different states as they could, their organizational commitment to appeal all adverse trial verdicts, and their development of a coordinated strategy with other organizations that sympathized with their plight, in particular the ACLU. The above considerations lend support to the argument that broader strategic concerns, beyond simply winning a case, occupied a central place in the conduct and management of their litigation agenda. Manwaring himself describes the close relationship that developed between the Witnesses and the ACLU, which viewed the Witnesses' status in the constitutional universe as dovetailing well with their expanding organizational portfolio of First Amendment concerns.[24]

In fact, as Manwaring notes, although it was the ACLU, not the Witnesses, who were directly responsible for moving the early flag salute litigation out of the state courts and into the federal courts, each group was eager to "get the flag-salute issue before the United States Supreme Court."[25] The ACLU believed that the Witnesses stood a much better chance of having their claims vindicated in the federal

courts, since the state courts were more likely to reflect local senti-
ments and prejudices. In contrast to the conservative posture common
in state courts, the lower federal courts had begun to follow the Supreme Court's lead on the incorporation doctrine and thus to declare
unconstitutional any state statute that violated the free speech and
press clauses of the First Amendment. This, in turn, created a more
hospitable legal environment for innovative litigation.

Since numerous states had prosecuted church members and their
children for their refusal to comply with laws that compelled them to
violate their religious beliefs, the Witnesses were able to choose cases
that best positioned the facts before the most suitable judicial forum.
This allowed them to pursue a litigation strategy that, when understood in context, did indeed possess the core characteristics of test-
case litigation. In *Cantwell v. Connecticut, West Virginia v. Barnette*, and
numerous other important but much less well-publicized cases, the
Witnesses enlisted the cooperation of sympathetic and sophisticated
cause-oriented organizations to help them develop a litigation strategy,
consolidate amicus curiae support, and select cases for appeal with
discretion and care. The Witnesses pursued their goals with an uncom-
mon persistence and resilience in a period when the Court had just
begun to signal its receptiveness to adjudicate and expand claims involving civil and constitutional rights. While dependent in part upon
accident and fate for their litigation agenda, and perhaps not as solici-
tous of external help as they should have been, the Witnesses nonetheless demonstrated that, as litigants, organizations could bring advantages to the pursuit of constitutional claims that were beyond the scope
of individuals.

The Court's decisions in *Cantwell* and *Barnette*, which made the free
exercise clause applicable to the states and in the process greatly expanded the constitutional definition of religious freedom, are lasting
testaments to the Witnesses' persistent and intelligent litigation campaign. But there were important long-term consequences for organizational confluence in the sphere of constitutional law and politics more
generally as well. As they watched the Witnesses use the courts so
deftly to their advantage, several other organized interest groups, both
religious and secular, while perhaps more integrated into the mainstream of the American social fabric than the Witnesses, were quick
to absorb their lessons. In turn, these organizations began an equally
determined campaign to transform the scope and application of the

Court's establishment clause jurisprudence, which proved to be the next step in the nationalization of the Bill of Rights.

The Establishment Clause

Everson v. Board of Education, which nationalized the establishment clause, also marked the first time the Court gave an authoritative judicial interpretation to the constitutional principle of the separation of church and state. Cortner has written that *Everson* offers a clear example of how organized interests, following the model established in cases concerning freedom of expression and equal protection, used litigation in a planned, strategic fashion to advance their group objectives in the area of church-state separation. But unlike other landmark constitutional litigation involving First and Fourteenth Amendment freedoms that had been sponsored and controlled by such established, skilled, and powerful public interest and constitutional rights organizations as the NAACP, the ACLU, and later the AJCongress, *Everson* did not materialize because a high-profile interest group believed it would make an ideal test case with which to challenge the status quo interpretation of the establishment clause. In fact, quite the opposite is true, as *Everson*'s origins have much more modest roots than other, better-known developments in constitutional law and litigation.

In 1941 the New Jersey legislature, following the lead of sixteen other states and the District of Columbia, enacted a statute that permitted the expenditure of state funds to subsidize bus transportation for school-age children to "any schoolhouse," including private and parochial schools.[26] The statute received widespread popular support among New Jersey citizens, who submitted petitions in favor of the transportation subsidies program that boasted approximately half a million signatures. This popular support did not, however, deter several religious and secular organizations, including the New Jersey Taxpayers Association, the League of Women Voters, numerous mainline Protestant churches, and the state chapter of the ACLU, from vigorous opposition to the bus subsidies program for parochial school students.

Some of the staunchest legislative opposition to the New Jersey bus law did not come from among these sophisticated organizations with national reputations but from a small fraternal group called the Junior Order of United American Mechanics (JOUAM). The JOUAM, of which some twenty thousand people were members, listed among its chartered purposes the vigorous support for and maintenance of the public school system and the strong commitment to the principle of the separation of church and state. Immediately after the passage of the New Jersey bus law, the JOUAM put the wheels in motion for a concerted legal challenge to determine whether a public program that provided financial assistance to parochial schools was constitutional. It secured representation from a local law firm, which agreed to handle the case at a reduced cost through the trial and appellate stages of the litigation. The JOUAM also provided the plaintiff in the litigation, Arch R. Everson, who lived in Ewing Township, a suburb of Trenton, and had long been an active member of the organization. Ewing Township made a particularly attractive target for a constitutional attack: after the state legislature's action, the Ewing Board of Education enacted an additional special resolution that authorized the use of public funds to reimburse the parents of children attending local parochial schools for out-of-pocket costs associated with their children's transportation.

Even with these tactical advantages in hand, the JOUAM had to resolve an important but tricky question of litigation strategy. Should it proceed with the litigation at the state or federal level? *Cantwell* and the *Flag Salute Cases* had firmly resolved question of whether the free exercise clause applied to the states, but in none of those cases had the Court mentioned whether the same held true for the establishment clause. Plus there was the Court's 1930 decision in *Cochran v. Board of Education* to consider. In *Cochran*, a unanimous Court upheld a Louisiana statute that provided free textbooks to students in public and private, including parochial, schools against the charge that the statute was unconstitutional. The Court held that such an expenditure of tax funds advanced a legitimate secular welfare objective directed at children and was not intended to benefit parochial schools or to contribute to the financial coffers of religious organizations.[27] Given that neither in *Cantwell* nor in the *Flag Salute Cases* had the Court indicated that it had any intention of reversing its ruling in *Cochran*, the JOUAM decided to err on the side of caution and mount the challenge against the New Jersey bus law in state court on state constitutional grounds rather than pursue a First and Fourteenth Amendment argument at the federal level. The JOUAM did not envision *Everson* as a vehicle for nationalizing the establishment clause; instead, it doggedly pursued the more immediate objective of having public subsidies for parochial schools declared unconstitutional.

In the fall of 1943 the New Jersey Supreme Court struck down the bus subsidies on state constitutional grounds, rejecting as irrelevant to New Jersey's case the "child-benefit" theory that Louisiana had advanced successfully in *Cochran* to uphold its textbook loan program. The New Jersey law, the court held, authorized the expenditure of state education funds for purposes other than the support and maintenance of the public school system. State expenditures on private and parochial schools were permissible as long as they advanced the general welfare of the students, as opposed to simply filling church coffers. The decision pleased the coalition of religious and secular organizations that had lobbied against the passage of the bus subsidy in the legislature several years before, particularly the ACLU, which—with the JOUAM's encouragement—had filed an amicus curiae brief in the New Jersey Supreme Court in support of Arch Everson. The ACLU continued to work closely with the JOUAM as amicus curiae through to the litigation's resolution in the United States Supreme Court.[28]

When, however, the New Jersey Court of Errors and Appeals reversed the state supreme court's decision in the fall of 1945, the pieces fell into place for Arch Everson's historic march to the United States Supreme Court. After extended discussions with their house lawyers and external counsel, the JOUAM decided to pursue the First and Fourteenth Amendment arguments in *Everson*, hoping that the Court would complete the nationalization process of the religion clauses that it had begun in *Cantwell*. The JOUAM's counsel also pursued an aggressive amicus curiae strategy, soliciting briefs from several mainstream secular and religious organizations opposed to government expenditures for parochial institutions, including, in addition to the ACLU, the Joint Baptist Conference Committee on Public Relations and the Seventh-Day Adventists. Because the JOAUM had secured appellate counsel with substantial experience in the Supreme Court to argue *Everson*—an impressive sign of organizational sophistication—it too was able to write and submit a separate amicus brief on behalf of itself.

When the Court decided in May 1946 to hear *Everson*, the major American Jewish organizations were well aware of the potential significance the outcome held for the constitutional development of church-state law. The AJCommittee, the AJCongress, and the ADL had each expressed opposition to public funds for parochial schools, released time from public schools for religious education, and religious exercises in the public schools. Even so, real and sometimes stark differences existed among the three groups over how to engage the public debate on these issues, whether to use litigation as an organizational vehicle to advance their position, and how absolute their commitment should be to the principle of church-state separation.[29] As I will discuss further in chapter 3, in the mid-1940s the AJCommittee, the AJCongress, and the ADL were just beginning to develop in earnest their policies on church-state matters, a phase in their respective histories that helped to sharpen the philosophical differences between these increasingly independent-minded and powerful organizations. Although it was well concealed from public view, bitter disagreement existed among the AJCommittee, the AJCongress, and the ADL over how to engage the church-state debate disagreement that indeed helped to cement the lasting rivalries among the three groups for the unchallenged leadership of organized American Jewish opinion on these as well as other matters.

While *Everson* attracted some attention from the organized Jewish community, it did not inspire the AJCommittee, the AJCongress, or the ADL to support the JOUAM's challenge to the New Jersey bus law, even though each organization was on record as opposing the use of public funds for such purposes.[30] For the JOUAM, the final decision of the AJCongress not to submit an amicus curiae brief in *Everson* was especially disappointing. An interfaith coalition of amicus support, the JOUAM felt, would help deflect criticism of the challenge to the New Jersey bus law as unsympathetic to the need for religious education and/or hostile in general to organized religion. Moreover, the JOUAM considered the AJCongress, which had begun to trumpet itself as the self-appointed "private attorney general" for the American Jewish community, the most progressive and visible of the Jewish organizations when it came to constitutional controversies.[31] Indeed, counsel for the JOUAM had actively sought the support of the AJCongress, having issued it a personal invitation to submit an amicus curiae brief.[32]

Had the AJCommittee, the AJCongress, and the ADL agreed to participate in *Everson*, they would have done so under the auspices of the National Community Relations Advisory Council (NCRAC). The NCRAC was a joint policy-making committee that had been created by the major Jewish organizations along with local community relations bodies shortly after World War II to coordinate and represent American Jewish opinion on matters of public policy. But in the late 1940s this umbrella organization was still reluctant to challenge the dominant pan-Christian civic culture as Jews qua Jews and consequently had no desire to intervene in *Everson*. This reluctance to take a public position in *Everson* ran highest within the leadership of the AJCommittee and the ADL. Each agency viewed open and concerted Jewish opposition to state-supported programs and policies that supported Protestant and Catholic educational objectives, whether in public or private schools, with much more trepidation than did the AJCongress because of their fear that such involvement would produce an anti-Semitic backlash, a view the AJCongress did not share. Since the NCRAC required unanimous approval from its constituent organizations in order to intervene in litigation, the failure of the AJCommittee, the AJCongress, and the ADL, as well as various less powerful but still influential rabbinical bodies and local federations, to reach a consensus on the advantages of such action prohibited NCRAC's involvement in *Everson*.[33]

The AJCongress did not, however, decide to refuse the invitation from the JOUAM to submit an amicus brief in *Everson* because it shared the concerns of the AJCommittee and the ADL that such concerted Jewish involvement would produce an anti-Semitic response from Christian organizations and in public opinion at large. Leo Pfeffer, whose name later became synonymous with the epochal changes in church-state law that occurred in the 1960s and 1970s, was in 1946 a neophyte staff lawyer who worked for the law and litigation arm of the AJCongress: the Commission on Law and Social Action (CLSA). Pfeffer, who had been placed in charge of research on church-state issues, recommended to Will Maslow, the CLSA's director, that the AJCongress submit an amicus brief on behalf of the NCRAC in *Everson*.[34] Maslow duly forwarded Pfeffer's proposal to the appropriate decision-making authorities at the higher levels of the AJCongress. But for reasons that were, according to Maslow, "political" rather than ideological, the NCRAC refused to accept the CLSA's recommendation that it participate in *Everson*.[35]

The "political" reason, according to Maslow, was that the president of the AJCommittee, Joseph K. Proskauer, was concerned that collective opposition on the part of the major American Jewish organizations in *Everson* would alienate the Catholic Church and other Catholic groups. The AJCommittee, which had close ties to Catholic institutions through its interfaith work and other organizational activities, had no desire to risk undermining a relationship that it so carefully cultivated over time. Given the AJCommittee's concerns and the fact that the NCRAC needed unanimous consent to submit an amicus brief, the AJCongress's position did not prevail. Pfeffer, who in all likelihood would have written the NCRAC brief had it decided to file one, believed that the AJCongress had frittered away an excellent opportunity in *Everson* to put the organization on record as a force with which to be reckoned in church-state politics, calling the CLSA's decision not to intervene a "pity" because it could have made "really worthwhile contribution."[36]

While the AJCongress later acknowledged there was probably little it could have done to bolster the case put forward by the JOUAM and its amici, it still viewed *Everson* as an opportune moment to assert the position of American Jews on religious freedom issues. Pfeffer, in particular, was itching for the AJCongress to take a public stand—even if only as part of a broader coalition of religious or secular organizations—on some issue involving the separation of church and state, whether it be released time from public schools for religious education, the recitation of Bible scripture in public schools, or government assistance to parochial schools. Even after the NCRAC had denied Pfeffer's overture to participate in *Everson,* he persisted, suggesting later that year that the AJCongress come out against the recitation of the Lord's Prayer in New York public schools, even though he knew that it, along with the other major Jewish organizations, believed the time was not quite right to do so.

Pfeffer's motives were twofold. For one thing, he believed that the CLSA had to become more assertive on church-state issues if it hoped to live up to its promise to represent the Jewish community in important constitutional litigation involving civil rights and liberties. Second, in his opinion the AJCongress should seize the moment from the AJCommittee and the ADL by adopting a more aggressive public posture—an approach, as I will describe in chapters 3 and 4, that the latter organizations then frowned upon. But Pfeffer—and the AJCongress— would have to wait until after *Everson* to enter the ever more confrontational and group-dominated environment of Supreme Court church-state litigation. When that chance came the following term in *McCollum v. Board of Education,* the major Jewish organizations, led by the AJCongress, did finally cast their line into this fractious debate, an action that changed the complexion and tone of Supreme Court church-state litigation for the next several decades.[37]

In February 1947 the Court handed down its much anticipated decision in *Everson*, which by then had attracted attention on a national scale. After all, the case offered an aperture through which the justices could extend the incorporation doctrine to the establishment clause and refine or even overturn the 1930 *Cochran* decision, which permitted states to loan government-purchased textbooks to parochial schools. The JOUAM and its amici, as well as other like-minded organized interests that watched from the sidelines, hoped that the Court would strike down the bus subsidies as an unconstitutional expenditure of public funds for religious purposes under the establishment clause. In contrast, New Jersey and six other states that had passed similar statutes, along with the Catholic Church and its lay supporters, wanted such programs to remain in place. As it turned out, the Court would disappoint both sides in *Everson*, but for very different reasons.[38]

In upholding, by a vote of five to four, the decision of the New Jersey Court of Errors and Appeals to sustain the bus subsidies program, the Court ruled that public authorities were *not* prohibited from enacting public welfare measures that included among the beneficiaries parochial school children or their parents. Writing for the Court, Justice Hugo Black held that New Jersey had done "no more than provide a general program to help parents get their children, regardless of their religion, safely and expeditiously to and from accredited schools."[39] Had Justice Black simply followed the line of reasoning familiar from *Cochran*, there would have been no reason for surprise at *Everson*'s outcome. But Justice Black did not. In fact, Justice Black made but a passing, oblique reference to *Cochran* in his opinion, one that served to support his view that it was "too late to argue that legislation intended to facilitate the opportunity of children to get a secular education serves no public purpose."[40] *Everson* was not, in Justice Black's view, a case that involved the unlawful expenditure of public funds for private religious purposes, as the JOUAM and its amici had argued before the Court. Rather, the Court held that the New Jersey bus law was a legitimate public welfare expenditure that potentially benefited all school-age children, regardless of their religious affiliation. Justice Black's opinion drew sharp dissents from Justice Robert H. Jackson and Justice

Wiley Rutledge, which suggested that perhaps somewhere down the line the Court would correct itself. Still, that did little to assuage the JOUAM and their allies' disappointment over *Everson*'s outcome.

But what baffled the plaintiffs, as well as later commentators, most about Justice Black's conclusion in *Everson* was its inconsistency with the analysis of the establishment clause that he set forth in the first thirteen pages of the Court's fifteen-page majority opinion.[41] Justice Black began his opinion with a historical review of religious persecution in Western European countries and how the lessons from those experiences led the framers of the Constitution to adopt the establishment clause. From there, Justice Black explained the theoretical and philosophical basis for the Madisonian conception behind the First Amendment's command that Congress—and, as he interpreted it, the states as well—"shall make no law respecting an establishment of religion." Justice Black concluded this discussion with an enthusiastic endorsement of the Jeffersonian metaphor that the establishment clause erected "a wall of separation between church and state [that] . . . must be kept high and impregnable."[42] In what A. E. Dick Howard has correctly called "the most famous *dictum* in any Supreme Court opinion on the meaning of the Establishment Clause," Justice Black wrote that the clause's intent and language

> must mean at least this: Neither a state nor the Federal Government can set up a church. Neither can pass laws which aid one religion, aid all religions, or prefer one religion over another. Neither can force nor influence a person to go to or remain away from church against his will or force him to profess a belief or disbelief in any religion. No person can be punished for entertaining or professing religious beliefs, for church attendance, or nonattendance. No tax in any amount, large or small, can be levied to support any religious activities or institutions, whatever they may be called, or whatever form they may adopt to teach or practice religion. Neither a state nor the Federal Government can, openly or secretly, participate in the affairs of any religious organizations or groups and vice versa.[43]

Indeed, the conceptual dissonance between Justice Black's interpretation of the clause and his subsequent argument that the *Everson* case did not in fact involve the use of public funds for private religious purposes could hardly escape notice.

The *Everson* dissenters, who, in addition to Justices Jackson and Rutledge, included Justice Felix M. Frankfurter and Justice Harold H. Burton, agreed with Justice Black's interpretation of the establishment clause, notably his conclusion that the limits it placed on government's power to support or aid private religion applied to state as well as federal laws. Granted, the incorporation of the establishment clause into the Fourteenth Amendment had not been the chief motive behind the JOUAM's decision to sponsor *Everson*. Even so, the fact that the Court used the case, at least in theory, to equalize the scope and application of the religion clauses—which had remained uneven since *Cantwell*—and did so without dissent on this point made the case of landmark consequence in the annals of constitutional law.

But the Court's doctrinal innovation in First and Fourteenth Amendment law was not greeted with universal acclaim, but instead with universal confusion. Catholic organizations, while relieved that the Court ultimately upheld the right of parochial schools to claim some access to public funds, would later criticize Justice Black's *Everson* dicta as a misguided construction of the framers' intent and charge that it, along with Justice Rutledge's dissent, built a much more imposing wall of separation than Jefferson or Madison had ever imagined. Even the immediate winners, then, feared that, over the long term, they would wind up as losers.[44] Critics of *Everson*'s holding had a much different reaction. Protestant, Jewish, and other religious and secular organizations that opposed government assistance to parochial schools, although pleased with the Court's unanimous theoretical endorsement of the strict separationist principles that animate the establishment clause, feared that in future such cases public funds might fall through the cracks of Jefferson's—and now the Court's—metaphorical wall.[45] Thus, while *Everson* completed the incorporation of the religion clauses, the schizophrenic qualities of Justice Black's opinion, along with the dissatisfaction with which it was received by all the parties that participated in the case, provided copious proof that the constitutional contours of the establishment clause were far from complete in their definition.

Pleased that the Court had upheld a public subsidies program for religious schools despite such strict separationist rhetoric, *Everson* encouraged Catholic organizations to press ahead with their political campaign in an effort to obtain additional public aid for their parochial schools, as well as to secure legislative support for released-time instruction in public schools (a subject that I will address at greater length in chapter 4). The leaders of several mainline Protestant churches, however, were concerned that *Everson* had established an unfavorable precedent for future establishment clause cases involving the transfer of public funds to religious institutions. Together with the Washington-based agencies that represented their interests in public affairs, they consequently convened a historic meeting in the nation's capital later that May to create a new organization, Protestants and Other Americans United for the Separation of Church and State (POAU).[46]

POAU soon became an influential, if controversial, voice in church-state politics, known for its consistent and vitriolic attacks on the efforts of the Catholic Church to persuade Congress and state legislatures to subsidize its parochial school system.[47] POAU's first order of business was to organize support for a proposed amendment to the Constitution, introduced by Representative Joseph R. Bryson of South Carolina, that would prohibit all government aid to religious schools. Second, POAU wanted to develop legislative and litigation strategies that in the meantime would discourage state legislatures from enacting additional programs that provided such assistance to parochial schools.[48] In 1964, though, the organization dropped the "Protestants and Other" from its name to quell what was, as it would later acknowledge, legitimate criticism from other religious and civil liberties organizations that it tried too hard to appeal to anti-Catholic sentiment. Thus, by the late 1960s—some twenty years after the *Everson* decision—Americans United (AU), as it now called itself, had shed much of the anti-Catholic animus associated with its public persona and had become a respected and forceful advocate on behalf of the separationist position in church-state politics.[49]

Everson also forced the major Jewish organizations to reevaluate their collective strategies on church-state issues. While the constituent bodies of the NCRAC remained divided over the appropriate strategic and tactical vehicles with which to engage the ever more public church-state debate, little communal disagreement existed within the NCRAC, or among the AJCommittee, the AJCongress, and the ADL, over Leo Pfeffer's general statement regarding the public schools. "Our non-sectarian public educational system," Pfeffer wrote in a 1956 retrospective on the church-state wars, "represents one of the most valuable contributions made by America to western civilization," and constitutes "the finest fruit of the principle of separation" that "better than anything else ... manifests democracy in action." Pfeffer also cautioned that, because of the central role of public schools in shaping and transmitting the values of American culture, "it [should] be expected that they will be subjected to sectarian pressures to a greater degree than perhaps any other agency of society." Since the public schools and the separation principle had served American Jews so well, Pfeffer believed that the major Jewish organizations should remain forever vigilant and uncompromising in their defense of both.[50]

The AJCommittee and the ADL shared Pfeffer's conviction regarding the importance of public schools as mediating structures and the need to keep them universal, secular, and free of sectarian intrusion. Rabbi Arthur Rosenbaum, director of interfaith relations for the AJ-Committee, said at a NCRAC meeting held as far back as June 1947 that the "sectarian control of education must be resisted" so that public schools could "perform their proper function in American democracy."[51] At the same meeting, Frank N. Trager, national program director of the ADL, contended that "public schools offered the best environment in which to advance "cultural pluralism." While not ignorant of religious values and their importance in the educational curriculum, "cultural pluralism," as the ADL envisioned it, recognized the important function of universal public education to advance the core democratic values of American pluralism and encourage mutual respect for children of all religious and cultural backgrounds. To secure these crucial social objectives, the ADL agreed with the AJCongress and the AJCommittee that it was absolutely necessary to honor the separation principle in the public schools.[52] Even before the decision in *Everson* was handed down, the AJCongress, the AJCommittee, and the ADL were on record as opposing federal and state funds for parochial schools, whether Catholic, Jewish or Protestant. The Court's decision to uphold the New Jersey bus subsidies program simply strengthened their collective resolve.[53]

But *Everson* did not strike the same visceral nerve within either the AJCommittee or the ADL leadership that it did within the upper reaches of the AJCongress. *Everson* erased whatever doubts still lingered among the leaders of the AJCongress over whether the time was right for a major American Jewish organization to take a bold, uncompromising position on the issue of church-state separation. In a speech delivered before the June 1947 NCRAC meeting, David W. Petegorsky, the executive director of the AJCongress, expressed his organization's disagreement with the position held by both the ADL and the AJCommittee that common elementary school practices such as the joint celebration of religious holidays or the teaching of religious principles "belong in the category of intercultural education rather than religious instruction."[54] Petegorsky also argued that the major Jewish organizations should stand firmly against the imposition of such practices in the public schools. But the discrepancies in the organizational philosophies of the AJCongress, on the one hand, and the AJCommittee and the ADL, on the other, were best illustrated when Petegorsky announced that "the Jewish community must do more than simply record its verbal position. It must be prepared actively to participate in rendering the principle of separation of church and state inviolate, despite whatever unfavorable short-term consequences may be indicated."[55] For reasons that I will discuss in chapter 3, the constituencies of the AJCommittee and the ADL did not yet support the direct-action approach of the AJCongress—which included not just a more active amicus role in important litigation but the sponsorship of lawsuits to challenge government support for religious schools and religious practices. Nor did either organization, while in agreement with the fundamental principle of church-state separation, then advocate the absolutist position that later became synonymous with the AJCongress, and in particular Leo Pfeffer.

In the end, *Everson* fundamentally reordered both modern establishment clause doctrine and the interest group politics that came to dominate subsequent church-state litigation. The Court's decision to nationalize the establishment clause meant that disputes over church-state relations that were once confined to state legislative corridors and local school boards would now assume a national character. Organized interests entered this new arena of battle determined to replace the varied customs, traditions, and rules of specific states and localities with new, sweeping constitutional doctrines that would transform the status of religious minorities in the American cultural and religious milieu. Neither the establishment clause nor the politics that soon enveloped it would ever be the same.

Organized Interests and
the Litigation Process

Legal scholars and political scientists have argued that the importance organized interests have come to place on law and litigation reflects their more sophisticated awareness of the power residual in the judicial process to effect substantive change on matters that involve the definition and application of public law. The literature on interest group litigation has, for the most part, focused on the efforts such groups have made to convulse the settled law on constitutional questions in order to further social change—although organized interests have also used the litigation process to refine, expand, or narrow the statutory definition of federal and state laws that involve constitutional rights. What little debate did exist within the literature on whether organized interests considered litigation as more than simple dispute resolution, namely, as an effective and powerful vehicle with which to advance their organizational objectives, has long been resolved. We know much more now about the role of interest groups in the litigation process than we did a generation ago when David Truman, and then Clement Vose, published the first conclusive evidence that organized interests did not in fact exempt the courts from the push and pull of the factional pluralism that characterizes organizational pressure on the political branches of government but sought rather to engage them as part of a more general advocacy strategy.[56]

What still intrigues scholars about the relationship of organized interests to the courts are no longer questions about litigation technique. We know that organized interests, through their financial and human resources, their legal expertise, and their knowledge of particular areas of law and litigation, are able to sponsor cases of import to their constituencies, to participate as an amicus curiae, or to provide other specialized assistance to less experienced attorneys who find themselves in an unfamiliar, complex litigation environment. But what still remains unanswered in the literature is how, on a relative scale, the multiple social, political, and intraorganizational forces that influence the behavior of organized interests at the most general level combine to condition their strategic choices on a more specific level—in this case, the litigation process.

Mark Tushnet has argued that when organized interests engage in litigation to advance an objective on behalf of their constituencies, the manner in which a given organization reaches a decision and how it carries out that decision must be viewed as a social process. Tushnet praises Richard Kluger's *Simple Justice* (1975) for its rich detail and elegant description of the series of events in the NAACP LDF's legal campaign that led to the Supreme Court's historic 1954 decision in *Brown v. Board of Education*. But Tushnet also argues that the predominant view in the public interest law literature, whereby the NAACP LDF's litigation campaign to abolish legally mandated segregated public education in the South prior to *Brown v. Board of Education* is depicted as a rational, internally ordered, and planned process, is inaccurate.[57]

True, the NAACP LDF did utilize and even help to define the test-case model of interest group litigation that came to be emulated by subsequent social reform movements. Tushnet argues, however, that proponents of this view "seriously overestimate deliberate design as a characteristic of the NAACP campaign." Once the NAACP had agreed to attack legally supported segregation through a conscious plan and had decided to use litigation as the chief weapon with which to tear it down, the organization found that, in some cases, the continual flux in the political and legal environment and, in other cases, changing organizational needs frequently required it to adjust the strategic choices it had originally conceived. How organized interests adapt to such internal and external disruptions, Tushnet argues, can best be understood by viewing litigation designed to achieve constitutional reform as a social, rather than strictly a legal, process. According to Tushnet, when clients articulate new and different demands to the organizational leadership, or when organized political and legal opposition enters the litigation process, or when staff preferences change, or when the ideological composition of the courts change, or when new questions arise over the allocation of financial resources, how organized interests resolve and respond to these internal and environmental shifts in the course of a litigation campaign ultimately amounts to a social process.[58]

On one level, the purpose of this book is to describe and explain how organized interests view the litigation process and what internal and environmental constraints influence their behavior. I agree with Tushnet and other scholars who have argued that organized interests—even such an experienced, sophisticated, and pioneer practitioner of public interest law as the NAACP LDF—that embark on a litigation campaign intended to advance an organizational goal often find the rational and predictable execution of an ideal, planned litigation agenda impossible.[59] What I find of greater interest, though, and by extension a potentially more useful theoretical exercise, is not the issue of whether organized interests are capable of rational, planned litigation, or even whether organized interests have a demonstrable empirical effect on judicial decisions. Rather, what intrigues me is how these internal and environmental forces—acting independently and in concert—influence the behavior of organized interests during the litigation process and what their behavior can tell us, more generally, about how organized interests practice public interest law. Through an examination of the internal and environmental forces that led the major American Jewish organizations to resort to law and litigation to redress their grievances against the legal dominance of majoritarian religious values and practices in the civic culture, I thus hope to contribute to the broader theoretical literature on the relationship of organized interests to the judicial process.

On a more specific level, I hope that this book will resurrect an important but heretofore neglected chapter of the Jewish experience in America. While American Jews today do not lack for organizational sophistication or political power, this was not always the case. As we have already noted, from the initial arrival of Jews in significant numbers in the middle 1800s until the close of World War II, the major American Jewish organizations were extremely reluctant to assert their interests in politics or through the law. The millions of European Jews who had come to America to escape the political persecution and economic impoverishment of state-sponsored anti-Semitism embraced their new, if fragile, freedom in America. But their escape from the evils of old world European oppression and their efforts to work themselves into the mosaic of American society did not relieve them of the yoke of prejudice and discrimination. Indeed, it was waiting for them, albeit in subtler forms, in their adopted home.

This new generation of American Jews, thankful just to be free from openly sanctioned discrimination and terror, was not eager to challenge the private sources of anti-Semitism that characterized prejudicial behavior in America—such as exclusion from public accommodations, discrimination on the part of major employers and educational institutions, defamation in the media, or the common and often coercive use of public institutions to promote Protestant teachings. Still unsure of the boundaries of their acceptance in their new homeland, American Jews understandably internalized much of their bitterness and resentment at these reminders of their second-class citizenship for fear that whatever success they might have in securing remedies for their grievances would eventually backfire, leading to more overt expressions of anti-Semitism. Naturally, the horror of the European Holocaust further intimidated American Jews from asserting their rights. Assimilation, not ethnocentric demands for equal rights, consequently became the operative norm among the American Jewish leadership, even if it meant that Jews would have to cast aside their aspirations for equal citizenship and hide their identification with their cultural and religious heritage from the larger Christian culture. Thus when American Jews, on the advent of the post–World War II era, decided to challenge the prevailing constitutional definition and application of the First Amendment religion clauses through a sustained organized drive that relied centrally on law and litigation, it represented a epochal transformation in their self-image. That the major American Jewish organizations assumed such a visible role and became so closely identified with the dramatic changes that took place in the constitutional and cultural relationship between religion and the state further testified to their unwillingness to remain forever confined to an inferior class as citizens. The activism of these organizations signaled that American Jews, as a community, no longer considered themselves unequal in the scheme of American religious and political pluralism.

Commenting in 1963 on the new public commitment of the major American Jewish organizations to the separation principle, Robert F. Drinan, the prominent Catholic cleric and commentator, attributed the intensity with which they pursued their objectives in court to the "long experience [of Jews] in cultural pluralism that made it theologically, institutionally and emotionally easier for Jews than Christians to be absolutely consistent ... in their practical implementation of the American principle of the separation of organized religion from the state."[60] Father Drinan (whose views have since changed) was correct in the sense that Jews—having found refuge and in some cases prosperity in America, due in no small part to the constitutional principle of religious disestablishment—were in a better position to assert their communal interests without creating dissonance. After all, it was the theological and cultural heritage of the Christian faiths that was bound together with American political institutions, not that of the Jews. But

I will argue in this book that the reverse case can also be made: the precariousness of the Jewish existence throughout history, both in the United States and abroad, worked simultaneously to prevent the organizational structures that came together to represent the interests of American Jews from adopting a strongly ethnocentric posture and aggressively pursuing their interests through concerted group pressure.

Moreover, even after American Jews had sufficiently overcome their insecurities to organize with the intention of defending and asserting their civil and religious rights, profound disagreements existed within the still nascent Jewish leadership over how best to gain their objectives without provoking an anti-Semitic response from the dominant Christian culture. The stark ethnic, social, religious, and even class differences that emerged within the American Jewish population in the early twentieth century as a result of the mass immigration of European Jews to the United States proved to be crucial forces in the creation of not one but several major organizations to represent Jewish interests in public and private spheres of influence. How these differences led to the formation of the AJCommittee, the AJCongress, and the ADL, colored their organizational personalities, and influenced their group strategies in the postwar environment of church-state litigation and politics are questions I shall address in the next chapter.

2

The Political Organization of
American Jewry, 1906–1947

As powerful voices within the American Jewish community, the AJCommittee, the AJCongress, and the ADL have all proved themselves potent defenders of the civil and religious rights of Jews. But while it is now commonplace to perceive of these organizations as similar in origin and purpose, each has its roots in different segments of American Jewry—segments that cut across ethnic, social, and political lines. The underlying differences were in turn pivotal forces that led to the transformation of the AJCommittee, the AJCongress, and the ADL from social service agencies to sophisticated practitioners of modern American interest group politics.

Jews first began to settle in America during the colonial period, but not until approximately the mid-nineteenth century did the first great wave of Jewish migration to the United States take place. Early Jewish immigrants to the United States, who hailed primarily from Germany and Austria, came to America not to flee political persecution—although such persecution was not unknown—but to pursue new, more open-ended economic opportunities. For most of the 1800s American Jews remained "loosely and autonomously organized, closely following the American pattern of decentralization and voluntarism" that characterized the organizational structure of the political and civic associations of that era.[1]

This stable pattern of American Jewish life was, however, destined to be completely upset by the mass exodus of Jews from Russia, Poland, and Austria-Hungary to America during the late 1800s and early 1900s. Approximately one third of all Eastern European Jews left their countries of origin for the United States between 1881 and 1914, a migration comparable in modern Jewish history only to the flight of Spanish Jews from the Inquisition. This influx of Eastern European Jews into the United States constituted perhaps the most spontaneous expression of a collective impulse among a people not unaccustomed to wandering the globe in search of "new modes and possibilities of life." By the turn of the twentieth century over a million Jews had emigrated to the United States, and by the end of World War I, the Jewish population in America had more than doubled. The sudden appearance in their midst of mostly poor, uneducated Eastern European Jewish immigrants startled the established Jews of Germanic descent, most of whom were thoroughly assimilated into the mores and customs of American life. This unplanned expansion of the American Jewish population had the effect of spawning two culturally, religiously, economically, and ethnically distinct Jewish communities—one German and one Russian.[2]

Even before the outbreak of World War I, these internal divisions within American Jewry were quite clearly drawn. But a subsequent series of tumultuous events, both at home and abroad, forced American Jews to begin thinking about laying the groundwork for a method of articulating their communal interests that would allow them to influence public policy and to defend themselves against the rise of domestic and international anti-Semitism. Historically, American Jews have been exceptionally conscious of their minority status. Now they would show themselves equally facile at developing political strategies aimed at advancing their interests through the established channels of American government.[3]

Organized American Jewish interests are today considered among the foremost religiously oriented lobbies in American politics. Representatives of Jewish civil rights and social agencies frequently intervene in litigation, actively lobby Congress, and pressure executive agencies, all in order to advocate their specific organizational interests and, in their eyes, the viewpoint of the American Jewish community.

But open, systematic, and concerted Jewish political action in American politics is a comparatively recent development. As we have seen, prior to World War II American Jews were divided over the issue of using organizational pressure to advance and to protect their interests, as well as the appropriate political and legal strategies to pursue. The remainder of this chapter will address the institutional and social forces at work within both the American Jewish community and the society at large that fueled the remarkable transitions in the organizational structure and purpose of the AJCommittee, the AJCongress, and the ADL that took place between 1906 and 1947. These years, which witnessed the metamorphosis and maturation of these three historic civil rights organizations, constituted a crucial formative period for Jewish representation and group influence in American politics.[4]

The American Jewish Committee

In February 1906, after having received disturbing reports from Czarist Russia of the pogroms directed at Russian Jews, several of New York City's most prominent Jewish citizens convened to consider forming a national organization to assist their brethren in foreign countries who had fallen victim to government persecution. After several meetings necessary to resolve disagreements over membership, funding, and organizational goals, the American Jewish Committee was created "to prevent the infringements of the civil and religious rights of Jews, and to alleviate the consequences of persecutions."[5] Originally, the AJCommittee's founders planned no more than a streamlined, skeletal organization that, while capable of expanding to meet emergencies, would have as its principal purpose to work discreetly on behalf of Jews.

Central to the strategy of behind-the-scenes pressure and backstairs diplomacy that soon became the AJCommittee's trademark were the political and social contacts its leaders enjoyed with high-level government officials and foreign dignitaries. Louis Marshall, the first president of the AJCommittee, in fact rejected the notion of an ethnocentric Jewish lobby in American politics: a wealthy and influential New York lawyer, he was active in numerous social and political causes during his lifetime. Marshall achieved such a formidable reputation as a master of the levers of American politics that each president with whom Marshall met, from Woodrow Wilson to Franklin D. Roosevelt, considered him the chief spokesperson for American Jewry. Marshall personified the type of member the AJCommittee sought out—the "uptown" affluent and educated Jew, preferably of German descent, capable of exploiting personal connections in Congress and with well-placed officials in the executive branch in order to call attention to Jewish concerns.[6]

The founders of the AJCommittee viewed themselves as the most successful and assimilated of the small number of Jews that had settled in America and were accordingly "undemocratic and elitist" in their selection of members and operational methods.[7] Pursuing a self-selected membership from the group's inception, its leadership never envisioned the AJCommittee as a mass organization. They also believed emphatically that American Jews should not view themselves as a group with interests that differed from those of other Americans. Political neutrality thus became a cardinal principle of the AJCommittee, "in line with the regnant creed of the founders that since Jews differed from their fellow Americans in religion only, it followed axiomatically that there was no distinctly Jewish behavior."[8] Marshall himself was most emphatic on this point:

> I disagree that the Jews of this country should unite for political action. The thought cannot be tolerated that the citizens of this country shall form racial and religious groups in the exercise of their civic and political functions. The citizens of the United States constitute one people, and there can be no divergent interest among them so far as government is concerned. For centuries their ancestors in foreign lands suffered from the consequences of an enforced segregation of this character, and they would not be so fatuous to create voluntarily a condition which in effect would establish an American ghetto.[9]

Other AJCommittee leaders shared Marshall's view that discreet lobbying would best serve the interests of American Jews. Oscar S. Straus, a prominent figure in New York business circles and Washington politics, who served as secretary of commerce and labor in Theodore Roosevelt's administration, likewise believed that the AJCommittee should act as a "benevolent patrician" to the less fortunate Jews in America and abroad. Straus was as adamant in his belief as was Marshall that American Jews should not isolate themselves as a "manipulat[ive], political pressure group," a strategy he believed would have negative ramifications for the Jews. Furthermore, Straus argued, such a strategy would have the undesirable consequence of increasing the exposure and public scrutiny of Jewish efforts to influence American politics. It would appear to link them to the bad reputation associated with "special interests" during the Progressive Era. The AJCommittee leaders, ever cautious about their social and political acceptance in non-Jewish circles, wanted no part of such a conspicuous fate.[10]

The decision of Marshall and Straus to downplay their Jewishness doubtless reflected their fear that the AJCommittee would be perceived as a Jewish lobby with interests at odds with those of other Americans. After all, the committee's founders had either immigrated to the United States before the Civil War or were the sons of prosperous Jewish families whose generational roots in America extended as far back as the Revolutionary War. Their encounters with governmental persecution and societal discrimination in America had been minimal, which had in turn enabled the formative generations of American Jews to achieve a comfortable level of economic affluence. Having entered into the social and political elite of American life, they had left much of their old world, traditional Jewishness behind. Louis Marshall, in particular, had an almost romantic attachment to American democratic values, remarking once that "prejudices would before long disappear in the gloriously free and tolerant atmosphere of America."[11]

Prudent politics and practical guidance were not alone among the considerations that influenced the early direction of AJCommittee. According to James Reichley, "religious and cultural forces at work within Judaism in the late 19th and early 20th centuries had important political effects" on Jewish life in America, both in terms of how Jews viewed themselves as a people and in their approach to group advocacy. The AJCommittee's leadership had strong ties to the Reform Judaism movement that had swept Germany during the early 1800s. The reform movement, which broke with Orthodox Judaism over the proper role for Jews in modern societies, advocated that Jews adopt the secular, philosophical values associated with Western democratic systems. Conversely, Orthodox Judaism stressed the traditional view of the Jews as a people in exile who were to live according to Old Testament commands and adhere to a strict interpretation of Talmudic law until the restoration of Israel made possible their return to Zion.[12] During the first quadrennial of the AJCommittee's existence, its leadership firmly believed that the promises of individual liberty and political equality for Jews in America were linked to emancipation from

Orthodox Judaism, with little attention being given to the question of whether American Jews should give serious thought to political organization for the purpose of securing their interests.[13]

Moreover, as we have seen, several AJCommittee leaders, especially Marshall and Straus, were politically well connected at all levels of the American political system. As a rule, however, they shunned partisanship in the political arena—a policy that proved to be exceptionally wise since, in its early years, the AJCommittee was in fact only rarely subject to partisan attacks from non-Jewish quarters.[14] The AJCommittee confined its agenda to issues having a direct impact on American Jews or those abroad. For example, in 1917 the AJCommittee embarked on a discreet campaign to pressure Congress and the executive branch into relaxing immigration restrictions that, if enforced, would have limited the number of Jews that could have emigrated from Europe. Efforts proceeded with great success and little fanfare despite the fact that the more established American Jews "had qualms about the influx of these people and regarded them as a threat to their own status . . . and feared that the peculiar customs of the Eastern Europeans would reflect adversely upon all Jews" in the United States.[15]

Putting their apprehensions aside, the AJCommittee continued to encourage immigration because of the moral obligation it felt toward other Jews in distress, especially those who had fled their countries of origin to escape religious and political persecution. Upon their arrival, the AJCommittee provided financial assistance to such immigrants and also helped them acclimate to the ethos of American culture. But even the lavish succor that the AJCommittee had arranged for the Eastern European Jews was motivated in equal parts by altruism and self-interest. The AJCommittee realized that the Russian Jews would have a dramatic impact on the future of American Judaism. To maintain the good reputation of the established, assimilated American Jews, the mass of new Eastern European immigrants, ignorant of the ways of modern life, thus needed to be taken by the hand and shown how Jews lived in their new country. The AJCommittee consequently expended massive resources to acculturate the Eastern European Jews who arrived in America between 1906 and 1918, although it had to struggle to keep pace with their arrival: from 1900 to 1914 Jewish emigration to America totaled almost two million. Most of these immigrants were of Russian origin and were, in addition, poor and uneducated. The settlement of large numbers of Jews in such a short period of time produced a social backlash that reached even into the ranks of the elite, established Jewish community. Unrest was particularly high in New York City, where, until 1925, three-fourths of all American Jews lived. For the first time, American Jews encountered open anti-Semitism, leaving both the religious and secular leadership of American Jewry unsure of the requisite steps to eradicate it.[16]

Louis Marshall served twenty-three years as the AJCommittee's president, from 1906 to 1929, an era in which a discreet, "insider approach" dominated organizational efforts on behalf of Jewish interests. Confronted with a new, unexpected challenge to the security of American Jewry, however, the AJCommittee had to reconsider that strategy, to assess whether it would be effective in combating anti-Semitism. But the committee could find no better alternative. Its leadership thus concluded that American anti-Semitism could be eradicated through community relations programs and coalitional educational work with non-Jewish organizations that stressed how Jews differed from other Americans in religion only.

Marshall rejected the use of litigation to attack anti-Semitic practices or to enforce the civil rights of Jews—a view shared by the disproportionate number of lawyers that belonged to the AJCommittee. Marshall, himself a renowned constitutional attorney, decided against litigation because he believed that it would bring the dissatisfactions of American Jews out into the open, thereby risking an even more intense anti-Semitic response. Ironically, Marshall litigated several cases on behalf of the NAACP when, in 1915, it began to challenge the common discriminatory racial policies practiced by governmental and private entities. For example, Marshall was instrumental in developing the legal strategy utilized by the NAACP when it first challenged electoral rules that excluded blacks from voting in state primaries, submitting an amicus curiae brief that became the model argument used in subsequent cases brought to protect voting rights.[17] Marshall in fact worked closely with the NAACP throughout his professional career. In addition to litigating cases and providing general counsel from its inception in 1909, Marshall served on the NAACP board of directors from 1923 until his death in 1929. Marshall was also directly involved in several other major constitutional cases concerning civil rights, including *Pierce v. Society of Sisters*, which established the right under the Fourteenth Amendment of children to attend parochial schools, and *Portersfield v. Webb*, which overturned a state law that prohibited Japa-

nese aliens from entering into enforceable property contracts.[18] Nonetheless, Marshall refused to use litigation to attack discrimination
against Jews, arguing that the peculiar nature of American anti-
Semitism must be addressed not in a court of law but in the court of
public opinion. Not even the tragic Leo Frank case, which exposed
the limits of the Marshall approach, persuaded the AJCommittee to
consider more direct action.[19]

In September 1913 Louis Marshall began receiving a stream of let-
ters from Atlanta Jews who were upset over the prosecution of Leo
Frank, a New York native who had lived and worked in Atlanta for
most of his life. Frank had been accused of murdering thirteen-year-
old Mary Phagan, who worked as a clerk in Frank's company. One
such letter drew a parallel between the violent anti-Semitic forces that
had mobilized against Frank in Atlanta and the French Dreyfus affair.
After sifting through other material that suggested Frank had been
framed, Marshall decided to organize a legal assistance campaign on
his behalf. But Marshall refused to use the Frank case to mobilize
American Jews to come to the defense of one of their own, declaring
instead that "it would be most unfortunate if anything were done from
the standpoint of the Jews." He insisted upon treating the unfounded
prosecution of Frank as a miscarriage of justice, a matter that should
concern all Americans, regardless of race or religion. Fearful that anti-
Semitism in the Deep South would intensify if an organization identified with wealthy, northern Jews led the fight to acquit Frank, Marshall
counseled the AJCommittee that "there is only one way of dealing
with this matter and that is in a quiet, unobtrusive manner to bring
influence to bear on the Southern press [to encourage a] wholesome
public opinion which will free this unfortunate young man from the
terrible judgment which rests against him."[20]

In short, Marshall decided against offering the direct assistance of
the AJCommittee. Rather, Marshall provided private legal counsel and
financial assistance to Frank's attorneys in support of his defense and
encouraged other able Jews to do the same. For example, Marshall
persuaded Adolph Ochs, the publisher of the *New York Times* and a
member of the AJCommittee, to use his newspaper to publicize the
injustices surrounding the Frank trial, but he also insisted that Ochs
not mention Frank was Jewish or suggest that anti-Semitism had influenced his prosecution. But even given this level of cautiousness, the
Times's campaign on behalf of Frank backfired. It gave southerners the

impression that outsiders, namely, northern forces, were interfering in a matter about which they knew nothing, an action southerners interpreted as both unwarranted and hostile. In all fairness, xenophobic southerners, fearful and resentful of outside involvement in their internal affairs, could hardly have been expected to be influenced by a Jewish-owned, New York newspaper. Nor could the AJCommittee, a parochial, self-enclosed organization unfamiliar with the customs and traditions of the South, have foreseen the consequences of the backlash that arose against Frank.[21]

The Leo Frank case had two important ramifications: it signaled the rise of American anti-Semitism resulting from the massive Jewish immigration to the United States, and it highlighted the growing difficulties that American Jews would face in trying to counter the spread of domestic anti-Semitism. These problems were further compounded by the now frequent defamation of Jews in the American news media and, in some cases, their exclusion from public accommodations.[22] Even so, despite these and other problems confronting American Jews, the AJCommittee failed to change its conservative approach to defending Jewish interests. In fact, the AJCommittee's lack of assertiveness and aristocratic qualities led other American Jews to form new organizations that sought to attack discrimination against Jews through more aggressive means. In 1913, as a direct response to the Frank case, B'nai B'rith created the Anti-Defamation League. Then, in 1918, a group of newly immigrated Russian Jews, who viewed the AJCommittee as "cowardly autocrats and appeasers," founded the American Jewish Congress with the goal of defending the interests of Jews both in America and abroad in a more forthright manner.[23]

As the Louis Marshall era drew to a close, relations between the AJCommittee and the upstart Jewish organizations were cool. Competition for financial resources and political machinations over the control of communal representation exacerbated the ideological differences that existed among the organizations. But the AJCommittee took no steps to discourage this trend, nor did it ever seriously consider how it could exert any substantial influence over the future social and political direction of American Jews. Even in the wake of major demographic realignments among American Jewry, the AJCommittee remained "aloof, ever the beneficent patrician" until the death of Louis Marshall and the rise of Nazi Germany forced it consider new methods of defending Jewish interests.[24]

From Marshall's death in September 1929 until the end of World War II, the AJCommittee placed domestic issues on the back burner to concentrate on the consequences of Hitler's rise to power and the resettlement of European Jews in Palestine. Despite the darkness that had descended over European Jews in Europe, however, the AJCommittee continued to believe that the American version of anti-Semitism was a less compelling problem, one that could be conquered through community relations and educational programs designed to correct negative perceptions of Jews. To take one example, the AJCommittee worked with prominent New York Catholic and Protestant clerics to build support among non-Jews for the condemnation of Father Charles E. Coughlin, the infamous "radio priest" of the Great Depression. In his radio broadcasts, Coughlin openly linked Jews to the worldwide spread of communism while, with unknowing irony, also accusing them of monopolizing control over international banking and finance. Coughlin also reprinted sections of the anti-Semitic book *Protocols of the Elders of Zion* in his newspaper, *Social Justice.* Unfortunately, the co-alitionist efforts of the AJCommittee and the mainline Protestant and Catholic organizations failed to temper Coughlin. Opponents of Coughlin would have to wait for public enthusiasm to die out on its own.[25]

A major turning point in AJCommittee philosophy came in 1943 when it elected John Slawson to the position of executive vice president, which, after Marshall's death, had become the most powerful policy-making office within the organization. Slawson adhered firmly to the AJCommittee's tradition of viewing civil rights for Jews as indicative of a larger struggle for the vindication of the rights of all minorities. But Slawson recognized that the selective and low-profile approach of the AJCommittee to important public policy issues had become outdated. He was consequently determined to transform the AJCommittee into a vibrant and socially relevant civil rights organization. Until Slawson entered the high levels of its policy-making apparatus, the AJCommittee had defended the civil rights of Jews essentially through reactive measures. In the assessment of one scholar, such as strategy lacked the "element of daring that could prompt intergroup reciprocity or financial contributions and often exposed the AJCommittee to the charge of doing 'too little, too late.'"[26] Slawson also believed that the AJCommittee needed to develop a positive and sustained social action program geared toward securing the full civil rights and liberties of all Americans, regardless of race, religion, or national origin. Although the committee remained uncertain about the most appropriate blend of strategies with which to combat societal and governmental discrimination, it had decided that an effective social action program must encompass the use of legal and legislative remedies, a decision influenced by the large number of attorneys that staffed its policy-making hierarchy.[27]

The fact that the AJCommittee took a more aggressive posture during the mid-1940s did not, however, translate into a wholesale revision of its traditional approach of private negotiation through the back channels of power. The AJCommittee did not seek to make courts and legislatures around the country a battleground for the advancement of civil rights, as it believed the AJCongress was doing, or to narrow its agenda of international concern to concentrate on domestic politics. Instead, the AJCommittee believed that its legal department should encourage stronger enforcement of existing civil rights laws, as opposed to engaging in protracted statutory or constitutional litigation.[28] In contrast to the "test case" approach favored by the NAACP, the American Civil Liberties Union, and the AJCongress, the AJCommittee never considered planned litigation as a strategic option to achieve its organizational goals. The AJCommittee entered litigation on a selective basis, usually only after all other forms of advocacy had been exhausted. Its involvement in state and federal litigation was limited to the submission of amicus curiae briefs, which it would not file until a case had reached the appellate level.[29]

The reluctance of the AJCommittee to enter litigation stemmed not from the conviction that it was ineffective; to the contrary, the new generation of leadership, particularly Slawson and Joseph Proskauer, who succeeded Louis Marshall as president, encouraged the AJCommittee to explore the possibilities of legal advocacy. Rather, even though it had grown in membership, expanded its organizational structure to include regional offices, and increased its financial resources, the AJCommittee remained the province of the Jewish upper class. When weighing a decision whether to become involved in litigation, the AJCommittee still regarded member reaction as its most important criterion, and an overwhelming number of members still resisted a visible Jewish presence in controversial public policy issues. That influence remained strong within the policy-making hierarchy of the AJCommittee until the middle 1960s. AJCommittee initiatives were accordingly constrained by a concern for how concerted Jewish political action in public affairs would be perceived by the larger public.[30]

By the end of World War II, though, the AJCommittee began to shed some of its inhibition against the concerted use of law and legislation to attack discrimination. In May 1947 John Slawson testified before the Select Committee on Civil Rights, which President Harry S Truman had commissioned to study American race relations. Speaking on behalf of the AJCommittee, Slawson sought to persuade the government to enter the cause of civil rights by attacking discrimination through education and the law. In 1948 the AJCommittee, along with the ADL, filed an amicus curiae brief supporting the NAACP in the landmark civil rights case, *Shelley v. Kraemer*, in which the Supreme Court ruled that the use of restrictive real estate covenants to bar the sale and rental of property to persons on the basis of race, religion, or national origin was unconstitutional.[31] The AJCommittee's intervention in *Shelley* also marked the beginning of a long working relationship with the NAACP in civil rights litigation. It continued to offer its support as an amicus curiae in the major racial segregation cases brought by the NAACP during the 1950s and early 1960s. This approach contrasted sharply with that of the Louis Marshall era. When Marshall argued cases and prepared briefs for the NAACP during its first antirestrictive covenant litigation back in the early 1920s, he did so as an individual lawyer, not as a representative of the AJCommittee. Though tempered by its historic cautiousness, this new forthrightness of the AJCommittee to participate in important civil rights causes signified an important break with its past.[32]

At the state and local level, the AJCommittee also entered into intensive diplomatic negotiations with the presidents of northeastern state colleges and professional schools in an effort to end the use of restrictive racial and religious quotas in their admissions policies. Moreover, the AJCommittee recommended that "discrimination be fought in private confrontations with college authorities and publicly by [the] denunciation of quotas and an educational campaign to win popular support for admissions based on merit."[33] Drawing on the good relations that it had built with Christian groups, the AJCommittee spearheaded an interfaith drive with numerous Christian denominational representatives to persuade their churches to reexamine their Sunday school textbooks and parochial school lesson plans for anti-Semitic references.[34]

But most illustrative of the AJCommittee's organizational metamorphosis was the dramatic growth that it experienced in financial resources. In 1939, when the fight against domestic anti-Semitism was at its peak, the annual operating budget of the AJCommittee totaled approximately $700,000. By 1949, when the overt threat to the security of world Jewry had decreased substantially, the annual budget of the AJCommittee had grown to just over $2 million. The organization had also increased its number of regional offices to seven and now sustained a membership of eighteen thousand. In just four decades, then, the AJCommittee had made the transition from an elitist civic organization to a mature, politically powerful interest group capable of vigorous organizational advocacy across the entire spectrum of governmental and private channels.[35]

The American Jewish Congress

Founded in 1918, the AJCongress began with two original goals: providing humanitarian relief for European Jews who had suffered from the carnage of World War I and restoring the State of Israel in Palestine. Even though the AJCommittee had formed a decade earlier with the similar objective of protecting the human rights of international Jewry, the founders of the AJCongress, who consisted largely of Eastern European and Russian émigrés, felt that they had been shut out of the other Jewish organizations. In their opinion, the "uptown Jews" of the AJCommittee viewed them in condescending and patronizing terms and were more concerned with ridding the "downtown" Eastern European Jews of their crude ways and cultural peculiarities in order to protect both their own privileged social status and the overall image of Jews in the larger Gentile world. The AJCongress was not intended to be "a Russians against the Germans movement" but rather an organization of American Jews who believed in a more "democratically representative" approach to protecting Jewish interests. The early advocates of an American Jewish "Congress," including Louis Brandeis and New York Rabbi Stephen Wise, believed that an organization based on a "democratic philosophy and structure would make possible maximum participation by a general Jewish population." It would better reflect the needs of all Jews, not just the privileged few.[36]

Ironically, Brandeis was a second-generation American of German-Jewish ancestry, but he never considered himself a member of German-

Jewish aristocracy that comprised the AJCommittee. The handful of individuals who exercised control over the AJCommittee were the same people whose money and influence helped "shape American Judaism in a Reform Jewish assimilationist, pro-business and anti-Progressive image"—a move that ran counter to the social democratic ideals at the heart of Brandeis's own political philosophy. In addition, a sizeable number of Jews who belonged to the AJCommittee were allied with the large corporate interests that were themselves the targets of the progressive reform movement led by Brandeis during the early twentieth century—thus rendering any potential alignment with the AJCommittee even more remote. Another factor distancing Brandeis from AJCommittee Jews was his status as a newcomer to the American Jewish elite. Whereas the AJCommittee represented the wealthy and influential descendents of the American Jewish establishment, Louis Brandeis was a self-made man whose family had struggled to maintain a middle-class existence during the fledgling years of Reconstruction in the South. His ascent to a position of national political influence by no means led him to forsake his deeply felt personal obligation to assist the Eastern European and Russian immigrants who had come to America, an obligation rooted in memories of his own upbringing. Brandeis viewed the Eastern European immigrants—which the AJCommittee held in disdain as inconvenient if not outright embarrassing to the American Jewish establishment—as a positive force in a vital, increasingly plural society.[37]

Not only did Brandeis and other AJCongress leaders find the elitist and autocratic structure of AJCommittee an anathema, they also fervently rejected the belief that Jews should not organize along ethnocentric lines. In their view, American Jews should no longer restrict their lobbying to the "behind the scenes" approach that had long characterized the organized Jewish approach to resolving social and political grievances.[38] To AJCongress leaders, the stark reality that Jews now lived in a plural society, one in which numerous social groups competed for economic and political resources, meant that their interests needed to be articulated through the appropriate organizational channels, and not merely by a few powerful, well-connected individuals. In the words of one AJCongress leader, American Jews needed to "organize . . . so that our resources may become known and made available . . . organization, thorough and complete can alone develop the necessary support."[39]

Orthodox Judaism prevailed among the Eastern European Jews who had emigrated to the United States between 1905 and 1920, but the leadership of the AJCongress had fallen under the influence of the emancipationist ideology identified with the Reform Judaism movement. Indeed, as one scholar has contended, the strength of Orthodox Judaism among the new immigrants "may have fed the trend among American Jews to break with religion altogether."[40] Large numbers of the Russian immigrants found the requirements of Orthodox Judaism too burdensome to maintain in their new country as well as inconsistent with the secular values associated with American cultural pluralism.

AJCongress leaders, particularly Stephen Wise, had thus begun to view American Jewry as a community that was both religious and ethnic, a dual identity that has persisted throughout the modern Jewish experience. In Wise's estimation, as a people possessing a distinct cultural history, American Jews should stand up and openly advocate their interests. He accordingly preached national consciousness and ethnocentrism as the philosophy that should guide the organized, political advocacy of American Jews.[41] As far as the AJCongress was concerned, Wise believed that organized Jewish advocacy in the American political process should concur with the secular value scheme of modern democratic nations. Contending that America afforded Jews a place "which at last finds the people resolved to rise to the dignity of self-mastery and self-determination" as full members in a plural society, Wise announced that the AJCongress would make it its mission to "end the old regime of the autocratic few over the affairs of the multitudes."[42]

As dedicated as Wise had become to making the AJCongress a more democratically operated institution than the other Jewish agencies, financial and organizational problems throughout the 1920s hampered its development. Instead of concentrating on problems facing American Jews, the AJCongress was forced to spend far more time raising money and seeking new contributors than it had anticipated in order to remain financially viable. In contrast to the AJCommittee, the AJCongress had relatively few wealthy members able to make large donations, a problem due in part to its organizational structure. The AJCongress began as a loose confederation of smaller, primarily Zionist organizations; it did not start enrolling individual members on a mass basis until the early 1940s. Consequently, the AJCongress relied for most of its operating expenses upon its constituent organizations, from which it often had a hard time collecting money.[43]

In addition to its financial difficulties, from 1918 to 1945 the AJCongress suffered from minimal organizational focus. Although Wise wished to make the AJCongress a force in American politics, his efforts were forced to take a backseat to developing an international agenda. Fueling the internationalism of the AJCongress was the urgent need to rescue European Jews from the tightening noose of Hitler's Nazi regime, a cause that took "precedence over a domestic situation which, however urgent, did not include the physical and economic destruction of American Jewish citizens." As a result, the AJCongress was reduced to fighting American anti-Semitism with a slingshot. Granted, the AJCongress leaders continued their call for American Jews to recognize and act upon their collective interests. Still, the dominant tactical motif among the AJCongress membership remained the conviction that educational and public relations campaigns were the most effective tools with which to fight anti-Semitism. Reflecting the mind-set of the organized American Jewish community, the AJCongress shied away from direct intervention in American politics until confronted with the consequences that communal silence had wrought for European Jewry. Only then did the AJCongress leadership begin to recognize that an active , rather than reactive, domestic program of law and social action could better protect and preserve the constitutional rights of American Jews.[44]

During the organization's formative years, the notion that planned litigation could advance the collective interests of American Jews received no serious consideration. The AJCongress, articulating the prevailing view of American Jewry, maintained that American anti-Semitism manifested itself in the private realm, not through government action. It further believed that if educational efforts failed to eliminate private discrimination against Jews, then it could do so simply by securing legislation that barred such practices. In other words, the AJCongress rejected the use of planned, test-case litigation as a method to eradicate private discrimination. After all, Jews faced a different plight than African Americans, who were battling state-enforced racial segregation as well as private discrimination and thus were more dependent upon litigative enforcement of the equal protection components of the Constitution and the few existing, if ignored, federal civil rights statutes.[45]

From 1915 to 1947 relations among the major American Jewish organizations grew more tense, but the source of that tension stemmed less from disagreement over the fundamental political agenda of American Jewry than over the issue of overt political action. The AJCongress rejected the assimilationist politics of the AJCommittee and, to a lesser extent, of the ADL. Yet, for all its theoretical obstinacy, the actual methodological differences dividing the AJCongress from the latter two organizations were far more rhetorical than real. As we have noted, like the AJCommittee and the ADL, the AJCongress relied on a reactive posture when it intervened in political affairs, until the Holocaust forced it to reconsider that approach.

For example, the AJCongress, in tandem with the AJCommittee and the ADL, joined a public campaign to delegitimize the anti-Semitic propaganda machine of Father Coughlin. In an attempt to reach Coughlin's core constituencies, AJCongress members canvassed churches and other public places in cities and towns in which the "radio priest" enjoyed sizeable followings, where they would distribute pamphlets refuting Coughlin's allegations. The AJCongress also organized interfaith commissions to build support among Christian clerics to convince them to combat Coughlin, as well as preparing a weekly digest containing reprints from the anti-Semitic press for distribution to the general news media. Combining its resources with the other major Jewish organizations, the AJCongress mounted a "thorough, well-planned and very effectively executed" campaign against Coughlin, one that had a major role in discrediting his message.[46]

By 1938 the AJCongress had also created several intraorganizational committees to study the barriers to Jewish advancement in American society. One, the Commission on Economic Discrimination, investigated discriminatory practices against Jews in housing and employment; another, the Commission on Law and Legislation, examined the utility of litigative action to secure "the constitutional or quasi-constitutional protection of the *factual* equality of men from private encroachments which are the essence of the American variety of anti-Semitism."[47] These innovations served to underscore the self-image of the AJCongress as a the most creative and aggressive advocate for Jewish interests. In reality, though, the AJCongress differed little in substance from the AJCommittee and the ADL even through World War II.

Major changes in fact did not take hold within the AJCongress until the early 1940s, when it first began putting in place the strategic elements associated with modern "pressure group" advocacy.[48] Moreover, the AJCongress did not look to model itself after other Jewish organizations. Instead, the AJCongress sought to emulate the techniques of the NAACP and the ACLU, both of which had implemented programs of legal action that made "the importance of appearances before courts and executive agencies" central to their organizational advocacy. In 1945, after much internal debate, the AJCongress combined the Commissions on Economic Discrimination and on Law and Legislation to form the Commission on Law and Social Action, which has remained its legal arm ever since.[49]

Somewhat ironically, by the late 1930s Rabbi Stephen Wise, the major leadership figure during the AJCongress's formative period, had become too consumed with what the future held for European Jewry to give serious attention to addressing the growing problem of American anti-Semitism. Fortunately, the AJCongress was able to fill the leadership vacuum created by Wise's new preoccupations rather painlessly. Several talented individuals, many of whom later became pioneers in the practice of public interest law, had been drawn to the AJCongress because of the innovative changes taking place within the organization. With the moment to shape the future path of the AJCongress wide open, a new vanguard of leaders emerged, the most important of whom were Alexander Pekelis, Shad Polier, Will Maslow, and Leo Pfeffer.

Alexander Pekelis, an Italian refugee jurist, became the intellectual force behind the creation of the CLSA.[50] Using the distinction between European and American anti-Semitism as the building block from which to construct a model of legal action, Pekelis argued that whereas the European version inhibited the social and political advancement of Jews through government sanction, American anti-Semitism originated and maintained itself through patterns of social behavior that were private or communal in nature, rather than public or governmental. Pekelis also believed that American Jews must not allow their collective identity to wither but urged them to recognize their place in American society by vigorously pursuing the right to self-expression that came with their citizenship:

The American philosophy of cultural pluralism offers the opportunity for a new solution [to] the age old problem of Jewish autonomy. Not as an "official" institution, but as a private group, the Jewish community has a legitimate place. . . .

The Jewish cause in America thus depends on the traditional American aversion to a levelling centralized government. And it partakes of all the difficulties and complexities inherent in a pluralistic conception of society. Congress' philosophy of Jewish life rejects the three simple "total" solutions of the Jewish problem: total assimilation, total emigration or total isolation. It claims our right to be, at the same time, Americans and Jews; a right inestimable to free men who strive towards a full affirmation of their manifold potentialities, and unthinkable in a simplified, unified society.[51]

According to Pekelis, moreover, the AJCongress should not limit its work to attacking governmental infringements on the constitutional rights of Jews. Instead, it should actively fight discriminatory practices by large, private organizations, including universities, corporations, and real estate associations—institutions that Pekelis called "private governments" because of their pervasive influence in American life. Pekelis encouraged the AJCongress to enter into an alliance with other like-minded organizations, such as the NAACP and the ACLU, to advance the cause of civil rights for all Americans, "whether or not the individual issues involved touched upon so-called Jewish interests."[52] To the CLSA leadership, the educational tactics and legal approaches used to attack discrimination should not be viewed as separate solutions. The CLSA believed the most effective education on "equality, group relations and civil rights is that which emerges from practical action, concentrates on a single issue, and points to practical methods of correction. When masses of people work together on a specific problem by which they are affected, they begin to develop the habit of cooperation."[53]

Will Maslow and Shad Polier, the two attorneys primarily responsible for CLSA legal policy over the next decade, agreed with Pekelis that the direct action method must concentrate on fighting legal discrimination, not just prejudicial attitudes. In their view, CLSA efforts must focus on obtaining a favorable constitutional interpretation of existing laws, securing new legislation to bar state and private discrimination, and persuading the courts to recognize new legal rights. In 1945 the notion that Jewish organizations should fight discrimination through law and enlist governmental power in that effort came as a novel idea within the Jewish community. Indeed, the CLSA, along with the NAACP and the ACLU, was on the cutting edge of a new interest group approach to vindicating the rights of minorities. During the 1940s the concept of using planned, strategic litigation to advance the cause of civil rights was still in its incubation period. But the CLSA, although it stumbled at bit at the outset, was committed, like the ACLU and the NAACP, to making legal action work. To augment this commitment, in 1946 the CLSA expanded its New York staff to seven full-time lawyers and opened a Chicago office. It also opened regional offices in Boston, Philadelphia, and Washington, D.C. Having put in place an impressive intraorganizational network, the CLSA could thus expand its scope of operations to include major Jewish population centers throughout the nation, which in turn enabled it to broaden its knowledge of the anti-Jewish discrimination that existed outside of New York and how best to take action against it.[54]

Initially, the CLSA devoted most of its work to fighting religious discrimination against Jews on the part of colleges and professional schools. It relied heavily on a multifaceted, interdisciplinary approach to attacking discrimination, one that took the "trained sociological research necessary to uncover discrimination and [the] legal skills and community pressure necessary to fight it" and combined them to create a single force. In contrast to the "insider," diplomatic approach that the AJCommittee and the ADL had long favored to address this problem, the CLSA filed legal complaints with government agencies that had jurisdiction over civil rights enforcement, published studies that described the techniques, both subtle and overt, universities used to identify racial and religious minorities in order to exclude them, and brought lawsuits challenging the tax-exempt status of public educational institutions that practiced discrimination. The CLSA's multipronged attack in a concentrated area led several universities to clean up their discriminatory admissions policies by removing from their application forms questions about race, religion, and national origin. In the legislative arena, the CLSA secured laws through the New York state legislature that prohibited colleges and professional schools from using those methods in the future to exclude minorities from admission, the first such laws enacted in the United States.[55]

Other CLSA efforts were directed toward securing employment and housing legislation. It filed repeated complaints with the New York state Commission Against Discrimination, a campaign that succeeded in bringing government pressure to bear on the discriminatory hiring practices of private employers. The CLSA also initiated litigation in New York state courts to prevent private insurance and real estate companies from barring blacks from moving into low-cost housing developments in New York City and to abolish the use of restrictive covenants that prohibited Jews and blacks from purchasing and leasing other properties, an example soon followed by its regional offices. In a widely respected article on the evolving field of public interest law, the *Yale Law Journal* praised the CLSA as probably the most active and effective organization seeking the enforcement of state laws guaranteeing nondiscrimination in housing and employment.[56]

Pekelis and Maslow subscribed to the theory that the rights of Jews would only remain secure when discrimination against all minorities had been eliminated.[57] Thus, having successfully attacked discrimination against Jews, the CLSA, "realizing perhaps more than any other group that a legal principle established by one minority group will often accrue to the benefit of others," expanded its agenda to take affirmative action on behalf of black Americans.[58] It entered into a cooperative effort with the National Urban League to root out housing and employment discrimination commonly practiced against minorities and bring such cases to the attention of the proper enforcement authorities. Like the AJCommittee and the ADL, the AJCongress decided to file an amicus brief in support of the NAACP in *Shelley v. Kraemer*. Originally, the CLSA was chosen by the National Community Relations Advisory Council, the national umbrella group of major Jewish organizations and local community relations councils, to draft the brief outlining the position of the Jewish community.[59] However, the AJCommittee and the ADL declined to associate themselves with the CLSA-drafted NCRAC brief and split off to file their own separate brief in *Shelley*. In addition to entering *Shelley* the AJCongress leadership successfully lobbied the Department of Justice to file an amicus brief with the Supreme Court on behalf of the NAACP. The CLSA continued to back the NAACP in its litigation drive to eliminate legal discrimination against blacks in housing, employment, and education, providing some of "its best work in support of the direct campaigns [for black civil rights] of other organizations."[60]

By 1948 the CLSA had firmly cemented into place the "pioneering methodology" of administrative enforcement, litigative intervention, and the utilization of social science techniques to advance civil rights as the centerpiece of its domestic fight against discrimination. Once a "loose, haphazard federation of Zionist groups concerned with the affairs of international Jewry," the AJCongress had matured into a sophisticated, well-heeled civil rights organization. In Will Maslow, Shad Polier, and Leo Pfeffer (Alexander Pekelis had unfortunately died in a plane crash on December 27, 1946), it, along with the NAACP, possessed quite possibly the most creative and talented legal staff of any national public interest group. All three attorneys were instrumental in making the CLSA the "first civil rights organization to clearly formulate and extensively publicize [a] positive approach" that made available "to all civil liberties organizations the most effective program yet suggested for meeting the complex civil rights problems of the future."[61] That notwithstanding, the most innovative and controversial decision, one that would affect the CLSA's future in the public interest field, came later that year, when the committee resolved to focus more exclusively on litigation involving the First Amendment religion clauses.

The CLSA leadership decided to move full force into the thicket of church-state politics for two reasons. First, the evolution of the NAACP and the ACLU into sophisticated organizational litigants with ambitious agendas of their own necessitated a division of labor among the three groups. Since each organization was a strong advocate of planned, test-case litigation to advance their respective goals, parceling out informal control to each group over its area of expertise made sense from a financial and strategic point of view. Thus, the CLSA carved out a special niche in church-state litigation partly for reasons of organizational maintenance.

But more important to the CLSA's decision to formulate a strategic attack on the settled interpretation of the religion clauses were the growing sectarian influences in elementary and secondary public education, along with the ever-increasing flow of government aid to parochial schools. Other Jewish organizations, chiefly the AJCommittee and the ADL, were horrified at the idea of a Jewish organization openly questioning the time-honored tradition of religious observances in the public schools and, to a lesser extent, government aid to private religious schools. They feared that such an effort would irreparably damage Jewish relations with the denominational representatives of the Christian churches, many of whom supported the establishment of the State of Israel in Palestine, and provoke greater anti-Semitism. The CLSA chafed at that charge. In the words of Leo Pfeffer, "the greatest danger [came] from those who believe in the separation principle 'but'—; those who urge a 'realistic' or 'practical' approach; those who deprecate a 'doctrine' position; those who plead compromise for the sake of good interfaith relations and the avoidance of anti-Semitism."[62] Undaunted, the CLSA went forward with its decision to mount a judicial campaign against what it believed to be an unacceptable compromise of America's first freedom, strongly guided by the belief that Jews would never be able to consider themselves equals in the scheme of American pluralism if they continued to view themselves as guests in a Christian nation.

The Anti-Defamation League of B'nai B'rith

In 1913 B'nai B'rith created the Anti-Defamation League to target and combat anti-Semitism in the United States. The B'nai B'rith leadership believed that the defamation of Jews in the news media and the disparaging characterizations of Jews on the stage and on the screens of movie theatres nationwide had grown to intolerable levels. Consequently, B'nai B'rith, itself originally founded in 1843 as a Jewish fraternal order, decided that a separate organization was needed to work full-time for the sole purpose of protecting the integrity of the Jewish name, largely by correcting misleading stereotypes about the history of the Jewish people through a public education campaign.[63]

For years, B'nai B'rith, which considered itself representative of the growing American Jewish middle class, had considered creating an organizational spin-off specifically devoted to combating the defamation of Jews. It had been particularly distressed over the denigration of Jews by entertainers. In response, B'nai B'rith had organized boycotts of theatres that presented "scurrilous and debasing impersonations" of Jews in movies, plays, and other live performances.[64] Furthermore, in the assessment of B'nai B'rith, the AJCommittee had shown no inclination to mount a campaign against this novel, but debasing, form of anti-Semitism in American culture. Much like the leaders of the AJCongress, moreover, the B'nai B'rith leadership viewed the AJCommittee as having a callous attitude toward less-established

American Jews, remaining distant and removed from the prejudice that Jews encountered on the grass- roots level.[65]

The idea for the ADL was originally kindled within the German-Jewish contingent of the B'nai B'rith leadership. Sigmund Livingston, a German-born lawyer who grew up in Indiana, and Adolph Kraus, a German who had immigrated to the United States after the Civil War and who eventually became the owner and editor of the *Chicago Times,* assumed the early responsibility for formulating the core principles behind the ADL's approach to combating anti-Semitism. Like Louis Brandeis, Livingston and Kraus felt uncomfortable among the powerful elites of the German-Jewish aristocracy and thus never considered joining the AJCommittee. However, both men were reluctant to embrace the Eastern European immigrants; in fact, there are suggestions that Livingston held the "obnoxious characteristics" of the new immigrants as partially responsible for the rising tide of American anti-Semitism, which included the public defamation of Jews.[66]

If Livingston did in fact view the Eastern Europeans with some trepidation, then it never showed in his recruitment of a membership base. B'nai B'rith believed that it could tap into the ethnic spirit of the gradually expanding Jewish middle class, a group that otherwise felt snubbed by the older, self-appointed Jewish elite yet alienated by the mass of poor, ill-mannered, and uneducated Eastern European Jews new to America. The organization thus sought to cultivate a constituency of American Jews who had no interest in cloaking their Jewish identity to win acceptance in an American culture dominated by pan-Protestant values but who also did not want to wear their ethnicity on their sleeve.[67]

In short, Livingston and Kraus envisioned the ADL as a pioneer civil rights organization, one committed to erecting an impenetrable institutional shield that would protect the collective reputation of American Jews against defamatory attacks. This was a void the B'nai B'rith leadership felt morally compelled to fill. Still, B'nai B'rith did not act on that promise until 1913, when the Leo Frank case in Atlanta made the consequences of continued inaction painfully visible to the leadership in New York and Chicago. In its explanation, the blatant anti-Semitism that permeated the Frank case, together with the failure of "Jewish and non-Jewish citizens alike" to attack defamation through "quiet criticism," necessitated the establishment of the ADL.[68]

The decision of the ADL to choose a "strikingly brazen name," one that did not obscure its purpose and intent, and to link its founding to the Frank case departed sharply from the AJCommittee's response to that incident.[69] In contrast to the stance taken by the AJCommittee, Kraus, who served as president of B'nai B'rith when it created the ADL, wrote in the founding statement of the new group that it was imperative for Jews to take collective action against American anti-Semitism:

> Remarkable as it is, this condition [anti-Semitism] has gone so far as to manifest itself recently in an attempt to influence the courts of law where a Jew happened to be a party to the litigation. This symptom, standing by itself, would not constitute a menace, but forming as it does but one incident in a continuing chain of occasions of discrimination, it demands organized and systematic effort on behalf of all right thinking Americans to put a stop to this most pernicious and un-American tendency.[70]

For a good decade after its founding, the ADL rejected the model that Louis Marshall had made synonymous with the AJCommittee to prevent anti-Jewish defamation. As described earlier, Marshall rooted his and the AJCommittee's lobbying strategies in the language and values of the Constitution—chiefly, that the Constitution protected the rights of individuals, not groups, to freedom from prejudicial action. Conversely, the ADL rarely employed the rhetoric associated with American constitutional values in its work, issuing instead statements to newspaper editors, advertisers, entertainers, and others that said "Jews *qua* Jews" were offended. Such procedural differences between the ADL and the AJCommittee led to a fractious relationship between the two over the best approach to protecting Jewish civil rights, a tension that would persist for almost a decade. However, bad feelings between the ADL and the AJCommittee ebbed by the mid-1920s, a rapprochement that, ironically, was due in part to an ideological consensus that developed between them on the nature of American anti-Semitism and how to fight it.[71]

Still, that does not mitigate the important institutional differences that the ADL had with the AJCommittee during the first decade of their dual existence. Chief among them was the ADL's conviction that Jewish agencies should focus on eliminating prejudicial remarks against the Jewish people, as opposed to the de facto discrimination against Jews practiced by private clubs, resorts, and large corporations.

Sigmund Livingston, who headed the ADL from 1913 to 1946, believed that American Jews had every right to resent the insult of group defamation. Moreover, he simply was not convinced that discriminatory behavior toward Jews could be ended through concerted legal action. Like Louis Marshall, Livingston viewed public opinion as the most important social barometer of American tolerance for minorities, and he adjusted the ADL's focus accordingly. If the ADL took positive steps to stop defamation against Jews, then public opinion might eventually change. To Livingston, legal remedies had marginal impact in a pluralist society whose mores and customs were formed through the social pressures of public opinion more often than through the language of the Constitution.[72]

In the eyes of the ADL, it mattered little whether a private social organization or large corporation chose to discriminate against Jews: the organization felt that lobbying campaigns aimed at compelling the inclusion of Jews in places where they were not wanted to begin with were unlikely to produce socially redeeming results. Louis Marshall, in contrast, lobbied diligently behind the scenes throughout the 1910s and early 1920s for antidiscrimination legislation in New York state designed to bar resorts and hotels from refusing Jewish patronage. Marshall, of course, worked not on behalf of the AJCommittee but through his own private network to bring about such legislation. This was the very combination of hidden-hand politics and coercive social legislation that produced the invidious double helix the ADL viewed as antithetical to the advancement of Jews in America. Writing in a 1913 newsletter, Julius Morgenstern, president of Hebrew Union College in New York, openly criticized Marshall for his efforts to shepherd a civil rights act through the state legislature:

> It is safe to say there is a Jewish influence behind this bill. It is not the Negro, nor the Chinese, nor the Indian, who seeks to force their way into hotels where he is not wanted. . . . It is the Jews, and Jews alone. I believe it to be a natural and inherent right of the individual to determine just whom he likes and wishes to associate with and whom he dislikes and does not want to associate with.[73]

As mentioned above, though, relations between the two organizations did eventually improve. After the initial sparks that had flown between them had been doused, over the next several decades the

ADL and AJCommittee never competed with one another for preeminence as the voice of American Jews in public affairs, nor did serious personality clashes develop between their respective leaderships. Acting in contravention to its earlier criticism of the AJCommittee, the ADL moved more into line with the lobbying strategies used by the AJCommittee during the late 1920s. It even went so far as to emulate the "insider approach" that Louis Marshall had pioneered years before. Sigmund Livingston, once a skeptic, grew increasingly convinced that respected ADL members could shape public opinion through the political leverage that their personal prestige had brought them. In a deliberate effort to enter the mainstream of American interest group politics, the ADL slowly backed away from the tactics of consumer boycotts and mass protests that it once used in favor of quiet pressure and backstairs diplomacy.

These changes within the organization did not, however, mean that the ADL intended to abandon its charter purpose. Well aware that not all anti-Semitic action could be countered through personal diplomatic initiatives or the use of discreet community pressure, the ADL remained ready to react to anti-Jewish defamation by making a public response. Having carved out a place in the emerging scheme of organized Jewish interests as the defender of the Jewish name, the ADL had come to take quite seriously its self-appointed role of ferreting out information on individuals and groups that threatened the physical well-being and emotional integrity of American Jews.[74]

One major factor that contributed to the ever-increasing vigilance of the ADL in this area was the rise of organized racism during the 1920s. Characteristic of this development was the success of the Ku Klux Klan in local southern politics and the anti-Semitic strain evident in the populist rhetoric of Father Coughlin and Huey Long, the demagogic governor of Louisiana from 1928 to 1932, not to mention other ominous signals from across the nation that forebode the upsurge of prejudicial hate movements.[75] The ADL's concern manifested itself at both the state and local level, as is evident from a major legal initiative it undertook in the early 1920s. This consisted of first drafting model antidiscrimination statutes that would impose criminal penalties against individuals found guilty of prejudicial conduct resulting in personal defamation or the destruction of property, and then working for the passage of such statutes in state legislatures around the nation, a practice the organization has since continued. The ADL also began building up extensive files on the personnel and politics of various extremist groups in the United States, gathering extensive information to document the forces behind the expanding number of American Nazi and neo-Nazi groups that had formed in sympathy to Hitler. The ADL compiled such a thorough repository of intelligence on domestic political extremism—and developed such a reputation as an authority on the subject—that the United States Departments of Justice and State soon relied upon the ADL's files for their own purposes.[76]

By the late 1930s the ADL had arrived as a permanent force within the organizational power structure of American Jewry. With its distinctive focus on attacking anti-Jewish defamation, the ADL "spoke effectively to the growing insecurity of . . . middle-class Jews by appealing for an American-style defense of Jews and endowing that effort with ethical Jewish overtones." In other words, the ADL had established itself on a middle ground between the elitist, assimilationist politics of the AJCommittee and the assertive, ethnocentric approach of the AJCongress. Like those organizations, the ADL also found its self-image evolving as a result of the influence of the reform movement in Judaism. As it continued to weave its way into the fabric of American Jewish life, this movement encouraged such organizations to steep their group strategies in the secular values of American democratic pluralism.

So, too, did the events of World War II, coming at a time when the ADL had just settled into a period of stability, force it to reshape its organizational strategy. The Holocaust brought home to the ADL the fact that American Jews could neither achieve equal civil rights nor ensure the protection of those rights through polite appeals to public opinion. The fight against invidious state and private discrimination now mandated the use of more creative strategies, chiefly hinging on law and legislation. In the words of one ADL activist, "There is not enough demand for the American way of life, the right to be different under the common law of the land. Once the Jew compromises with the American principle which grants him the right to be himself, he is lost. The Jew should consider himself as a natural partner in a government of the people and by the people."[77]

The ADL's conversion to a more aggressive civil rights posture paralleled similar permutations taking place concurrently within the AJCommittee and the AJCongress. In the case of the ADL, these were related to both an internal restructuring and a changing perception of the domestic political environment. A turnover in ADL leadership had infused the organization with individuals possessing new ideas, who were intent on making the ADL an important and effective representative of American Jewish interests. Foremost among the new leaders was Benjamin Epstein, a social psychologist formerly on the faculty of the University of Pennsylvania. Epstein believed the ADL had to take that important next step away from the tactics of enlightened public persuasion toward the more effective trilogy of education, community action, *and* legal action.[78]

But the changes taking place within the ADL were not nearly as far-reaching as those reconfiguring the future path of the AJCongress. The ADL had no interest in pursuing its organizational agenda through litigation, but, like the AJCommittee, gradually found itself drawn into it. Instead, the ADL had followed the lead of the AJCommittee; that is, it was now willing to engage more openly in public policy debates and to commit its organizational resources to legislative, litigative, and grass-roots efforts aimed at attacking discrimination. Inaugural steps in that direction included ADL support for President Truman's civil rights initiatives and, in combination with the other major Jewish civil rights groups, an extensive campaign to force institutions of higher education to cease their imposition of restrictive quotas as part of their admissions policies. Testing the waters of litigation politics for the first time, the ADL joined with the AJCommittee to file an amicus curiae brief in support of the NAACP in *Shelley v. Kraemer.* Even though litigation had little inherent appeal to the ADL or the AJCommittee, politics helped overcome their normal reluctance to become embroiled in controversial civil rights litigation. With the National Community Relations Advisory Council lined up behind the NAACP, the failure of the ADL and the AJCommittee to enter *Shelley* would have made them the only major national Jewish organizations not involved in the case.[79]

By 1947 the ADL's annual budget had reached $1.5 million. Having begun with the elemental purpose of giving Jews a public voice in the fight against defamation, the ADL emerged after World War II as a fully grown and sophisticated political interest group determined to represent the interests of its constituents in American public and private life. Although B'nai B'rith had originally planned the ADL as an organization with a large, mass-based membership drawn from its lodges, over time the ADL abandoned the notion of becoming such a group. It had instead organized itself along hierarchial lines, with an emphasis on delegating policy-making responsibilities to an intricate web of committees, made up primarily of major financial contributors and prominent professionals from Jewish communities around the nation. The ADL also opened offices in cities with significant Jewish populations, which enabled it to advance its organizational agenda through state legislatures and local governing bodies, while also providing it with important governmental contacts at all levels of the American political system.[80]

Even possessed of a strong organizational infrastructure, considerable financial and human resources, and a new political sophistication, however, the ADL nonetheless retained serious misgivings about the decision of the AJCongress to attack government-endorsed religious practices in the public schools through a comprehensive litigation campaign. It feared that the AJCongress's decision would lead to a deeply felt backlash among Christian organizations and the non-Jewish population at large and, in the process, damage Christian-Jewish relations for years to come.[81] Like the AJCommittee, the ADL believed that Jews would inevitably have to confront the issue of sectarian religion in the public schools. But in its view the most effective strategy was to work through community relations channels—alerting school boards to religious practices offensive to Jews, educating school principals on the cultural and religious traditions of Judaism, and encouraging schools to include Jewish holidays in their seasonal celebrations.

The ADL understood that most public schools, versed in pan-Protestant religious values from time immemorial, had crossed the constitutional threshold from religious instruction to religious indoctrination long before Jews had come to America. For Jews to lead the assault on such a cornerstone of American culture bordered on the brash, if not the foolhardy. Moreover, forcing the public schools to abandon a long-standing tradition under court order risked inviting defiance, not to mention a special bitterness directed toward American Jews. Taken together, those risks did not appeal to the ADL. Though having overcome the political self-consciousness so common in the American minority experience, the ADL was far from convinced that the success of the still-fragile Jewish experiment in America depended upon their immediate liberation from sectarian religious practices in the public schools through judicial mandate.

The Political Transformation
of American Jewry

Will Herberg has correctly observed that by the mid-1920s American Jews, "despite their internal divisions," had become a well-defined ethnic group. The evolution of the major Jewish organizations into influential political forces within American politics was slower to follow. From the late 1930s until the late 1940s, the AJCommittee, the AJCongress, and the ADL each underwent a process of transformation. From their youthful years as parochial, social service agencies, they had grown into powerful ethnic defense organizations determined to vindicate their civil rights through all available vehicles of organized advocacy, a maturation process that mirrored the evolving self-image of American Jews. That self-image placed front and center the right of Jews to view their Jewishness as a correlate to their "Americanness" and, commensurate with that status, their right to an equal place in the American religious and civic culture.[82]

The AJCommittee, the AJCongress, and the ADL, having all originated ostensibly to represent and defend the interests of American Jews, initially appealed out of necessity to the same potential supporters, a factor that inevitably placed them in competition with one another. Moreover, the ethnic, religious, cultural, and class differences among them eventually led to sometimes bitter ideological and strategic disagreements over how best to advance the interests of American Jews. The AJCongress came to regard direct litigation as the most powerful tool with which to secure the constitutional rights of Jews and other minorities. In contrast, the AJCommittee and the ADL, while slowing losing their aversion to concerted legal action, still preferred to bank their organizational strategies on the less confrontational methods of intergroup negotiation and "insider" lobbying.

Not surprisingly, the AJCommittee and the ADL greeted the decision of the AJCongress to mount a frontal litigation attack on government-supported sectarian religious observances in the public schools with a resolute coolness. To some extent, the tension that arose reflected the ideological differences among the three groups. But it also served to highlight what had become fundamental institutional disagreements over the most appropriate methods with which to advance their respective goals as organizations. Without a doubt, the NCRAC's decision to make the AJCongress the "attorney general" for the organized Jewish community also contributed to this intergroup friction. With the notable exceptions of the AJCommittee and the ADL, the constituent groups of which the NCRAC was comprised were of the opinion that the AJCongress possessed the most sophisticated organizational apparatus to deal with the still formidable legal obstacles that stood in the path of Jews to full equality under the law. The AJCommittee and the ADL did not share this opinion.[83]

Feeling slighted by the glowing praise that the AJCongress had received for its innovative plan of direct legal action to attack discrimination, as well as resentful of the concomitant implication that they did not possess the same talent and vision, the AJCommittee and the ADL began to distance themselves from the NCRAC. The NCRAC's decision to make the AJCongress the lead counsel on behalf of the organized American Jewish community was, for both the AJCommittee and the ADL, an indication of the diminishing influence each could expect as a NCRAC member. Thus, the organizational rivalries that emerged during this formative period resulted not just from the historical and demographic differences among the AJCommittee, the AJCongress, and the ADL but also from their respective desires to become the true guardian of the civil rights and liberties of American Jews. The cultural, class, ethnic, and religious differences that resulted in the creation of multiple national organizations each claiming to represent American Jews left a lasting signature on the approaches the AJCommittee, the AJCongress, and the ADL would favor in their subsequent drive to reshape the law of church and state.

3

Challenging the Public Schools

The Released-Time Cases

The Supreme Court's decision in *Everson v. Board of Education* essentially upheld the power of state legislatures to authorize the use of public funds to subsidize the transportation costs of children attending parochial schools. But, given Justice Black's lengthy and vigorous preamble defending the separation of church and state, the ruling sent mixed signals to the religious and secular groups who had submitted amicus curiae briefs both in support of and in opposition to the New Jersey program. The Catholic organizations that had participated in *Everson* as amici advocating government financial assistance to religious educational and social welfare institutions were heartened by the Court's refusal to discard the child-benefit theory articulated in *Cochran v. Louisiana*. But official Catholic opinion—which included the powerful National Catholic Welfare Conference (NCWC, which in 1963 changed its name to the United States Catholic Conference) as the official representative of the Catholic Church in American politics and public affairs—was not at all pleased with the separationist tenor of Justice Black's opinion. The NCWC, as well as the major Catholic journals and newspapers, objected to Justice Black's conception of the proper relationship between religion and the state, which was steeped in Thomas Jefferson's "wall of separation" metaphor.[1]

The religious and secular civil liberties organizations that had argued for the invalidation of the bus subsidies program in *Everson* expressed the opposite reaction. In their view, it was the Court's decision that should be greeted with disdain, not Justice Black's dicta on the fundamental importance of the separation principle to the constitutional relationship between religious and civil institutions. In fact, the coalition of organizations that opposed the transfer of public monies to religious institutions found some solace for the future in Justice Black's impassioned exegesis on the importance of the separation principle— assuming that at some point that view would be translated into law.

The schizophrenic nature of Justice Black's opinion in *Everson* left not just the religious and civil liberties communities that had sought a more authoritative statement from the Court on this matter confused regarding the limits the establishment clause was intended to place on the power of government to aid religion. State legislatures, public school boards, private school authorities, and the other institutions that would be responsible for implementing the decision were equally puzzled. To be fair, even if Justice Black's opinion on the permissible scope of state power to provide financial assistance to religion had been more consistent in one direction or the other, *Everson*'s outcome was bound to disappoint someone. But what made *Everson* even more frustrating was that it left none of the relevant actors in this drama— whether lower courts, state legislatures, public school boards, parochial educators, or civil liberties and religious organizations—with any real clue about where the Court intended to draw the line marking the constitutional boundaries between religion and the state. What complicated this matter further was that the Court, in *Everson*, did not show the slightest sign that it was even close to a consensus on what the establishment clause meant, much less how it should be applied to disputes involving church-state relations. The Court was unanimous in the broad view that the states, as well as the federal government, were bound by the text and intent of the establishment clause. But what the clause actually meant, under just what circumstances it applied, and precisely how the government was constrained from sponsoring or advancing the interests of religion was obviously as unclear to the Court as it was to those government institutions, nongovernmental organizations, and individuals who stood to be affected by the decision.

The deep division within the Court over *Everson*'s legacy was visibly evident in the energetic, forceful, and ultimately prophetic dissents that Justice Black's justifiably famous and influential opinion provoked from Justice Robert Jackson and, in particular, Justice Wiley Rutledge. Justice Jackson acknowledged that as a Catholic he was sympathetic "with Catholic citizens who [were] compelled by law to pay taxes for public schools, and also feel constrained by conscience and discipline to support other schools for their own children." But whereas the Court's decision "marshals every argument in favor of state aid and puts the case in its most favorable light," Justice Jackson contended that its "reasoning confirms my conclusions that there are no good grounds upon which to support the present [New Jersey] legislation." In Jackson's view, the Court's opinion, "advocating complete and uncompromising separation of Church from State," was "utterly discordant with its conclusion yielding support to their commingling in educational matters." For Justice Jackson, the case that most paralleled *Everson* was "that of Julia who according to Byron's reports, "whispering 'I will ne'er consent,'—consented."[2]

For Justice Rutledge, who countered Justice Black's bow to constitutional history with his own vision of the Jefferson-Madison conception of the establishment clause, the Court's decision to uphold the New Jersey bus subsidies program was a direct repudiation of the desire of those who framed the Constitution to see a "complete division of religion and civil authority."[3] Justice Rutledge argued that *Everson* could have been the Court's chance to repair the breach in Jefferson's "wall of separation" that was created seventeen years before in *Cochran v. Louisiana,* when the Court upheld a state textbook-loan program to pupils in parochial schools on similar grounds. Given this chance to retire *Cochran*'s control over state efforts to aid religion, Justice Rutledge wrote, the Court's decision to uphold the New Jersey law instead amounted to a second breach that made "neither so high nor so impregnable today as yesterday . . . the wall raised between church and state by Virginia's great statute of religious freedom and the First Amendment."[4] The incentive for new and additional abuses would surely follow: "That a third, and a fourth, and still others will be attempted, we may be sure. For just as *Cochran* . . . opened the way by oblique ruling for this decision, so will the two make wider the breach for a third. Thus with time the most solid freedom steadily gives way before continuing corrosive decision."[5]

But Justice Rutledge saved the most prescient language of his dissent for the end. Assessing the current and future domain of establishment clause litigation, Justice Rutledge wrote: "Two great drives are constantly in motion to abridge, in the name of education, the complete division of religion and civil authority which our forefathers made. One is to introduce religious education and observances into the public schools. The other, to obtain public funds for the aid and support of various private religious schools. In my opinion both avenues were closed by the Constitution. Neither should be opened by this Court."[6]

In other words, just as *Everson* had made irrelevant the second question—of whether the Court should unlock the public coffers to grant financial assistance to parochial schools—so too would parallel controversies in communities across the nation involving religious instruction and religious observances in the public schools soon draw the Court into the first dimension of the establishment clause quagmire to which Justice Rutledge called attention.

At the time, such a conclusion seemed to run counter to common sense. After all, in view of the intensely emotional reaction to *Everson*, as well as the division among the justices on the issue, one might have expected litigation that challenged statutes and policies involving public assistance to parochial schools to dominate the Court's establishment clause docket for the foreseeable future. Accordingly, it would be from these such cases that the core principles of the establishment clause would evolve. But such a scenario never came to pass: the Court would not revisit the issue of public assistance to parochial schools for over two decades. Instead, a sequence of cases that involved an interrelated series of issues focusing on the power of states and localities to promote religious doctrine and instruction in the public schools became the intellectual core from which the Court would construct and define its post-*Everson* establishment clause jurisprudence. The Court's decision to concentrate on this area of establishment clause law confounded the expectations of lower courts, state legislatures, public and private educators, and secular and religious organized interests alike.

For the major American Jewish organizations, like numerous other concerned secular and religious groups, the Court's decision to hear

McCollum v. Board of Education the summer after it handed down *Everson* offered them a splendid, if complex, opportunity once again to engage the establishment clause debate in the courts. *McCollum* involved the question of whether state-supervised released-time for religious instruction on campus during school hours violated the establishment clause. On the upside, participation in *McCollum* would allow the Jewish organizations a chance to persuade the Court to strike down a practice they uniformly considered unconstitutional. This would in turn pave the road to future opportunities to address other religious practices in the public schools, such as Bible reading and state-prescribed prayers. On the downside, to support the constitutional attack on released time inevitably meant that the Jewish organizations would have their name associated with the lawsuit's plaintiff, Vashti McCollum, an avowed atheist who was not only hostile to religious instruction in the public schools but to religion in general. How the AJCommittee, the AJCongress, and the ADL proceeded in *McCollum*, and later in *Zorach v. Clausen*, reveals much about the relationship between the three organizations over the next decade, as well as how the pressures both internal and external to organized interests would influence their behavior in the litigation process.

McCollum: The Fractious First Step

When the Court agreed to hear *McCollum*, the AJCommittee, the AJ-Congress, and the ADL were divided over whether to participate as amici curiae in the case. The AJCongress had no hesitation whatsoever about submitting an amicus brief to the Court; in fact, the AJCongress, while naturally displeased that released time had won acceptance in the lower federal courts, viewed *McCollum* as a significant new opportunity to present the position of the organized Jewish community to the Court on a pivotal issue involving church-state separation. By so doing, the AJCongress hoped to recover some of the ground that it believed had been lost in *Everson*. Since released time was an issue that had attracted the attention of the AJCongress for quite some time, it was understandably eager for an appropriate case that would allow it to challenge what it resolutely felt was an unconstitutional practice. Moreover, the AJCongress had conducted a major investigation of released-time practices in school districts across the nation prior to the Court's decision to hear *McCollum*. With the data it had acquired on how released time was practiced in public schools, the AJCongress was convinced that it could present the Court with documented evidence of the serious abuses in how such programs were carried out. The chief architect within the AJCongress responsible for building the case against released time was Leo Pfeffer—for whom *McCollum* would serve as the first in an almost uninterrupted string of successful appearances before the Court over the next twenty-five years as an amicus curiae or as lead counsel in various church-state litigation.

Alexander Pekelis and Will Maslow, who coheaded the CLSA of the AJCongress upon its creation in 1945 until Pekelis's death in late 1946, had long been interested in the released-time problem and the search for an appropriate legal argument that could challenge how it was practiced in the public schools. But Pekelis and Maslow were also concerned with other civil rights and liberties issues, such as racial, religious, and ethnic-based discrimination in employment, education, and housing, as well as other private manifestations of American anti-Semitism. As a result, they had little time left to devote to the church-state problem.[7] For no other reason than convenience, then, that task was delegated to Pfeffer, who later confessed in a autobiographical note that his assignment to the released-time issue was most likely a matter of simply being in the right place at the right time. At least in Pfeffer's own view, it was not because he possessed any prior expertise or experience on such matters.[8]

Pfeffer's first formal legal inquiry into the released-time issue came in 1945, when, at the request of Maslow and Pekelis, he conducted a comprehensive investigation of school districts across the nation that engaged in the practice. Pfeffer prepared a memorandum for the AJCongress in which he outlined the extent to which released time was practiced nationally in public school districts, and how support for and participation in the program broke down on the basis of religious affiliation and the religious composition of local communities.[9] This memorandum later served as the foundation for a short but influential pamphlet entitled *Religion and the Public Schools*, which was widely circulated among religious and secular civil liberties organizations that were also opposed to released-time programs. The reasoning put forth on released time in *Religion and the Public Schools* helped to a considerable degree to shape the arguments that went into several of the amicus curiae briefs submitted in *McCollum*.[10]

In his initial memorandum, Pfeffer did not reach a definitive conclusion on the constitutional strengths and weaknesses of released time. He instead centered on the arguments for and against such programs, and on demonstrating how support for them varied by religious affiliation. While Pfeffer wrote that it was "impossible to gauge with any degree of accuracy" the number of students that participated nationwide in released time, he did note that "where there is a substantial Catholic population, the Catholics participate in the program to a very large extent," while Protestants did so far less and Jews almost never. In his initial memorandum, Pfeffer did not conclude, on the basis of disproportionate Catholic participation in released-time programs, that such practices were unconstitutional, but he did hasten to point out that almost "all Jewish communal organizations . . . expressed themselves in opposition to the plan," as did such secular organizations as the ACLU and the nation's major associations that represented public schools and teachers.[11]

Over time, however, Pfeffer's opinion on released time changed. During the period between his initial memorandum and the final draft of what later became *Religion and the Public Schools,* Pfeffer had concluded that released time as it was commonly practiced—with religious instruction taking place in public school classrooms set aside for such a purpose—was indeed unconstitutional. "For the Jewish community," wrote Pfeffer, "it is even more certain that the dangers and disadvantages [of released time] outweigh by far the benefits which may be derived from the program. Above all, and aside from questions of expediency, as a matter of principle released time in actual practice, if not in theory, comes dangerously close to weakening or even breaching the wall that in democratic America should separate church and state."[12] The AJCongress leadership ardently embraced Pfeffer's constitutional analysis of released time as the organization's official stance on the matter. The AJCongress was thus firmly positioned against released time and prepared to challenge state statutes and local programs that authorized the practice in the public schools. The next step was to persuade the NCRAC executive committee, which included members of the AJCommittee and the ADL, to enter the *McCollum* case in order to make known the position of the major Jewish organizations on this issue, as well as their willingness to fight it where and when necessary, including the United States Supreme Court.

The AJCongress made just that argument in an executive committee session of the NCRAC called in summer 1947 to decide whether there was an appropriate role for the major Jewish organizations in the *McCollum* case. Unlike the AJCommittee and the ADL, the AJCongress did not believe that interfaith goodwill and educational programs would convince Protestants and Catholics to abandon their support for released-time and other state-sponsored programs to assist religion. The AJCongress also rejected the central fear later expressed by the AJCommittee and the ADL—that the concerted, open confrontation, on the part of Jewish organizations, of state and local laws, policies, and customs that advanced the interests of Christian America in the public schools and other areas of American public life would fan the flames of anti-Semitism. David Petegorsky, the executive director the AJCongress, argued that such fears, while not altogether ill-founded, were exaggerated. Consistent with the approach to civil rights and liberties law that had evolved within the CLSA under Pekelis, Maslow, Pfeffer, and Shad Polier, Petegorsky was of the opinion that for American Jews to take the opposite path—to sit back and wait—entailed even greater risks:

> We are acutely conscious of the fact that few issues present more serious problems to the Jewish community in terms of its relationship to the non-Jewish world. Opposition to any or all of these [religious] practices carries with it the dangers of being falsely accused of indifference or hostility to the dissemination of religious faith and teaching. We submit, however, that Jews have always been, and will always be, far better advised to take their position on the basis of fundamental principle rather than of temporary or immediate considerations of expediency. The attitude of the non-Jewish community towards Jews is only one of the many factors determining the status and security of the Jewish community. A far more important factor affecting that status is the strength and health of the democratic system under which we live. In opposing any impairment of the separation of church and state, we stand firmly on sound and tested democratic principle.[13]

The AJCommittee and the ADL at this time did not share the opinion of the AJCongress that released time, as a concept, was necessarily unconstitutional. Moreover, even if the AJCommittee and the ADL found the manner in which released time was implemented in some public schools problematic, neither organization shared the AJCongress's enthusiasm for the use of litigation to advance an objective that, they believed, could be better achieved through the cultivation of public opinion. For several additional reasons, the AJCommittee was hesitant to endorse the firm belief of the AJCongress that released time for religious instruction in the public schools was a violation of the establishment clause and hence unconstitutional per se. As we have seen, long before the Court agreed to review *McCollum,* the AJCommittee had frowned upon direct and open confrontation with Protestant and Catholic organizations on church-state issues as a method of conflict resolution. High-level officials within the AJCommittee, such as its executive vice president, John Slawson, and Joseph Proskauer, its president, felt that such a "militant" approach to the problem of religion in the public schools would hinder the efforts of Jews to persuade their potential Christian allies of the need to monitor the possible abuses of such common practices as released time and Bible reading. Worse, such visible opposition would contribute to the common impression in the Protestant and Catholic communities that Jews were hostile toward religious education.[14]

In the view of the AJCommittee's leadership, a more delicate approach to sensitive church-state matters such as released time for religious education, which had the potential to ignite interfaith tensions, was likely to yield far more fruitful results. An alternative tactic, one that relied upon behind-the-scenes negotiation between high-level officials of the major organizations that represented American religious interests, was preferable to concerted mass-level confrontation, in which Jews might well be seen as intransigent and as distinct from other religious groups in America—a concern that dated back to the Louis Marshall era.

As Slawson maintained, it would be better if the major American Jewish organizations used their resources to persuade their Christian "friends" to safeguard the public schools from sectarian intrusion while working to create an acceptable alternative that would allow the schools to encourage and improve access to religious education for their students.[15] Rather than use litigation to force school districts to abandon released time, and thus incur the ill will of the powerful Catholic and Protestant organizations that supported it, the AJCommittee recommended the creation of interfaith councils to formulate and supervise guidelines that would encourage religious education but not encroach upon the fundamental principle of the separation of church and state. Should such an arrangement prove impossible or unworkable, the AJCommittee was prepared to support an interfaith effort to develop an alternative program called "dismissed time." Under this arrangement, public schools would permit early dismissal for students who wished to attend religious classes at their respective church or synagogue.[16] Above all, the AJCommittee stressed that American Jews could best represent their interests and protect their "good name" if they cooperated with Protestant and Catholic organizations to construct a workable approach to released time.

The ADL was also lukewarm to the AJCongress's endorsement of litigation to attack released time. Like the AJCommittee, the ADL believed that litigation was too confrontational and would ultimately damage the constructive relationships that Jews had built up with the Protestant and Catholic communities. Moreover, along with the AJCommittee, the ADL did not initially view released time as an encroachment on the principle of church-state separation. The ADL also shared the AJCommittee's view that the resolution of whatever tensions might arise in the implementation of a released-time program in a public school with respect to the separation of church and state would not come through litigation but through education.[17] If particular communities were determined to develop and implement a released-time program, the first reaction of Jewish organizations should not be to charge forward with a lawsuit. Rather, they should work with the Protestant or Catholic communities in question to ensure that Jewish values and culture were part of such a plan. Richard E. Gutstadt, the national director of the ADL, believed that an education program that stressed "cultural pluralism" and the inclusion of multicultural themes offered the best chance to ameliorate the potential sectarian abuses of released time and instead emphasize education about religion. "When you find yourself up against a situation which you cannot entirely correct," Gutstadt told the NCRAC executive council, "and an evil which you cannot eliminate, it is the part of sagacity and good judgment to temper, in so far as you can, whatever elements are in that program which you fear and which you feel may have an undesirable effect."[18]

Gutstadt did acknowledge that in those unusual instances when interorganizational, interfaith cooperation failed to produce a workable agreement on the implementation of a released-time program, the "oft-suggested measure of legal procedure" might serve some useful purpose provided such action was well prepared, possessed the unified support of the major Jewish organizations, and conducted under the most favorable auspices possible. In a less than subtle reference to Vashti McCollum, Gutstadt suggested that the Jewish organizations should not back a plaintiff who is greeted

> with the contempt and the detestation of the overwhelming number of the people whose consciousness we are trying to influence; that at least we get as plaintiffs those who have a right to expect a sympathetic hearing; but more important even than that, is that the basic issue be not confused by the needless creation of an atmosphere of mistrust and suspicion directed against an expected encroachment of a political ideology of a radical character upon an area where it has no genuine interest.[19]

While the AJCongress's support for litigation to attack the constitutional infirmities of released time intensified between the 1946 NCRAC conference on religious instruction and the public schools and the 1947 NCRAC executive council session called to debate the merits of joint participation in the *McCollum* case, the ADL's aversion to such legal remedies grew even stronger. Like his counterparts at the AJCommittee, Frank Trager, who directed the ADL's national efforts to promote intercultural awareness, believed that education offered a much stronger tool than litigation to address the "sectarian aspects of the [released-time] problem."[20] Trager, like Gutstadt, maintained that, from the perspective of public relations and simple self-interest, support for "cultural pluralism" was preferable to joining any effort to have released time declared unconstitutional. The major Jewish organizations courted disaster if they ignored the vital role of the religious tradition in American culture. Warned Trager:

> Make no mistake about it: Protestant America is determined, wrongly or rightly, to press this issue at this time. For reasons peculiar to itself, Catholic America is going along with Protestant America. This is the argument from a public relations point of view, which I could ignore if I did not truly believe that principle here supports expediency. We can afford to search out ways and means because we stand for sound principles in the field of social relations, principles derived from the theory and practice of cultural pluralism applied in the schools in terms of intercultural

education, education which welcomes the *whole* child and *all* aspects of community living.[21]

But much to their chagrin, the AJCommittee and the ADL found no support for their position within the NCRAC. Nor was sympathy forthcoming from the Synagogue Council of America, the umbrella representative of the Orthodox, Conservative, and Reform sects on the rabbinic and congregational levels, which had agreed as well to appear on the brief submitted in *McCollum*. The NCRAC's decision to participate as an amicus curiae in *McCollum* despite their protests left the ADL and the AJCommittee with two choices: to disassociate themselves with the NCRAC and thereby harbor the distinction of being the only two major American Jewish organizations not to appear on the brief or to put aside their objections and join the cause. Neither choice was especially attractive. But aware of the potential embarrassment, not to mention the negative political consequences, that would almost certainly result if they did not participate in what was otherwise a consensus decision by the nation's major American Jewish organizations, the AJCommittee and the ADL put aside their doubts about the wisdom of such an effort and joined in signing the NCRAC brief.[22]

Even so, the AJCommittee and the ADL held onto the hope that they could persuade the other constituent organizations within the NCRAC to hoe a moderate line. Neither the AJCommittee nor the ADL felt that it was in the best interests of American Jews to be perceived as rushing to support a professed atheist's attack on the well-established practices of the Protestant and Catholic majorities in the public schools. They accordingly argued that the NCRAC's brief should keep these considerations in mind. But whatever hopes the AJCommittee and the ADL held that such a temperate view would prevail among the major Jewish organizations were soon dashed when the NCRAC executive council voted to give the AJCongress, and thus Leo Pfeffer, the primary responsibility for drafting the *McCollum* brief.

Pfeffer's memoranda on released time and his subsequent , *Religion and the Public Schools*, which had received wide distribution among the major Jewish organizations prior to the NCRAC's decision to participate in *McCollum*, left no doubt about where he stood on the constitutionality of such programs. Pfeffer had used his chance assignment, when he joined the legal staff of the AJCongress in 1945, to investigate released-time practices in the public schools to cultivate an expertise on church-state issues. Of equal importance in his initial rise to prominence within the organized Jewish community was the fact that Pfeffer was the only professional staff member with legal expertise from the AJCongress, the AJCommittee, or the ADL to have developed such a single-minded focus on church-state issues. Compared to his colleagues at the AJCommittee and the ADL, Pfeffer's legal expertise on church-state issues was so authoritative that it would have been almost incomprehensible to consider giving anyone else primary responsibility to craft the NCRAC's amicus brief in *McCollum*. And while the ADL and the AJCommittee would continue to profess their uneasiness over Pfeffer's evolving "absolutism" on the establishment clause and his eagerness to confront the nation's major Christian denominations on such controversial matters, no professional in either group could match Pfeffer's intellectual dominance over the legal and constitutional issues at stake in the debate over released time. Thus the AJCommittee and the ADL were again forced to defer their objections to Pfeffer's selection as lead counsel on the *McCollum* brief since there was no larger support for their position within the NCRAC.

The released-time program challenged in *McCollum* was familiar to the AJCongress, the AJCommittee, and the ADL because it was among those that Pfeffer had described as constitutionally suspect in *Religion and the Public Schools.*"[23] To Pfeffer and the AJCongress, *McCollum* presented a classic case of the inescapable establishment clause trap into which released-time programs were destined to fall. Since 1940 the school district in question, located in Champaign, Illinois, had permitted Catholic, Protestant, and Jewish religious instructors, usually local clergy, to offer classes to public school students on campus during a period set aside during the regular school day. Students were not required to attend these classes. But the attendance of those who did was monitored by school administrators, whereas those students who declined to participate in released-time instruction were obliged to attend their regular classes. In Pfeffer's legal opinion, these facts made the subsequent argument quite clear: Champaign's support and direct assistance for religious education on the public school's watch violated the establishment clause.

While conceding Pfeffer's and the AJCongress's point on the constitutional problems with the Champaign program, the AJCommittee and the ADL saw in *McCollum* another dilemma that should be weighed carefully against the establishment clause concerns. The ADL, in particular, believed that what it called the "public relations" factors in *McCollum* might not warrant the nation's major Jewish organizations taking such an aggressive approach. Gutstadt warned his ADL colleagues prior to their final decision to enter the Champaign case of the risks inherent in supporting the claim of Vashti McCollum—who, he reminded them, had argued in her original complaint that religion was the opiate of the masses and a virus injected into the minds of public school children. Gutstadt also reminded them of how, in such an atmosphere, the basic issue upon which the original trial should have been based had already been buried beneath the outrage of an "aroused populace of the state of Illinois against a Communist attempt to do away with religious instruction."[24] How possibly could the interests of American Jews be advanced if their major representative bodies lined up behind someone like Vashti McCollum in the nation's highest Court at the expense of their need to maintain the support and goodwill of their Protestant and Catholic "allies"? Could the NCRAC's interests be served by walking on such delicate public-relations eggshells? Gutstadt, as well as high-level officers within the AJCommittee, insisted that Pfeffer make clear in the NCRAC's amicus brief the contempt with which American Jews viewed McCollum's atheism.[25]

Although Pfeffer did not agree with the AJCommittee and the ADL that there was any real need to draft such a disclaimer, one was included to ease their general discomfort of having to participate in *McCollum*. Into the brief's "Interest of the Amici" section, Pfeffer inserted what could almost be characterized as a disclaimer, writing that:

> We wish to make clear our regret that the appellant chose to use the case as a medium for the dissemination of her atheistic beliefs and injected into the record the irreligious statements it contains. We wish not only to disassociate ourselves completely from the anti-religious views of the appellant, but wish to deplore the fact that the sponsors of the original petition chose the case as a means of inscribing such matter on the public record and confusing the basic issues in the case by dragging into it the unrelated issues of atheism vs. religion.[26]

But in the same section Pfeffer countered this concession to the AJCommittee and the ADL with language of his own, stating that the principles at stake in *McCollum* required that "Jews overcome [their] natural reluctance to join in a case of which the record is replete with anti-religious matter . . . because the importance of the issues to Jews requires intercession regardless of the risk of defamation."[27] Pfeffer also included in the "Interest of the Amici" section a reference to evidence presented in the trial record that teachers in Catholic and Protestant released-time religion classes had on occasion taught that Jews were responsible for Christ's crucifixion, which resulted in the stigmatization of Jewish students.[28] This was a clear shot at what Pfeffer believed was the "cowardice" manifested by the AJCommittee and the ADL when it came to asserting their constitutional rights as Jews.

With the internal politics now resolved, at least for the moment, Pfeffer turned to the constitutional issues raised by the Champaign released-time program. Pfeffer's argument in *McCollum* built on the themes that he had first articulated in his original 1945 memorandum on released time for the AJCongress and then later in *Religion and the Public Schools*. The Champaign school district, Pfeffer argued, was in direct violation of the establishment clause because it essentially compelled school children to participate in religious instruction in the public schools. That compulsion resulted from the coercive atmosphere that was created when public school teachers and religious authorities joined together to pressure students to attend the on-campus religious classes. For one thing, such pressure induced students to attend religious classes when they might otherwise not want to do so. Perhaps even more to the point, it also encouraged students to attend classes outside their true religious faith for fear of being harassed or ridiculed, a situation that was most prevalent among Jewish students. But regardless of whether one combined or singled out these various considerations, the NCRAC brief argued, the conclusion was inescapable: school districts that participated in released time were providing financial and institutional support for the advancement of religious education in their classrooms, and such efforts violated the establishment clause.[29] For the NCRAC, as well as the other parties that participated as amici curiae in *McCollum*, it now remained to see whether the Court would condone released-time programs as the equivalent of public subsidies to religious schools—since their purpose was to aid the child and not the church, as the briefs of the Champaign school district and their amici argued—or view them as state support for religion and thus in violation of the establishment clause.

In handing down its verdict on *McCollum*, the Court followed the broad interpretation that it had given the establishment clause in *Everson*. But here the Court avoided the inexplicable, and logically inconsistent, about-face of that decision and instead struck down, by a vote of eight to one, the Champaign released-time program as unconstitutional state support for religion. Justice Black, who had authored the Court's much maligned opinion in *Everson*, this time made clear that no such confusion would detract from the business at hand in *McCollum*. Again writing the majority opinion, Justice Black stated that the Champaign released-time program was "beyond all question a utilization of the tax-established and tax-supported public school system to aid religious groups to spread their faiths. And it falls squarely under the ban of the First Amendment (made applicable to the states by the Fourteenth) as we interpreted it in *Everson v. Board of Education.*" Continued Justice Black: "Here not only are [the] state's tax-supported public school buildings used for the dissemination of religious doctrines. The State also affords sectarian groups an invaluable aid in that it helps to provide pupils for their religious classes through use of the state's public school machinery. This is not separation of Church and State." [30]

Concurring, Justice Frankfurter—joined by Justices Jackson and Rutledge, both of whom had written quite critical dissents in *Everson*—wrote that "the fact that [state] power has not been used to discriminate [in the administration of released time] is beside the point. Separation is a requirement to abstain from fusing functions of Government and of religious sects, not merely to treat them all equally." [31] Justice Frankfurter emphasized that the establishment clause did not, in contrast to the state's assertion, permit nonpreferential government support for and aid to religion. The clause, Justice Frankfurter argued, was intended to prevent government "inculcation of the religious tenets of some religious faiths, and in the process sharpens the consciousness of religious differences at least among some of the children committed to its care. These . . . are precisely the consequences against which the Constitution was directed when it prohibited the Government common to all from becoming embroiled, however innocently, in the destructive religious conflicts of which the history of even this country records some dark pages." [32] Together, Justice Black's majority opinion and Justice Frankfurter's concurrence left little doubt that the Court had rejected the old arguments on behalf of a nonpreferential interpretation of the establishment clause in favor of the principles articulated in *Everson* and *McCollum* that instead advocated strict limits on government power to aid and support private religion.

Not surprisingly, *McCollum* was received with mixed reviews among the religious and secular organized interests that had participated as amici in the litigation. This time, however, the reaction of the interested parties was reversed. Their internal differences aside, the AJCommittee, the AJCongress, and the ADL all hailed *McCollum* as a "milestone on the road to a full application of the traditional American principle of the separation of church and state." While there is no concrete evidence to support their contention that *McCollum* "followed closely the arguments advanced in the brief filed as 'friends of the court' by the constituent organizations of the SCA and NCRAC," the major Jewish organizations did believe that their presence had influenced the Court's opinion on the invidious nature of released time.[33] To bolster their claim, the AJCongress, the AJCommittee, and the ADL cited the footnote in Justice Frankfurter's concurrence that referred to "the divergent views expressed in the briefs submitted here in behalf of religious organizations, as *amicus curiae*," which "in themselves suggest that the movement has been a divisive and not an irenic influence in the Community."[34]

Catholic organizations, which had feared that Justice Black's lengthy dicta in *Everson* might soon pilot the Court's establishment clause jurisprudence, condemned *McCollum* as an irresponsible decision that cast aside with little remorse the custom and tradition that permitted the nation's public schools to accommodate and encourage the religious education of their students. But what made the attendant political reaction from *McCollum* so unusual was, as Robert Drinan later pointed out, the decision's ironic effect of reconciling the nation's leading Protestant denominational bodies—which had denounced *Everson* as a triumph for "the evil designs of the Catholic Church to grab ahold of the public purse"—with their longtime Catholic adversaries.[35] These were the same Protestant denominational bodies that had come together after *Everson*, as described in chapter 2, to create a new organization, Protestants and Other Americans United for the Separation of Church and State, whose original, shrill anti-Catholic animus was unmistakable. In fact, the manifesto issued on behalf of POAU urged its new members to "call out and unite all patriotic citizens in a concerted effort to prevent the passage of any law by Congress which allots to church schools any portion of a federal appropriation for education, or which explicitly or implicitly permits the states to make such allotment of federal funds."[36] For the major denominational bodies of American Protestantism to join forces with their long-standing Catholic rivals to confront what the Jesuit magazine *America* later called a new alliance of "secular humanist" and Jewish organizations, an alliance determined to secularize American public education and to thwart even indirect assistance to private education, was nothing short of astonishing.[37]

But if *McCollum* confirmed the darkest fears of the Catholic Church, it also sent a disquieting message to the upper reaches of organized American Protestantism to the effect that the Court was no longer prepared to accept the long-established relationship between the nation's religious and civic institutions simply for tradition's sake. Whatever the future might hold for the relationship between religion and American public life, Christian America could be sure that after *Everson* and *McCollum* its cultural preeminence in the nation's most fundamental public institutions was no longer secure. Indeed, the Court's authoritative rejection of released time as a permissible instrument whereby public schools could advance religious education among their students inspired the AJCongress, and to a lesser extent the AJCommittee and the ADL, to confront other offensive religious practices in the public schools. Newly confident of litigation's power to redress the constitutional excesses of the political process, the major Jewish organizations now turned their attention to released time's cousin, off-campus "dismissed time" for religious instruction.

Zorach and Its Consequences

The AJCommittee, the AJCongress, and the ADL each heralded the *McCollum* decision as a significant step toward the full application of the establishment clause to intrusions of the separation principle into public education. Even the ADL and the AJCommittee, both of whom had had to be dragged into *McCollum*, celebrated the Court's clear-cut condemnation of the Champaign released-time program as unconstitutional. That Catholic and Protestant organizations viewed *McCollum* as a signal that religious Americans "must guard against the establishment of atheism" did not, in the phrase of an unsigned editorial in the Jesuit publication *America*, compel either organization to retreat into

their usual defensive posture or apologize for their position on released time.[38] Upon reflection, the ADL and the AJCommittee each
thought that the decision in *McCollum* was right—that it established
an important principle whose time had come. But *McCollum*, while
boosting their self-confidence, did not diminish their basic desire to
maintain diplomatic ties with the major organizational forces in the
Catholic and Protestant communities. *McCollum*, they concluded,
should be allowed to settle in. Rather than immediately engage in
more litigation to force compliance with the Court's decision, and thus
risk further antagonism, the ADL and the AJCommittee believed that
the next step for the major Jewish organizations should be to encourage a peaceful dissolution of released-time programs through community relations efforts. After all, as far as public relations were concerned, the fallout from *McCollum* would give the major Jewish
organizations enough to handle. With these considerations in mind,
the AJCommittee and the ADL had no real desire to turn around and
head right back into court, this time to attack dismissed time—a popular and in their view less offensive alternative to released time—as
unconstitutional.

Here, as in *McCollum*, the AJCongress found the caution exhibited
by the AJCommittee and the ADL more recreant than prudent. In particular, Leo Pfeffer, whose commitment to litigation as the foremost
vehicle through which to effect constitutional change had become even
more intractable, argued that *McCollum* had established a solid precedent on which to base an attack on dismissed time, a position that
enjoyed the complete backing of the AJCongress. So whether the AJ-
Committee and the ADL were willing to join forces with it or not, the
AJCongress was determined to move forward on dismissed time. But
for this next battle in the legal arena Pfeffer wanted to persuade the
NCRAC that, rather than waiting around for a suitable dismissed-time
case to be brought by someone else, the major Jewish organizations
should take the initiative and sponsor such a lawsuit independently.
Direct sponsorship would enable the NCRAC to exert control over the
litigation process from the start, allowing it to choose and develop a
test case that would merit Supreme Court review, an objective that
would not be possible if it confined itself to an amicus curiae role.

Moreover, in Pfeffer's opinion, the visible weight of the major national Jewish organizations behind such a case would send an even
stronger message to the Protestant and Catholic communities—and

perhaps the Court—to the effect that the major American Jewish organizations were determined to push for constitutional reform through
litigation themselves. This time, they would not wait for someone else
to do it for them.

Once again, Pfeffer's suggestion that the Jewish organizations resort
to litigation encountered initial resistance from the AJCommittee and
the ADL. In *McCollum* the AJCommittee and the ADL had been fearful
that mere participation in a case as an amicus curiae would cause an
increase in anti-Jewish sentiment. Surely, then, to sponsor litigation
against dismissed time, which neither organization believed was as
odious as released time, would make them even more vulnerable to
harsh criticism in the Protestant and Catholic press and quite possibly
do serious damage to interfaith relations for the foreseeable future. But
the AJCommittee and the ADL soon realized that, as in *McCollum*,
their position had no support within the NCRAC. Thus, they quickly
dropped their opposition to the notion of a dismissed-time lawsuit
and agreed to cooperate with the AJCongress's recommendation to the
NCRAC executive council to cosponsor such litigation—on the condition, however, that their respective agencies have some defined role in
the process.

To soothe their concerns, the AJCongress agreed to form a strategy
committee whose members, in addition to Leo Pfeffer and Shad Polier,
would include representatives of the AJCommittee and the ADL. The
AJCongress also agreed to accept their request for a non-Jewish individual to serve as the lawsuit's lead plaintiff, although it saw no need
for such a precaution. But to leave no doubt as to who would be in
charge, the AJCongress insisted that Pfeffer conduct the investigation
into dismissed-time practices and be responsible for assembling the
factual record to present at trial. Since an appeal was certain no matter
what the trial court ruled, the AJCongress further demanded that Pfeffer have responsibility for directing the appellate stages of the litigation as well, with assistance from the AJCommittee and the ADL only
if Pfeffer requested their help. In June 1948, just three months after
McCollum was decided, the AJCommittee, the AJCongress, and the
ADL signed a joint memorandum at the annual NCRAC executive
council session, known in their subsequent correspondence as the "Atlantic City" agreement, that formally outlined these responsibilities.
With their respective demands satisfied, the three organizations could
now embark on what would become *Zorach v. Clausen*.[39]

In consultation with the ACLU, the Public Education Association, and the United Parents Association, each of whom would assist in the lawsuit, the three organizations settled on Tessim Zorach, the son of a Brooklyn sculptor, as lead plaintiff. Because Pfeffer wanted to have as much control as possible in building the case's factual record, the AJCommittee, the AJCongress, and the ADL agreed to seek out a local plaintiff to challenge New York City's dismissed-time program. Working in New York would make it easier to investigate dismissed-time practices, build a factual record, assemble affidavits and select witnesses, and respond to the day-to-day problems that arise in complex lawsuits without the burden of travel or the incurring of needless financial expenses. But far more important in Pfeffer's calculations were the resemblances that the New York City program had to the Champaign plan struck down in *McCollum*. Like the Champaign plan, the New York City Board of Education allowed religious organizations to cooperate with public schools in setting up a dismissed-time program; permitted such instruction to take place during normal school time; and required school administrators to monitor the student's presence or absence from religious instruction.[40] From Pfeffer's point of view, the Champaign and New York plans, with the exception of the latter's use of off-campus locations instead of on-site public school facilities for religious instruction, were thus virtually indistinguishable.

The next phase in the lawsuit's preparation involved the selection of the lead plaintiffs and the preparation of the trial record. Frederick C. McLaughlin, the executive director of the Public Educational Association, had suggested Tessim Zorach to Clifford Forster, the executive director of the ACLU, before the AJCommittee, the AJCongress, and the ADL had reached their formal agreement to pursue the lawsuit.[41] Forster, in turn, passed along McLaughlin's recommendation to Pfeffer, who submitted Zorach's name to the NCRAC strategy committee for approval. Zorach was especially attractive to the AJCommittee and the ADL because he was an Episcopalian active in church affairs. McLaughlin pointed out that, while Zorach's father, a well-known New York sculptor, had "been identified with left-wing groups, the son has no such record. He is presently employed by the Eastern Cooperative Wholesale, and the coops have been one group shunned and disdained by the Communists in this country."[42] Zorach's religious background and good standing in the community mitigated the concern of the AJCommittee and the ADL that another atheist with communist sympathies, like Vashti McCollum, would end up as the symbolic leader of the charge against the traditional religious practices of the Catholic and Protestant establishments. To strengthen the trial record, the AJCongress recruited a second plaintiff from within their local membership, Esta Gluck, but even this did not bother the AJCommittee and the ADL as long as Zorach's name identified the lawsuit.[43]

Public relations concerns and nervousness over the arousal of anti-Jewish sentiment also drove the second major strategic decision behind *Zorach's* conception. As part of the Atlantic City agreement, the AJCongress acceded not only to the request of the AJCommittee and the ADL that the principal litigants be non-Jewish, but that a non-Jewish organization, represented by a non-Jew, serve on paper as lead counsel in the dismissed-time case. Although the Jewish organizations would build the case, write the briefs and, in consultation with whoever "represented" Zorach, direct the litigation, their names would not go into the public record. Pfeffer was not pleased with this compromise, since he had conceived of the dismissed-time challenge before *McCollum* was even decided and envisioned *Zorach* as the chance to enhance his and the AJCongress's reputation as important forces in church-state litigation. But the AJCommittee and the ADL argued that Pfeffer had already accomplished that goal in *McCollum*—and in the process had set both himself and the AJCongress up as major targets of Catholic and Protestant criticism. For those reasons, as well as to keep the peace among the major Jewish organizations, Pfeffer reluctantly agreed to delegate the formal task of representation to Kenneth Greenawalt, a young Wall Street lawyer who had written the ACLU's amicus brief in *McCollum*. The ACLU's name also would appear on the principal briefs in *Zorach,* but Pfeffer, not Greenawalt, would actually prepare the case and outline the appellate stages of the litigation.[44] Thus, to shield the involvement of the AJCommittee, the AJCongress, and the ADL, the ACLU and Greenawalt appeared as the parties of record on behalf of the plaintiff, but it was the major Jewish organizations that designed and directed *Zorach.*

Pfeffer's brief for the New York trial court in *Zorach* stressed two major points, each of which centered on the inherent constitutional frailties of religious education that was conducted with governmental cooperation, regardless of whether such instruction took place on or off public school grounds. Pfeffer set up his case in *Zorach* by first arguing that the decision in *McCollum* had essentially declared all released-time programs to be unconstitutional. If released time was unconstitutional per se, as Pfeffer argued it was, then variations on that same theme most likely suffered from defects similar to those of the program invalidated in *McCollum.* This argument was a reach, and Pfeffer knew it, but he wanted to get it on record regardless of whether the lower courts would issue a favorable ruling so that ultimately the Supreme Court might consider it on appeal. Second, and more to the point, Pfeffer argued that the manner in which New York City operated its dismissed-time program was unconstitutional. Even though religious instruction under the New York City plan took place off campus, the state was still using its educational machinery to coerce schoolchildren through subtle, and in some cases not-so-subtle, methods to participate in dismissed-time education. The *Zorach* brief presented ample evidence, consisting of sworn statements and affidavits from parents, students, public schoolteachers, and even religious instructors collected by the AJCommittee during the investigation and fact-finding stage, that students who did not participate in the program were often subjected to ridicule by their classmates and, on occasion, by their teachers as well.[45] In general, the brief argued, the New York City school system had forged an unconstitutional alliance with area religious schools who wished to advance their interests in sectarian education. Worse yet, it had also created a coercive environment in which this all took place.

Despite what the major Jewish organizations believed was a strong factual and constitutional case, the New York trial court ruled to uphold New York City's dismissed-time program. The lower court gave scant attention to the factual record in *Zorach* that highlighted the alleged abuses in the operation of the dismissed-time program. Rather than pass judgment on the narrow question of whether New York City's dismissed-time program was unconstitutional as applied, the lower court instead focused on the broader contention raised in the plaintiff's brief—that the purpose and intent of dismissed time and released time were identical and hence, given the Court's analysis in *McCollum,* unconstitutional. Here, the lower court found the constitutional issues insignificant, concluding that the evidence presented in the plaintiff's brief amounted to nothing more than minor inconveniences that did not impugn the dismissed-time program.

On the constitutional question, the court held that dismissed time, in contrast to the released-time program struck down in *McCollum*, did not violate the establishment clause. No public school classrooms were used for religious instruction; no public school openly encouraged participation in dismissed time; and, despite the plaintiff's assertion to the contrary, no public school had created a coercive atmosphere that resulted in what was basically state sponsorship of sectarian objectives. The lower court concluded that released-time and dismissed-time programs bore substantial enough differences to each other so as to allow the latter to survive.[46] To worsen matters, the lower court judge excluded the affidavits from the students, parents, and teachers from the appeals proceedings, a decision that made it even more difficult to support the plaintiff's claim that dismissed time was unconstitutional in practice as well as in conception.[47] The lower court's decision was affirmed by divided courts in the New York appellate division and court of appeals.[48]

The major Jewish organizations and their cosponsors had not, however, expected to prevail in the New York courts. Indeed, it was on the assumption of an adverse decision in *Zorach* that they had developed their litigation strategy. As we have noted, their ultimate objective was not a final resolution of the case in the New York courts, but, through a judicious, step-by-step process, a decision from the United States Supreme Court that would extend the principles of *McCollum* to dismissed-time programs. Thus Pfeffer's two-tiered argument in *Zorach*—addressing the broad constitutional question of whether dismissed-time was unconstitutional per se and the narrower issue of whether New York City's program, as administered, contravened *McCollum's* requirement that public schools not cooperate with religious institutions to encourage students to participate in religious education—were designed to pique the Court's attention. So when the Court decided to hear *Zorach* during its 1951 term, Pfeffer considered this development as more than just a vindication of the litigation strategy he had conceived when the major Jewish organizations first considered a dismissed-time lawsuit in June 1948. More important, it offered a premier chance to broaden the scope of the Court's establishment clause jurisprudence even further.

Given the stakes now involved, Greenawalt proposed to Pfeffer that perhaps it would strengthen their case if they divided the responsibility for oral argument. Much as Pfeffer wanted to accept this invitation, the AJCommittee and the ADL rejected Greenawalt's suggestion for the same reasons they originally had agreed to participate in the lawsuit: neither organization wanted Pfeffer's name or that of a Jewish organization identified with the lead plaintiff.[49] For the sake of appearances, then, Pfeffer had little choice but to remain in the background, although he still was responsible for the plaintiff's briefs on which Greenawalt's name appeared. But on Pfeffer's suggestion, the AJCommittee and the ADL did agree to coauthor, in conjunction with the AJCongress, an additional amicus brief on behalf of the NCRAC and the Synagogue Council of America. The preparation of this brief would be a collaborative effort among the lawyers from all three agencies that served on the NCRAC strategy committee.[50] In their view, the joint amicus brief they had submitted in *McCollum* had weighed fairly heavily on the justices' conclusion that released time divided rather than united the nation's major religious denominations. The AJCommittee, the AJCongress, and the ADL, along with the other constituent organizations in the NCRAC and the SCA, consequently believed that a similar submission from them on the issue of dismissed time could have a crucial influence on the Court's decision in *Zorach*.

But rather than strike down dismissed-time instruction as an unconstitutional alternative to released time, the Court instead voted six to three to uphold the rulings of the lower courts. Indeed, it used *Zorach* to retreat from the broad establishment clause principles that it had articulated in *McCollum*. Writing for the Court, Justice William O. Douglas, a member of the eight-person majority in *McCollum*, declared:

> We would have to press the concept of separation of Church and State to . . . extremes to condemn the present law on constitutional grounds. We are a religious people whose institutions presuppose a Supreme Being. When the state encourages religious instruction or cooperates with religious authorities by adjusting the schedule of public events to sectarian needs, it follows the best of our traditions. For it then respects the religious nature of our people and accommodates the public service to their spiritual needs. To hold that it may not would be to find in the Constitution a requirement that the government show a callous indifference to religious groups. That would be preferring those who believe in no religion over those who do believe.[51]

In language carefully chosen to set apart released time's constitutional infirmities from the provisions of New York City's plan, Justice Douglas concluded that the government

> may not coerce anyone to attend church, to observe a religious holiday, or to take religious instruction. But it can close its doors or suspend its operations as to those who want to repair to their religious sanctuary for worship or instruction. No more than that is undertaken here. In the *McCollum* case the classrooms were used for religious instruction and the force of the public schools was used to promote that instruction. Here, as we have said, the public schools do no more than accommodate their schedules to a program of outside religious instruction. We follow the *McCollum* case. But we cannot expand it to cover the present released-time program unless separation of Church and State means that public institutions can make no adjustments of their schedules to accommodate the religious needs of the people. We cannot read into the Bill of Rights such a philosophy of hostility to religion.[52]

Not surprisingly, Justice Douglas's opinion devastated the major Jewish organizations. They had anticipated that the Court, having sealed in hermetic fashion the fate of released-time plans in *McCollum*, would be prepared to extend the principles articulated therein to off-campus instruction. Much to their dismay, in *Zorach* the Court instead took a giant and unexpected step backwards from its previous decisions, even though these had appeared to promise a bolder future commitment to separationist principles in its establishment clause jurisprudence.

Among those dissenting was Justice Black, whose opinion in *McCollum* all but constituted an outright admission of error in *Everson*.[53] Black now charged that New York City had done through its program precisely what the Court had ruled government could not do in the original released-time case: manipulate its compulsory education laws in such a way as to "channel children into sectarian classes."[54] Wrote Justice Black:

> Here the sole question is whether New York can use its compulsory education laws to help religious sects get attendants presumably too unenthusiastic to go unless moved to so by the pressure this state machinery. That this is the plan, purpose, design, and consequence of the New York program cannot be denied.

The state thus makes religious sects beneficiaries of its power to compel children to attend secular schools. In considering whether a state has entered this forbidden field the question is not whether it has entered too far but whether it has entered at all. New York is manipulating its compulsory education laws to help religious sects get pupils. This is not separation but combination of Church and State.[55]

Justice Jackson was even less impressed by the Court's effort to finesse the differences between released and dismissed time. In language as caustic as this usually most literate of jurists ever used, Justice Jackson commented:

It takes more subtlety of mind than I possess to deny that this [dismissed time] is governmental constraint in support of religion. . . . The distinction attempted between *McCollum* and this [case] is trivial, almost to the point of cynicism, magnifying its nonessential details and disparaging compulsion which was the underlying reason for invalidity. A reading of the Court's opinion in that case along with its opinion in this case will show such difference of overtones and undertones as to make clear that the *McCollum* case has passed like a storm in a teacup. The wall which the Court was professing to erect between Church and State has become even more warped and twisted than I expected. Today's judgment will be more interesting to students of psychology and of the judicial processes than to students of constitutional law.[56]

Needless to say, the AJCommittee, the AJCongress, and the ADL were gratified that Justices Black and Jackson—and, in a separate dissent, Justice Frankfurter—agreed with the position set forth in their briefs that the New York City program possessed all the unconstitutional qualities of the released-time program invalidated in *McCollum*. But the opinions of three dissenting justices were of little consolation when compared to the Court's majority ruling in *Zorach*. Pfeffer was especially stung by the Court's decision since he, more than anyone else, had prodded the major Jewish organizations into resorting to litigation to challenge the New York City dismissed-time program. In *McCollum*, the Court had issued an opinion that made good on the expansive establishment clause principles it articulated but then pulled back from in *Everson*. Thus, and reasonably enough, Pfeffer believed that *McCollum* created a more hospitable litigation environment for a second released-time case that would center on state-supervised off-campus instruction—in other words, a case like *Zorach*.

When one considers the two central principles that emerge in the Court's analytical framework in *McCollum*—whether tax-financed properties were used for religious instruction and whether the state's coercive hand had encouraged participation in religious activities— the decision of the major Jewish organizations to pursue the *Zorach* litigation makes good sense. Such a case was indeed the next logical step in their legal efforts to sever the cooperative relationship between the public schools and local churches that had long been used to ad- vance sectarian religious education. Their failure to persuade the Court to consider dismissed time a poor substitute for in-school released time and thus strike it down as violating the establishment clause did not, one can argue, result from a mismanaged litigation strategy or poorly conceived and executed constitutional arguments. The subse- quent revolution in the Court's establishment clause jurisprudence over the next two decades would make *Zorach* an anachronism. But, with their hopes pinned high on *McCollum's* promise, the AJCom- mittee, the AJCongress, and the ADL were naturally disheartened by Justice Douglas's opinion in *Zorach,* complete with its references to America's tradition as a "religious people whose institutions presup- pose a Supreme Being." His gavel crashed down on the still embryonic litigation campaign of the major Jewish organizations to reform the Court's extant establishment clause jurisprudence with a loud and un- mistakable thud, leaving them confused and in internal disarray over what, if anything, to do next.

From Cooperation to Conflict

The ties that had bound the major Jewish organizations together in their initial ventures into the realm of church-state litigation began to unravel in *Zorach's* wake. Ever since the NCRAC's coalescence in the late 1940s, the AJCommittee, the ADL, and the AJCongress had agreed to a marriage of convenience, one rooted in a concern for public ap- pearances and a once-common interest in concealing their pronounced philosophical differences from Christian America. But almost from the start, tension rather than accord dominated their internal relations re- garding what constituted appropriate policy and the most productive strategies for advocacy. The three groups differed over what the proper objectives to pursue on church-state problems were, whether litigation was an effective vehicle with which to correct constitutional deficiencies in the law and its application, and how to divide organizational responsibilities so as to represent the complete interests of the American Jewish community. The once strong but nonthreatening rivalries that had existed among the major Jewish organizations—each of whom wished to claim the mantle of the "true" representative of the American Jewish community in politics and public affairs—had, since the NCRAC's creation, devolved into an entrenched bilateral struggle between the AJCommittee and the ADL, on the one hand, and, on the other, the AJCongress for the Jewish community's allegiance and in turn their financial and political support. These differences, as we saw earlier in this chapter, became more pronounced during the debates over whether to participate in *McCollum*. But it was *Zorach*'s failure, and the events leading up to it, that finally led the AJCommittee and the ADL to break from the NCRAC and, by default, from the AJCongress.

While *Zorach* facilitated this split, the AJCommittee and the ADL had always struggled with their defined role in the NCRAC, in both a policy-making and a strategic context. Each group resented the NCRAC's decision, as expressed through its constituent organizations at the national and local levels, to make the AJCongress the de facto legal counsel for the American Jewish community in the church-state arena. The AJCommittee and the ADL believed that the AJCongress's anointment sent a clear message to their respective organizations that litigation, rather than improved community relations, education, or "insider" lobbying, had been chosen as the prime mechanism with which to effect constitutional changes concerning the place of religion in American public life. It was a decision they were reluctant to accept from the start, and one that in *Zorach*'s shadow had become even more untenable. Neither the AJCommittee nor the ADL had ever been comfortable with the AJCongress's doctrinaire absolutism on the establishment clause; neither had agreed with its immediate emphasis on litigation as the most fruitful tactic with which to challenge discriminatory religious practices and education in the public schools. Their differences on these fundamental issues, all of which had taken root prior to *Everson*, had changed little in the interim.

Even while *Zorach*, backed by their cosponsorship, was in litigation, the AJCommittee and the ADL had reached a stalemate with the AJ-Congress over the contents of a major policy statement being prepared for release by the NCRAC that centered on whether public school authorities could take a religious census of their students. The ADL and the AJCommittee believed that, under certain conditions, instructors might have a sufficient reason for conducting a religious census in the classrooms. Such "appropriate" reasons included scheduling time off for religious holidays if necessary, making referrals to family agencies, or implementing a program of intercultural education. The ADL and the AJCommittee each strongly objected to the AJCongress's view that such information is "altogether beyond the cognizance of public school authorities."[57] Nor had either agency retreated from their stance endorsing the celebration of religious holidays in public schools as a useful educational forum through which to promote religious pluralism, although this additional—and long-standing—rift with the AJCongress was also kept quiet for the sake of appearances. For these reasons, and out of a desire to assert their independence, the AJCommittee and the ADL refused to sign on to the NCRAC's "Memorandum on Church Affiliation Census in the Public Schools," thereby signaling that they would, when possible, distance themselves from the establishment clause absolutism of AJCongress.

All this was just fine with the AJCongress and Pfeffer, who had been assiduously working ever since *Everson* to assert their firm control over the legal and public policy strategies of the major Jewish organizations in the church-state arena. Never convinced of the ADL and the AJCommittee's commitment to wholesale constitutional change, Pfeffer sought to harden the NCRAC's position on the establishment clause and encourage aggressive litigation to enforce it. He knew full well that such a tactical posture might well drive the AJCommittee and the ADL out of the admittedly fragile NCRAC coalition—but such a development would have the distinct advantage of giving the AJCongress sole command over the policy-making structure of the NCRAC and over subsequent church-state litigation and other enforcement strategies. In response to the ADL's and the AJCommittee's complaint to the NCRAC executive council on the position of the AJCongress on the religious census, Pfeffer and CLSA cocounsel Phil Baum replied with a stinging letter, which perhaps better than any other document of this period epitomized the fundamental philosophical differences between the three major Jewish agencies:

Those who like us for our position on the religious census will not like us less for this argument. And those who condemn us as godless atheists will not condemn us any the quicker. It is important that our brief impress courts, school boards, lawyers, all who may chance to read it, with the fact that there exists an inflexible legal mandate requiring that Church and State be kept scrupulously apart. . . . We cannot continue to win support if we become too queasy even to state our position. . . . In conclusion, the AJCommittee denies there is reason to fear that data on religious affiliation may be used improperly in the schools. It expresses confidence that parents and school boards themselves "will know how to deal with public school officials who misuse their trust." . . . [But] the mere fact that we require legal memoranda on the distribution of Gideons' Bibles, on the circulation of religious questionnaires in the public schools and on other related incidents, is sufficient indication that we cannot comfortably delegate this problem to local authority. More is at stake here than a few paragraphs in a legal memorandum, else we should not have taken so much space and so much time. *There is at stake here a basic attitude on the part of the American Jewish community.* To us, that attitude is important.[58]

In addition to the original philosophical differences resulting from the social, political, ethnic, and class differences in the constituencies of American Jewry that the AJCommittee, the AJCongress, and the ADL had been formed to represent, internal forces of more recent vintage had begun to exacerbate organizational tensions. Thus their policies and strategies had been and would continue to be shaped by their varying perceptions of and reaction to external considerations—such as the Court's evolving position on specific legal doctrines, the reaction of Protestant and Catholic groups to their actions, and public opinion at large. By now, though, the degree of importance that the AJCongress, the AJCommittee, and the ADL attached to litigation stemmed as well from the divergent professional socialization of their respective staffs. Litigation as a vehicle for constitutional reform and innovative social change had become the paradigmatic norm within the AJCongress, which was propelled by its CLSA and the lawyers who dominated the staff in both numbers and influence. Will Maslow and Alexander Pekelis (who together created the CLSA in 1945), Leo Pfeffer, and Shad Polier were all firmly committed to law and litigation as the most effective means to bring about social change. Through their influence and conviction, they had successfully made legal reform the model on which the AJCongress built its organizational strategies and public policy agenda.

But the legal culture never came to exercise such influence over the AJCommittee and the ADL because their staffs, as well as their policy-making hierarchies, were never dominated by attorneys who embraced the activist litigation model of public interest law. To illustrate, while the AJCongress's New York–based CLSA legal staff grew from seven to ten between 1945 and 1952 and its regional offices hired staff attorneys to monitor local developments, the AJCommittee retained just one full-time lawyer, Ed Lukas, to act as director of its legal department, which it created in 1947. The ADL did not even create an in-house legal department until 1954; until then, Sol Rabkin, a community relations professional with a background in the law, served as its legal emissary to the NCRAC. The organizational norms of both the ADL and the AJCommittee were still rooted in the community relations model, which emphasized multicultural education, interfaith cooperation and networking, and elite-level negotiations over litigation and legal remedies. Thus, their preferences with regard to staff leaned toward sociologists, professional educators, and social psychologists whose professional background comported with the organizational accent on the social relations model.

Contributing as well to this ever-widening cultural divide between the AJCongress's commitment to legal reform and the AJCommittee's and the ADL's joint preference for the social relations model was the uncontested emergence of Leo Pfeffer as the organized Jewish community's chief strategist on church-state issues. Tension was no stranger when it came to the working relationship between the AJCongress and the AJCommittee and ADL, but Pfeffer's insistence on exercising almost complete authority over the NCRAC's growing litigation agenda in church-state cases became harder and harder for the latter two organizations to accept. Throughout *Zorach,* they disagreed with the AJCongress over organizational responsibilities, strategic choices, and even how "absolute" their position on the establishment clause should be. Much of this disagreement was inspired by Pfeffer's attempts to wrest control from his rivals by downplaying, and often outright ignoring, their input into the case. In turn, the ADL and the AJCommittee

lodged numerous complaints with the NCRAC executive council accusing the AJCongress and Pfeffer of usurping their roles in *Zorach*. In
one such letter, Arnold Forster, the director of the ADL's national civil
rights division, complained that:

> Pfeffer's approach, his tendency to be a stickler for formality and
> to split hairs as to the precise meaning of our understanding, is
> regrettable; especially in view of the fact that he has failed to
> keep our agencies apprised of important developments in the
> case, and has even, on occasion, seen fit to argue in opposition to
> positions previously agreed on by our agencies.[59]

By *Zorach's* conclusion, relations between the AJCongress and the
AJCommittee and the ADL had deteriorated to a point where rapprochement was impossible. From start to finish, in fact, confrontation
had marred almost every aspect of their efforts in the case. At one
point, Pfeffer even vetoed the AJCommittee's draft of the final joint
memorandum intended for distribution to local chapters and community relations councils that summarized their respective contributions
to the litigation, even though the changes he demanded did not alter in
the slightest the substance of the document—although they certainly
clarified whatever ambiguities had existed concerning his leading
role.[60]

Still, *Zorach's* negative outcome did not tarnish Pfeffer's by now considerable reputation as a scholar-advocate in the church-state arena,
which had spread beyond the circle of major Jewish organizations. Indeed, early the following year saw the publication of the first edition
of his well-received *Church, State, and Freedom,* a comprehensive history
of church-state relations and law in the United States that would prove
to have considerable influence in the academic and legal communities
over the next several decades. Nor did *Zorach* diminish the AJCongress's enthusiasm for litigation and legal reform or cause it to consider
abandoning its absolutist stance on the establishment clause, whereas
the case inspired an altogether different reaction from the AJCommittee and the ADL. For them, *Zorach* sent an uncomfortable but
needed signal that it was time for them to reassert their identities as
distinct organizations—identities that had been built on their commitment to the social relations model—and above all their independence
from Pfeffer's strong arm and an AJCongress-dominated NCRAC.
Consequently, in late 1952 the ADL and the AJCommittee officially

broke their ties to the NCRAC and withdrew from active involvement in church-state litigation over the next few years in order to pursue other interests.

This left the AJCongress right where it wanted to be: in a position to cast the terms of debate in the church-state battles yet to come in the courts. With the AJCommittee and the ADL off on their own, Pfeffer was no longer constrained by the need to satisfy their demands. Released time had been dealt a powerful blow in *McCollum*, and the ruling in *Zorach* was narrow enough that it could not restore the old relationship between private religion and the public schools. Moreover, *Zorach* could not even save other time-honored practices in the public schools, such as teacher-led classroom prayer and Bible reading, from eventual extinction. These were next up on Pfeffer's litigation agenda, and he was determined to have the AJCongress lead the way, with or without the AJCommittee and the ADL behind him. Now it was matter of finding the right cases with which to proceed—and the patience with which to do so.

4

Separation to the Fore

Torcaso, Engel, Schempp,

and Beyond

As we have seen, *Zorach* marked a turning point in the relationship among the three major Jewish organizations. Well over a decade would pass before the AJCommittee, the AJCongress, and the ADL would again collaborate in church-state litigation at the level of the Supreme Court—and even then, they would limit their cooperation to participation as amici curiae.[1] Never again would the AJCommittee, the AJCongress, and the ADL combine forces to cosponsor a religion case, as they did in *Zorach*, whereas the AJCongress would sponsor numerous landmark church-state cases over the next several decades, either alone or in cooperation with other organizations such as the ACLU. The AJCommittee and the ADL would, however, limit their role in such litigation to participation as amici curiae: neither organization ever independently sponsored another church-state case decided by the Court. But the AJCommittee and the ADL's decision to confine their involvement in church-state litigation to a supportive role should not be construed as a sign of disinterest. Between 1947 and 1969 the AJCommittee and the ADL participated as amici curiae in more church-state cases at the Supreme Court level than any other organized interest except for the AJCongress and the ACLU, surpassing such groups as the United States Catholic Conference, the National Council of Churches, and Americans United for Separation of Church and State.[2] Compared to organized religious interests outside the Jewish community, then the AJCommittee and the ADL remained visible, active participants in the church-state battles that were taking up more and more space on the Court's docket of cases involving civil rights and liberties. For reasons that shall be explained later in this chapter, the AJCommittee and the ADL believed that their organizational objectives in the church-state arena could be accomplished through participation as amicus curiae and thus saw no need to compete or cooperate with the AJCongress to sponsor litigation.

Having departed from the NCRAC, the AJCommittee and the ADL, which had often joined forces in an effort to mitigate the AJCongress's growing dominance over the NCRAC's policy and strategy, were now free to pursue their own agenda without the need for compromise with or reciprocal obligation to their once (and future) rival. In contrast to the AJCongress, which pursued its church-state agenda with vigor throughout the 1950s, the AJCommittee and the ADL took a momentary respite from the religious wars in the courts. They would return to the national church-state stage only in the early 1960s, when the Court decided the historic cases that outlawed state-sponsored prayer and Bible recitation in the public schools.[3] But for much of the 1950s, the AJCommittee and the ADL, having now created a more explicit partnership to promote their civil rights and liberties agenda, concentrated their efforts on community relations activities with a view to promoting the Court's mandate on racial desegregation and stimulating Jewish involvement on behalf of the larger civil rights cause.[4] Religious issues were not ignored; indeed, each organization continued to monitor ongoing problems in the public schools. But the ADL and the AJCommittee were content, for the time, to resolve such controversies via their traditional tactics of social relations work, education programs, and interfaith negotiation.

Driven by Pfeffer's uncontested emergence as the organized Jewish community's preeminent scholar, advocate, and, despite *Zorach*, strategist on church-state relations, the AJCongress reaffirmed its commitment to effecting constitutional change through the legal reform model by developing an extensive program of law and litigation. Much of its immediate post-*Zorach* effort during the 1950s took place in state, not federal, courts. However, in no sense was the AJCongress's decision to use state courts a retreat from its commitment to establishment clause reform through the federal litigation process. Rather, it was a corollary strategy of attack intended to create additional opportunities for possible Supreme Court review.[5]

One such case to originate in a state court but whose aspirations were more ambitious was *Engel v. Vitale,* which contested the New York Board of Regents's power under the state constitution to compose and prescribe a nondenominational prayer for "voluntary" recitation in the public schools. While the AJCongress did not sponsor *Engel,* Pfeffer played an instrumental role behind the scenes directing the litigation strategy of the ACLU, which financed the case and provided lead counsel to the plaintiffs. Pfeffer also coordinated the submission of amicus curiae briefs by other supportive parties and, when the case reached the Supreme Court in 1962, wrote and submitted amicus briefs on behalf of the AJCongress and the NCRAC. A similar pattern is evident in *Abington v. Schempp,* decided the following year, in which the Court struck down state-sponsored "voluntary" Bible reading exercises in the public schools as violative of the establishment clause. *Schempp* was another instance in which Pfeffer controlled much of tactical and strategic decisions involved in the litigation process, although he appeared on record only as having submitted an amicus curiae brief on behalf of the AJCongress and the NCRAC. Other cases that Pfeffer and the AJCongress either sponsored or supported as an amicus curiae and that were crucial in setting the stage for the Court's establishment clause decisions of the 1960s abound.

What is remarkable about the AJCongress's decision to continue with its ambitious litigation campaign designed to attack settled religious practices in the public schools was not simply that it forged ahead despite the obstacle posed by the precedent set in *Zorach.* If anything, more striking is its willingness to proceed even in the face of the negative and often strident reaction that its participation in previous cases and its public statements on the separation of church and state had aroused in the Catholic and Protestant press. Shortly after *Zorach,* the Jesuit magazine *America* issued the first in what became a consistent line of critical editorials directed toward the major American Jewish organizations in general and Pfeffer and the AJCongress in particular, a practice that would continue up through the Court's decisions on school prayer and Bible reading.

The first shot was fired in response to a year-end resolution of the

AJCongress in which the organization, despite *Zorach*, reaffirmed its complete and uncompromising opposition to religious instruction in the public schools and government aid to private and parochial schools. *America* faulted the AJCongress for "taking issue with both the N[ational] C[ouncil] of C[hurches] and the Catholic hierarchy." Even more suspect, the editorial continued, was the Jewish organization's ideological distance from mainstream American public opinion on government accommodation for religion. Editorialized *America*: "The AJC[ongress] simply fails to join issue with the Christian, *and traditionally American*, position that if religion is indispensable to American society, then our public schools must somehow give instruction it. And if absolute 'separation' is the lesson of Jewish experience, it seems strange that the State of Israel did not adopt it. Christians have learned from history that absolute separation is the slogan of anti-religious government, the USSR's use of it being the most alarming example today."[6] Influential Protestant magazines expressed similar criticism but did so without the rhetorical coarseness exhibited by *America*.[7] Indeed, the Jesuit magazine developed an even more antagonistic editorial stance toward the major organizational representatives of American Jewry as the decade wore on.

Prominent conservative Jewish commentators also voiced dissent from the AJCongress's absolutist position on the separation principle and its equally steadfast determination to advance that vision through the legal reform model. Sociologist Will Herberg, the prominent academic whose 1955 book, *Catholic, Protestant, and Jew*, would profoundly influence the study of religious sociology in America, wrote in the AJCommittee's then still somewhat liberal magazine *Commentary*, that while it was possible to understand Jewish sympathies for a strict reading of the establishment clause, such a stance would not, over the long run, prove beneficial. "American Jews, even more than Protestants," Herberg wrote, "must rid themselves of the narrow and crippling minority-group defensiveness" that dominates the secular and religious bodies who claim to represent their "interests" in this pivotal national debate.[8] Herberg's criticism, however, must not be viewed as an extension of the AJCommittee's differences with the AJCongress. *Commentary*, like *Moment*, the other magazine published by the AJCommittee, retains editorial independence from whatever the official position the organization takes on a given public policy issue.[9]

Granted, Herberg's article did not represent dominant Jewish opinion on the separation of church and state. Nonetheless, that a respected Jewish scholar would publicly question the wisdom of the major Jewish organizations' commitment to separationism and the tenacity with which some, like the AJCongress, pursued their related objectives did nothing to encourage more accommodationist Jews to assert themselves on a constitutional matter of the utmost importance. Will Maslow later characterized the 1950s as a period of retrenchment for many American Jewish organizations. Their members were now more inclined toward a submissive attitude regarding the policy interests of the major Catholic and Protestant groups so as not to be considered unfaithful to America's stance as the defender of religion in the Cold War with the Soviet Union. This was the period when Congress enacted resolutions to inscribe "In God We Trust" on coinage and to insert "under God" into the Pledge of Allegiance, which was dutifully recited in the nation's public schools every morning. Thus, concerted opposition to state support for religious practices in the public schools required a certain boldness that several major Jewish organizations, such as the ADL and the AJCommittee, decided just was not worth the cost.[10]

But as the 1950s drew to a close, the AJCommittee and the ADL began to question how effective their emphasis on the social relations model had been in educating their Catholic and Protestant colleagues to their concerns—about the uncomfortable position that Jewish schoolchildren still found themselves in when teachers led Bible reading and prayer exercises before class each day, for example, or their objections to the religious tests still commonly administered to elected officials as a condition for holding state or local office. Progress had been made on Christmas and Easter celebrations in the public schools, not to proscribe their observance but to persuade principals and teachers to include Chanukah and Passover in their holiday calendar. Recognition of "multicultural pluralism," not a ban on the celebration of religious holidays, was what the AJCommittee and the ADL, in contrast to the AJCongress, had long advocated—and each group was glad for whatever improvements had been made on this front.

But despite repeated complaints from students and parents, the AJCommittee and the ADL could not persuade local school boards to cease their prayer or Bible reading periods. Nor had they been able to convince Protestant and Catholic groups that such practices raised serious constitutional problems, quite apart from the personal discomfort these customs caused for Jewish students or other students whose religious faith differed from mainline Christianity. Thus, while the AJ-Committee and the ADL still had some serious misgivings about what they perceived as the brazenness of the AJCongress's—and Pfeffer's—confrontational strategies and were still somewhat reluctant to be allied with their reputation as absolute separationists, they saw little choice but to support litigation, albeit as amici curiae, not sponsors, that challenged these practices in the courts. Gradually, then, they came to view education and interfaith negotiation as complements to—but not substitutes for—a program of law and litigation designed to vindicate their constitutional rights.

For most of the 1950s, though, Leo Pfeffer remained the dominant individual force in managing the flow of church-state litigation in state and federal courts intended to test the constitutionality of the religious oath requirement, school prayer, and Bible reading—a role Pfeffer retained well into the early 1970s. Moreover, by the late 1950s, Pfeffer had made the AJCongress into the unrivaled organizational force behind the mobilization of church-state litigation up the judicial ladder to the Supreme Court. No other organized interest active in this field, not even the ACLU, could then claim to match the combination of Pfeffer's expertise and the organizational commitment of the AJCongress to constitutional reform, with litigation as the chief weapon, of the law of church and state. The AJCongress used this mixture of staff expertise and organizational commitment to constitutional change through the litigation process in the three historic establishment clause cases decided by the Court in the early 1960s, all involving the appropriateness of government sponsorship of religious practices in various aspects of public life: *Torcaso v. Watkins, Engel v. Vitale*, and *Abington v. Schempp*. How it did so is the question to which this chapter now turns. In turn, this chapter will also examine the supportive and extralitigation efforts of the AJCommittee and the ADL in these cases, the points of cooperation and conflict between them and the AJCongress, and the external concerns—both political and legal—that influenced their individual and collective behavior.

Torcaso v. Watkins

Pfeffer had been hopeful, but never optimistic, that the Court would extend *McCollum*'s core principles to *Zorach*. He had even offered such a view when the major Jewish organizations, along with the ACLU, were considering whether to encourage the plaintiffs in *Doremus v. Board of Education*—a 1950 New Jersey case challenging two state statutes that required Bible reading and recitation of the Lord's Prayer in the public schools—to appeal their case to the Supreme Court.[11] As Pfeffer counseled the other Jewish agencies and the ACLU, it was not an opportune moment to present such emotional, as well as untested, issues to the Court, because of the "terribly effective job the Catholic church has done in making the *McCollum* decision unpopular," plus the Cold War environment. Not only were such conditions not conducive to the success of a lawsuit challenging Bible reading and prayer in the public schools, Pfeffer argued, but to give the Court a ready-made excuse to retrench on *McCollum* would mean suicide for the long-term agenda that the AJCongress and the ACLU had in mind for litigation designed to encourage the Court toward an even more expansive interpretation of the establishment clause in the future.[12]

The ACLU, however, ignored Pfeffer's advice and appealed the case up the judicial ladder—a decision, for reasons to be discussed below, that the AJCongress had no choice but to follow. But it ultimately confined its participation to filing an amicus brief with the Court asking it to declare such religious exercises unconstitutional, and it was the only Jewish organization to do so.

Later, to the relief of all the major Jewish organizations, the Court dismissed the case on procedural grounds, a ruling that had little constitutional significance or impact on policy because it simply left undisturbed a state supreme court decision. The Court's decision came as a great relief to Pfeffer, as well as the AJCommittee and the ADL, all of whom had foregone involvement prior to the litigation's appellate stages. I will have more to say about the importance of this case vis-à-vis the litigation and policy strategies pursued by the AJCongress, the AJCommittee, and the ADL on future cases involving in-school Bible reading and prayer. For now, though, the Court's unfavorable decisions in *Zorach* and *Doremus* discouraged whatever support existed for litigation designed to attack religious exercises in the public schools. Those concerns would be revisited, with much greater success, in the late 1950s and early 1960s.

But in the meanwhile, the AJCongress was still on the lookout for a case pertaining to the separation of church and state that would enable it to litigate a substantial establishment clause question, with the hope that the Court was now prepared to pick up where it had left off in *McCollum.* Evidence that the Court was again prepared to engage controversial issues that could result in bold and often unpopular decisions mounted in abundance as the 1950s pressed on. Besides the historic school desegregation decisions that began in 1954 with *Brown v. Board of Education,* the Court issued several opinions that broadened the rights of political dissenters, including avowed members of the American Communist Party and others under investigation by the Department of Justice, under the First and Fifth Amendments.[13] Backlash against the Court for the tenor of its decisions was considerable. Senator Joseph R. McCarthy, for example, declared that Chief Justice Earl Warren had become a "hero to the *Daily Worker*," a noted communist newspaper. Similarly, a report issued by the Senate Internal Security Subcommittee, whose charge it was to root out and investigate suspected communists in the government, media, and universities, attacked the Court as "an instrument of Communist global conquest."[14]

For the Court to receive such harsh criticism for its "Black Monday" and "Red Monday" decisions, as the critics called the school desegregation and right of conscience cases, and yet show no sign of buckling under encouraged the AJCongress to return to the federal litigation arena. Now all the AJCongress needed to do was find a suitable case. It would prefer one that presented a significant constitutional issue but did not raise further controversial questions pertaining to the Court's other recent civil rights and liberties decisions. That the Court had become more sympathetic to rights of unpopular individuals and classes in American society that had long been discriminated against did not automatically imply that the AJCongress, not usually an organization to back off when controversial issues were involved, wanted to count itself in such company. In *Torcaso v. Watkins,* the AJCongress found what it was looking for.

In July 1959 Pfeffer came across some information on the Religious News Service wire that he believed had the potential to make an excellent establishment clause test case. Citizens in Maryland could not become notary publics unless they professed a belief in God, a requirement that Pfeffer believed so fundamentally violated the principle of separation of church and state that the Court would have no choice but to accept the case and declare such a practice unconstitutional. From the outset, Pfeffer did not want to limit the AJCongress's involvement in *Torcaso* to participation as an amicus curiae. Prior litigation experience, staff resources, and his own expertise, Pfeffer declared, made "religious liberty . . . an area in which the AJCongress has established its leadership," adding that "I strongly recommend that we pursue this matter further for the purpose of seeing whether a legal suit to test the statute is practicable." Pfeffer suggested to Shad Polier that the Baltimore-Washington area office of the CLSA investigate the matter further. If the opportunity presented itself, the AJCongress should make an overture to Roy Torcaso and offer to sponsor the litigation.[15]

Prior to the AJCongress's intervention, Torcaso had already engaged the services of a private firm in Washington, Sickles and Sickles, to handle his case, albeit one that had no real experience in constitutional litigation, much less on church-state issues in particular. Joseph Sickles had agreed to handle the case on behalf of the ACLU's Washington chapter but was left largely on his own to craft the arguments with which to challenge Maryland's religious oath requirement for public office. Thus when Pfeffer offered to intervene and have the AJCongress assume chief responsibility for developing the legal strategy in *Torcaso* from the trial through the appellate stages, including the absorption of financial costs, Sickles, with Torcaso's permission, consented. Thus, while Pfeffer permitted Sickles to write the original drafts of the briefs in *Torcaso*, it was he who ultimately determined the content and direction of the arguments. In his original draft, Sickles emphasized that the establishment clause, which had been made applicable to the states through the Fourteenth Amendment, barred the use of religious tests as a prerequisite to assuming public office. But he did not mention the equal protection issues that Pfeffer believed were also important to the case. Since Maryland's oath requirement exhibited a preference for religion over nonreligion, Pfeffer argued that such a distinction violated the Fourteenth Amendment's equal protection clause as well. Nor did Sickle's initial brief illuminate for the Court the original intent of the test oath clause of Article VI of the Constitution, which explicitly bans religious tests as a requirement for holding public office. Pfeffer accordingly asked Sickles to incorporate these two changes into his original brief, and Sickles agreed. Thus the arguments based on the equal protection and test oath clauses, along with that relating to the establishment clause, became integral components of the Pfeffer-Sickles brief in *Torcaso* when it reached the Supreme Court.[16]

While Pfeffer and the AJCongress worked closely with Sickles and the ACLU to mobilize *Torcaso*, no such assistance was sought from the

AJCommittee or the ADL. Neither organization was invited to cosponsor the case or to participate through the submission of an amicus
brief. Even so, in December 1959, after the AJCongress had reached an
agreement with Sickles to lend its organizational sponsorship to the
case, the Washington office of the ADL considered whether to submit
an amicus brief on behalf of the local or national office in *Torcaso*. The
local trial court and intermediate appellate panel had held that to secure status as a notary public was not an inherent right but a privilege.
As such, Maryland could require that citizens who aspired to that office take a religious oath. The case had been set for argument before
the Maryland Court of Appeals, the state's court of last resort, and
did involve a fundamental principle of church-state separation. Several
active members of the ADL community in Washington had consequently urged the local executive committee (the leadership body
within each regional office that votes on policy issues and offers recommendations for appropriate organizational action to take on the local or national level) to consider the submission of an amicus brief on
behalf of the plaintiff in *Torcaso*.

By a two-to-one margin, though, the Washington-area ADL executive committee voted not to submit an amicus brief in *Torcaso*. Said
one influential committee member, whose comments, according to the
executive committee's chairman, exemplified the thinking of the majority: "In my opinion the situation is so obviously unjust and unconstitutional that there is no doubt that [Torcaso] will succeed in establishing
the point without the assistance of the ADL. On the other hand, *an
interference in the case might be misconstrued as an ungodly attitude and,
therefore, be inadvisable.*"[17] This recommendation was also forwarded by
the Washington office to the national office in New York, which de-
ferred to local opinion and refused to override its independent judgment. And once the ADL had formally decided not to enter the *Torcaso*
case, there was no chance that the AJCommittee would consider action
without the support of its civic defense partner. Besides, the Washington offices of the ADL and the AJCommittee counted several of the
same individuals on their respective policy-making and executive
committees, so the voice of one regarding litigation of potential interest
was often the voice of the other.

The reluctance of the ADL and the AJCommittee to engage in public
support for an admitted atheist's right to hold an office of public trust
did not surprise the AJCongress. Sandy Bolz, the Washington-area rep-

resentative of the AJCongress who had monitored the debate within the ADL and the AJCommittee over whether to intervene in *Torcaso*, commented to Pfeffer that the ADL's efforts to rationalize its decision to stay out were "self-explanatory" and characteristic of "the kind of fearful thinking that still pervades the ADL on such problems." But Bolz was not concerned that the support of the AJCommittee or the ADL was somehow essential to *Torcaso*'s chances for success when the litigation reached the state supreme court, or even the U.S. Supreme Court, a sentiment that Pfeffer and the national office shared. Rather, his comments were intended to reaffirm the AJCongress's opinion of itself—that it was the only major Jewish organization with the courage to wage important battles over fundamental principles of religious freedom in full public view.[18]

Over a year later Will Maslow made a similar point to the ADL's national executive director, Benjamin Epstein, after *Torcaso* had been argued before the Supreme Court but six weeks before the Court ruled that religious oaths were unconstitutional. An ADL newsletter had featured a prominent article on the *Torcaso* case touting the importance of the amicus brief that it and the AJCommittee had decided to submit when the Court granted certiorari to hear the case during the fall 1960 term. The article, however, mentioned nothing about the AJCongress or the ACLU, the organizations that had brought the case through the trial and intermediate appellate stages. Wrote Maslow to Epstein: "No one would ever know from reading [the] otherwise excellent article [on *Torcaso*] of the role played by the American Jewish Congress and the ACLU. Perhaps that fact is not of interest to your readers but to the professionals in the field it seems like a studied omission. I have always found that agencies that are strong psychologically or otherwise have no need to withhold such facts and I flatter myself that Congress rarely, if ever, does that."[19]

Maslow's criticisms notwithstanding, when *Torcaso* reached the Supreme Court, the ADL and the AJCommittee did participate as amici in support of the plaintiffs and enlisted the Unitarian Church as a cosigner as well, a rare departure from its then-standard practice of filing on behalf of themselves alone. The AJCongress and the ACLU did not encourage the other Jewish organizations to submit an amicus brief in support of their own efforts but welcomed it nonetheless. Theodore Leskes, the legal director of the AJCommittee, had earlier explained to Lawrence Speiser, who headed the ACLU's Washington office and had been involved in *Torcaso* on the local level, that his organization was hesitant to participate for much the same reason as his colleagues in the ADL when the case was still in the Maryland state courts. Speiser assured Leskes that the AJCommittee and the others could remain assured "as to which side [would] be the beneficiary of [their] *amicus* appearance."[20]

There was nothing controversial in their brief: their arguments virtually paralleled those set forth in Pfeffer's main brief. But the long-standing concerns of the ADL and the AJCommittee over public backlash against the Jews for their absolutist (or, in their case, near-absolutist) position on separation of church and state still occupied the minds of numerous high-level officials in each organization. Thus their decision to reenter the national dialogue in the courts over the substance of the religion clauses of the First Amendment marked a significant internal transition within each organization regarding how and when to articulate their interests on a matter of historic concern to their respective constituencies. Reconciliation with the AJCongress and reentrance into the NCRAC fold were still far off, but, as *Torcaso* revealed, the forces within the AJCommittee and the ADL that saw the need for a strong and visible commitment to the separation principle had begun to overcome the older leadership, which still supported a more accommodationist public posture on matters of church and state. As we shall soon see, the willingness of the ADL and the AJCommittee to involve themselves in the concurrent litigation over in-school religious exercises was evidence of their rekindled desire for a public presence—a marked change from their post-*Zorach* period, in which such concerns had been relegated to the back burner.[21]

The Court's unanimous decision in *Torcaso* that Maryland's religious oath requirement violated the separation principle and freedom of religious conscience was a hopeful sign that it was prepared to return to its pre-*Zorach* position on the religion clauses. This was especially true in light of the four rather disappointing decisions concerning Sunday closings that it had handed down the month before, in which it upheld the rights of states and municipalities to enforce laws that made it illegal for certain businesses to open and operate on Sunday.[22] In *Torcaso*, though, Justice Black revisited his *Everson* dicta, writing that the Court again reaffirm[s] that neither a State nor the Federal Government can constitutionally force a person "to profess a belief in any religion." Neither can constitutionally pass laws or impose requirements which aid all religions as against non-believers, and neither can aid those religions based on a belief in the existence of God against those religions founded on different beliefs. . . . This Maryland religious test for public office unconstitutionally invades the appellant's freedom of belief and religion and therefore cannot be enforced against him.[23]

Such language was a welcome departure from the accommodationist tones the Court had sounded in *Zorach,* when it handed the same coalition of organizations responsible for *Torcaso* such a bitter defeat, compounding it further with references to the "religious nature of the American people" and their presupposition of the existence of a Supreme Being. No such references were present in the *Torcaso* decision.

But if the victory in *Torcaso* was especially sweet for anyone, it was for Pfeffer and the AJCongress, each of whom had staked so much on *Zorach* and lost. True, the ACLU had helped to coordinate *Zorach* and *Torcaso* and had contributed to their legal development in cooperation with the AJCongress, for which is due appropriate credit. But it was Pfeffer who had conceived and directed the litigation strategies in each case. And while Pfeffer's star as a scholar and as a brilliant advocate on church-state issues had long since risen in legal and academic circles—high enough that his detractors were now as numerous as his supporters—*Torcaso* was his first successful oral argument before the Court as lead counsel. It would mark the commencement of a spectacular line of successful appearances before the Court over much of the next two decades as either lead counsel, or more often, as an amicus curiae. The latter strategy allowed Pfeffer and the AJCongress the chance to participate more often in relevant litigation, thereby influencing the case's direction and outcome without having to absorb the financial costs associated with direct sponsorship. Moreover, even as an amicus, Pfeffer still commanded considerable attention because of his reputation as the outstanding presence in the field. In other words, Pfeffer and the AJCongress had successfully maneuvered themselves into a position where they could have a significant impact on the substance of church-state law and litigation even in an amicus role or through the informal direction of a case brought under the auspices of other organizations. This becomes much clearer when the litigation histories of the Court's two most historic—and most controversial—establishment clause decisions, *Engel v. Vitale* and *Abington v. Schempp*, are examined within the context of political jurisprudence and interest group politics.

The Constitutional Politics of
School Prayer and Bible Reading

The Court's decisions in *Engel* and *Schempp* were the most unpopular it made during the tumultuous era of Chief Justice Earl Warren.[24] When considered against some of the Warren Court's controversial landmark decisions on civil rights and liberties, such as *Brown v. Board of Education, Yates v. U.S., Mapp v. Ohio,* and *Miranda v. Arizona*—all of which convulsed settled constitutional doctrine as much or more than *Engel* and *Schempp*—that these decisions achieved most vilified status is no small accomplishment.[25] One cannot overestimate the influence that *Engel* and *Schempp* had on the development of church-state law or the extent to which these decisions shook the foundations of the majoritarian civic—and religious—culture. Ruling that Bible reading and the recitation of state-composed prayers, whether such recitation was coerced or "voluntary," violated the fundamental principles of government neutrality toward religion and respect for individual conscience, which are at the heart of the constitutional guarantee to religious freedom, the Court essentially redefined religious pluralism. In modern America, Jews, Catholics, Christian Scientists, Mormons, Jehovah's Witnesses, and members of the smaller, less established Protestant denominations could no longer be regarded as second-class citizens. This in turn made judicial protection for the traditional acknowledgment of religious traditions and customs associated with pan-Christian values in public schools impossible. *Engel* and *Schempp* were thus liberating decisions not only for Jewish school children but for others, some of whom were religious minorities and some of whom were not, who had long been subjected to the indignities associated with coercive, state-sponsored religious exercises in the public schools.[26]

The major Jewish organizations were well aware that mass public opinion would regard a Supreme Court ruling that such well established religious practices as school prayer and Bible reading were unconstitutional as the moral equivalent of a dagger through the heart of the traditional Christian values so long embodied in the American civic and religious cultural milieu. Precisely for this reason they approached the original question of whether to involve themselves in such litigation with extreme caution. As we have seen, there was concern that if the national American Jewish organizations did indeed confront head-on religious exercises in the public schools, an anti-Semitic backlash would result that might ultimately place both individual Jews and broader Jewish interests at risk. Moreover, were the constituencies of the major Jewish organizations in accord with the decision of their respective national offices to join in the crusade against the dissemination of pan-Christian values in the public schools? Did the national offices possess the financial resources and staff expertise to match wits with their opposition on a blow-by-blow, trial-by-trial, appeal-by-appeal basis? And even if these concerns could be successfully addressed, the AJCongress, the AJCommittee, and the ADL still had to face the less certain question of just how far the courts, and ultimately the Supreme Court, were prepared to venture in refashioning the metaphorical wall separating religion and the state. Implicit in this set of questions was a fundamental uncertainty over whether the Court was prepared to look mass public opinion right smack in the eye and refuse to blink on an issue that resonated so deeply and emotionally with the American populace.

For all these reasons and then some—such as the opposition they were sure to encounter from the same organized Catholic and Protestant forces that were so vocal in *Everson, McCollum,* and *Zorach*—the decision of the AJCongress, and the separate, joint decision of the AJCommittee and the ADL, to support litigation that would force a judicial resolution on the constitutionality of religious observances in the public schools took time. They were reached over a decade-long period that witnessed several such potential cases start and then stop, before the legal process culminated in *Engel* and *Schempp.* Fledgling cases that involved religious observances in the public schools, such as *Doremus v. Board of Education* and *Carden v. Board of Education,*[27] fizzled or ground to an abrupt halt because one of the supporting groups—or an influential individual within that group—decided the plaintiffs were undesirable; or that the trial record was insufficient; or that a particular jurisdiction should be avoided for fear that a court would return an adverse decision that would make a successful appeal to the Supreme

Court difficult. To understand how *Engel* and *Schempp* emerged as the chosen vehicles in this next, more delicate phase in the campaign to challenge religious exercises in the public schools, one must also understand why other cases were considered but not chosen, as well as the organizational politics underlying these decisions, in this attenuated litigation quest to find the appropriate test case.

If one can point to a single judicial milestone that first alerted the major Jewish organizations, as well as other separationist groups such as the ACLU, to both the possibilities and the concurrent difficulties of undertaking litigation to abolish religious practices other than released time in the public schools, it would be fair to consider *Doremus v. Board of Education* as that case. *Doremus* first came to the attention of the AJCongress, the AJCommittee, and the ADL in May 1950, after each group, along with the ACLU, was well immersed in the *Zorach* dismissed-time litigation. Such late notice on *Doremus* amounted to no great loss, though, since none of the Jewish organizations believed that constitutional doctrine or public opinion had matured to the point where a litigative attack on Bible reading or school prayer statutes was appropriate. Concern for the cultivation of favorable public opinion was something that Pfeffer, in particular, argued to his colleagues had been neglected after *McCollum* had been decided. Pfeffer would later charge that several of the other organizations supportive of *McCollum* as amici had failed to perform their follow-up duties in connection with initiating an education campaign to persuade the public that *McCollum* was a great moment in the progress of civil liberties. Instead, that battle was being lost to their Catholic and conservative Protestant opponents.

Rather than view *Doremus* as an extension or even a companion case to *Zorach* that would enable them to expand their line of attack, the major Jewish organizations backed away from it. In fact, when the AJCommittee and the ADL issued a joint memorandum that summarized the New Jersey lower court's decision to uphold the state's Bible reading statute, which required the recitation of an Old Testament verse before the beginning of each school day, the reaction within the NCRAC, including that of the AJCongress, was simply to let the decision stand, at least for the time. This collective and nonacrimonious decision, one that came as the fragile coalition between the AJCongress and the combined opinion of the AJCommittee and the ADL had begun to show more visible signs of strain, was not even altered after the New Jersey Supreme Court's dismissal of the plaintiff's appeal on rather conjectural grounds. The court declared that:

> the Old Testament and the Lord's Prayer, pronounced without comment, are not sectarian, and that the short exercise provided by the Statute does not constitute sectarian instruction or . . . worship but is a simple recognition of the Supreme Ruler of the Universe and a deference to His majesty; that since the exercise is not sectarian, no justifiable sectarian advantage or disadvantage flows therefrom; and that, in any event, the presence of a scholar at, and his participation in, that exercise is, under the directive of the Board of Education, voluntary.[28]

In deciding *Doremus*, the New Jersey court also brushed aside the import of the *Everson* and *McCollum* decisions, asserting that the issues in those cases—bus transportation and released time, respectively—were "not in point and not binding" because they were so completely different from the question of whether Bible reading was constitutional under the establishment clause. Still, the New Jersey Supreme Court's refusal to acknowledge *Everson* or, and of greater significance still, *McCollum* in its opinion, on top of its references to the assumed presence of "His majesty" (and "God, our father") were not enough to pique the interest of the Jewish organizations to point where they would intervene.[29] None had an interest in the appeal to the state supreme court, and none supported the next phase of the appellate process—a petition to the United States Supreme Court. As if to underscore their current hesitancy on the issues of Bible reading and school prayer, all three declined to pursue a complaint filed with the NCRAC by a rabbi in West Hempstead, Long Island, about the practice common in several of the town's public schools of observing a period of silent prayer.[30]

Within the Jewish community, the fiercest opposition to intervention in either the New Jersey Bible case or the West Hempstead complaint regarding silent prayer did not come from the ADL or the AJCommittee, as one might have expected, although neither supported such action. Rather, it came from Pfeffer and the AJCongress. Heyman Zimel, the attorney representing the plaintiffs in *Doremus*, met with Pfeffer soon after the New Jersey Supreme Court upheld the Bible reading statute to discuss the merits of a possible appeal to the Supreme Court.

Prior to their conference, the executive committee of the AJCongress's CLSA had voted to recommend that the plaintiffs in *Doremus* forsake such an appeal because, as Pfeffer put it, the committee believed that the Court would not grant certiorari on such a sensitive question, "which would be bad, or would take the case for the purpose of retreating from *McCollum,* which would be worse."[31] Zimel agreed with Pfeffer that further litigation on the Bible reading matter was not, at this point, in their interest, but he pointed out that his clients, two malcontent atheists whose concern for public relations and the nuance of political jurisprudence was nil, were insisting that the case go forward. With Will Maslow's knowledge, Pfeffer told Zimel that the NCRAC, as well anyone else that he could persuade to do so, would pressure his two clients through "various sources" to withdraw their appeal. But these backdoor attempts to coerce them into agreeing were unsuccessful.[32]

Until the Court sorted out the consequences of *McCollum,* Pfeffer was resolved that no litigation other than the released-time issue should move forward in the federal courts. What concerned Pfeffer so much was what he perceived as the unfavorable climate of opinion that the Catholic Church had been able to generate in *McCollum's* wake, an environment that he did not think was conducive to a second consecutive innovative decision that would further strengthen the separation principle. In Pfeffer's opinion, the Catholics had succeeded in portraying *McCollum* as a "blot like the *Dredd Scott* decision [*sic*]" when it instead could have been regarded as "one of the great landmarks in civil liberties like *Yick Wo,*" and thus placed the separationist organizations on the defensive. After *McCollum,* Pfeffer had urged the other constituent members of the NCRAC, as well as non-Jewish organizations such as the ACLU, the Public Education Association, and the United Parents Association, to undertake a comprehensive public relations campaign to publicize the decision. But no major effort on behalf of this recommendation materialized, even when the need for such a campaign to counteract the efforts of the Catholic Church to influence public opinion had become even more critical than before. A favorable climate of public opinion about the *McCollum* decision, Pfeffer argued, would "strengthen the U.S. Supreme Court and lower courts and administrative bodies when they are faced with the issue." Now, with the ante up yet further, such an effort was "far more important . . . than seeking out additional cases."[33]

Before this new, reconstituted public relations drive could make some headway, the Court granted certiorari to hear *Doremus* during its 1951 term. Pfeffer was pessimistic that the Court would overturn the New Jersey decision and allow the Bible reading statute to stand, and he feared the consequences of such a negative decision. This dour outlook was reinforced by his belief that the AJCommittee and the ADL, which the NCRAC had delegated after *McCollum* to educate public opinion on the importance of separation of church and state, had failed miserably in their task. Backed into a corner, and with little control over the next sequence of events, Pfeffer now felt that the AJCongress was left with no choice but to file an amicus brief in *Doremus* asking the Court to strike down the New Jersey Bible reading law. Rather than having the AJCongress pursue this objective alone, however, Pfeffer would attempt to organize an interfaith coalition of religious organizations, such as the Seventh-Day Adventists, the Baptist Joint Committee, and even POAU, to participate as amici in *Doremus.* The coalition's purpose would be to inform the Court that Bible reading offended the principles of non-Jewish citizens as well. Although this was a legitimate strategic objective, Pfeffer was unable to fulfill it, as he acknowledged beforehand would probably be the case.[34] In contrast to the AJCongress's decision to reverse course and participate as an amicus curiae in *Doremus,* the AJCommittee and the ADL held fast to their earlier decision to maintain their distance. Both groups took an active behind-the-scenes role in the public relations campaign, but each remained neutral on other aspects of the *Doremus* litigation, such as the unsuccessful NCRAC-led effort to persuade New York City not to side with the New Jersey school board in defending the Bible reading statute. Neither group was thus willing to interfere with the AJCongress's attempts to influence the litigation process.[35]

While these events were unfolding in *Doremus,* the New York Court of Appeals decided *Zorach,* whereby it reversed the lower court and upheld the New York City released-time program as constitutional. But instead of remanding the case and ordering a new trial, a decision the NCRAC and the ACLU had anticipated, the New York appeals court issued an opinion on the constitutional issues. Thus the state supreme court paved the road for an appeal to the United States Supreme Court. In light of the New York court's decision in *Zorach,* Pfeffer, Ed Lukas of the AJCommittee, and a representative from the ACLU met in July 1951 to consider how all these cases fit together and whether this unexpected change in the course of events required them to reevaluate their present litigation strategy.

The ACLU was much more committed to pushing *Doremus* up the ladder than was the AJCongress, and it was also much more optimistic than Pfeffer that the Court would declare the New Jersey Bible reading law unconstitutional. In fact, the ACLU disagreed with Pfeffer's stated objections all the way down the line. As the ACLU saw it, *Doremus* was stronger than *Zorach*, since it involved the actual teaching of religion by the schools rather than the mere facilitation of such teaching. It further believed that the Court was in a receptive mood and thus prepared to strike down state-directed Bible reading in the public schools; it did not believe the Court wanted to retrench after *McCollum* because of what Pfeffer perceived as a negative environment resulting from public objections to such a bold decision. Rather than let *Doremus* wither, the ACLU wanted to schedule it for argument with *Zorach* and present both cases together before the Court. Assessing *Doremus*, the ACLU concluded: "Unless we want to withdraw our released-time case [*Zorach*] as well, it seems to [us] that there is no reason whatever why we should have this case withdrawn. Certainly, the court will not improve within the foreseeable future."[36]

Although the twist in *Zorach*'s expected fate made Pfeffer less vociferous in his objections, he was still less than thrilled with the prospect of *Doremus* going forward. Nonetheless, Pfeffer and the AJCongress agreed to support *Doremus* when it was argued before the Court by filing an amicus curiae brief, a strategic choice the ACLU had planned to pursue as well. It was the ACLU's categorical objection to the withdrawal of *Doremus* that had the heaviest influence on Pfeffer's eventual decision to lend the institutional support of the AJCongress to the case. Again, it was a question of public relations: the AJCongress and the ACLU could not afford to be united in *Zorach* but split in *Doremus*, for this would constitute a not-so-subtle discrepancy that the national and religious press would be sure to pick up on and report.[37] In contrast, the ADL and the AJCommittee felt no such obligation to lend their support to *Doremus*, regardless of what the press and the public might think. Each had committed to *Zorach* simply to maintain the appearance of unified Jewish agreement evident in *McCollum*—but neither had the slightest desire, especially not in the current political environment, to associate themselves with another cadre of defiant atheists who were adamant about attacking such a sensitive and emotional issue as Bible reading.[38]

Thus the ACLU and the AJCongress were left alone in their amici support for the plaintiffs in *Doremus*. Even the Junior Order of United American Mechanics, the fraternal order that had sponsored the challenge to New Jersey's bus transportation program for parochial schools in *Everson*, filed an amicus brief in support of the state's Bible reading statute. As the Jewish organizations were to discover when *Engel* and *Schempp* began to take shape in the late 1950s and early 1960s, the major organizations that represented the nation's chief Protestant denominations were not prepared to extend their unequivocal opposition to government assistance for parochial—read Catholic—education much beyond that point. Certainly, they were unwilling to support a similar demand that public schools cease their traditional practice of state-sponsored Bible reading and prayer.

All this intricate negotiation, concerned debate about public relations, and strategic manipulation among the Jewish organizations, the ACLU, and the *Doremus* plaintiffs—ultimately intended, of course, to place the case in the most favorable light—turned out to be for naught. In March 1952, about six weeks before it handed down *Zorach*, the Court dismissed *Doremus* on procedural grounds and thus allowed the state court's decision to stand. This decision was fine as far as the AJCongress was concerned. After all, it had held all along that when the time came to mount a challenge to state-sponsored religious exercises in the public schools, a much more extensive effort than had gone into *Doremus* would be required. Basically, the AJCongress wanted only to escape from *Doremus* unscathed, and its wish was granted.

But the ACLU was not prepared to let the issue rest. In May 1952, after the *Zorach* decision had come down, the ACLU called a conference with the AJCongress, the AJCommittee, and the ADL to consider a proposal by its New York chapter to challenge the newly written prayer adopted by the state's Board of Regents for recitation in the public schools. Pfeffer, on behalf of the three Jewish organizations, advised against such litigation, for what he assumed were obvious reasons: *Doremus* and *Zorach*. Plus, having just been hit over the head twice in two months, the Jewish organizations had no desire to allocate any of their scarce financial resources for yet another round of litigation that none thought had the slightest chance of succeeding. But the

ACLU wanted the Jewish organizations not only to collaborate on the legal preparation of the case but to supplement the financial costs of the lawsuit. Since this was something they were not willing to do, prospects for litigation were all but eliminated.[39]

In short, another round of litigation on the school prayer and Bible reading issues was not, in the view of the major Jewish organizations, a viable option, not with the twin shadows of *Zorach* and *Doremus* looming over them. Even the ACLU, after some deliberation, seemed resigned to the current environment of law and politics. Rather than to the pursuit of litigation, the AJCongress, the AJCommittee, and the ADL agreed that for the time being their resources should be devoted to a public education campaign designed to foster a more conducive atmosphere for a better planned lawsuit down the road. But such an effort, in Pfeffer's view, should not have the ACLU at its center, since the major Protestant organizations associated it with radical secularism and consequently would not be responsive to its leadership. Nonetheless, the foundations were now in place to launch a comprehensive, full-bodied campaign that would culminate in a challenge to the constitutional place of Bible reading and prayer in the public schools. For the major Jewish organizations, this campaign would turn out to be an enormous success. But it did not quite arrive at its destination through the careful, step-by-step litigation process that the Jewish organizations had envisioned after narrowly averting disaster in *Doremus*.

In November 1951 the New York Board of Regents composed a one-sentence nondenominational prayer that read: "Almighty God, we acknowledge our dependence upon Thee, and we beg Thy blessings upon us, our parents, our teachers and our country." The board encouraged, but did not require, its local public school districts to begin each regular school day with the recitation of this prayer. But the response of the public schools was not as enthusiastic as the regents had hoped. By the mid-1950s the New York education department estimated that only somewhere between 10 and 20 percent of its local school districts had adopted the prayer; some schools had opted instead for another recommendation of the regents, namely, that students sing the fourth verse of "America," which opens with, "Our father's God to thee, author of liberty, to thee we sing." The board had made it clear, moreover, that school districts that did choose to adopt either the prayer or the verse from "America" could not require their students to participate.[40]

As we saw above, from the time the Board of Regents first issued the prayer for possible adoption by school districts until the first legal complaint was filed that questioned whether the state was authorized under the establishment clause to promote religious observances and worship, the major Jewish organizations, unlike the ACLU, were not eager to take this matter to court. They had instead concentrated on a public education campaign to discourage school boards from incorporating either of the regents' suggested devotional practices into their school day.

To the AJCongress, public education was a vehicle through which to communicate its now well-known message that commitment to a secular state would allow private religion to flourish and thus promote the integrity of the public education system, making it hospitable to students from all religious backgrounds. But the cultivation of diffuse public support was not the final objective of the AJCongress. It knew that the ultimate determination regarding the constitutionality of the religious practices that commonly took place in the public schools—such as Bible reading, prayer, and holiday celebrations—would come about through litigation, regardless of whether the AJCongress itself was behind the lawsuits that forced the resolution of these issues. Although the Court's record thus far gave no indication that it was presently prepared to invalidate one or more of these practices, the AJCongress believed that when the atmosphere of hyperpatriotism and gratuitous religiosity inspired by the Cold War ebbed, the Court would limit or ban altogether the power of the public schools to require or even to encourage religious observances on school time and with their endorsement. When that moment arrived, the AJCongress, in particular, wanted the constituencies responsible for the implementation and enforcement of the decisions—governors, school boards, and other responsible institutions on the state and local level—to understand the principles behind the new laws and abide by them, as well as doing what they could to secure the support of the public. But constitutional change through litigation was the ultimate objective; education and public relations were a means to help achieve that end.[41]

For the ADL and the AJCommittee, caution was still the watchword, even when it became more and more obvious that a constitutional confrontation on the power of the public schools to promote religious worship was no longer a matter of if, but when. During the mid-1950s, the ADL and the AJCommittee still favored a much more behind-the-scenes, accommodationist approach to mediating conflicts over religion in the public schools, one which stressed education and public relations as competent vehicles in their own right, rather than considering litigation the end of the rainbow. While much of this hesitance on the part of the ADL and the AJCommittee was rooted in the demands and orientation of their respective constituencies, some of it was also due to the geographic extent of their constituent base. Unlike the AJCongress, whose regional expanse during the 1950s was, with the exception of Washington and Chicago, confined for the most part to the urban Northeast, the ADL and the AJCommittee each had a strong and influential presence in several southern and midwestern cities and smaller communities. Concern for the needs of their respective constituencies led to several clashes between the AJCongress and the ADL and AJCommittee in such diverse cities as Miami, Minneapolis, Nashville, Indianapolis, and Gary, Indiana, over how to press their objections to religion in the public schools.[42] In each of these cases, the AJCongress wanted to encourage litigation as the means to resolve a problem with religion in the public schools, while the ADL and the AJCommittee wanted to pursue nonlitigative approaches. With the exception of a major lawsuit that the AJCongress initiated with the ACLU in Miami to complement *Engel* and *Schempp,* a lawsuit that commenced despite the objections of the other two major Jewish organizations, the ADL and the AJCommittee were able to discourage litigation in these communities. Disagreement over the appropriateness of litigation was especially open and volatile in Miami, where the AJCongress intervened to challenge several religious practices in the Dade County school system. This decision was not well received by the Jewish newspapers in Miami, which criticized the AJCongress often and harshly for its selection of a southern city, albeit not one that shared quite the same demographics as its Bible Belt cousins, in which to launch such a major lawsuit. Given that Miami was very much the province of the ADL and the AJCommittee, established Jewish opinion there supported their more accommodationist approaches (which included a compromise on how certain religious practices should be conducted) over the confrontational tactics of the AJCongress.[43] *Engel* made the ultimate outcome of the AJCongress's lawsuit in Miami pro forma, since the Supreme Court did not to rule on it until after the case involving the Regents' prayer was decided. But the competing organizational philosophies of the three major national Jewish agencies were on full display all throughout the range of Bible reading and school prayer litigation that took place in the late 1950s and early 1960s.

In general, though, the national ADL and AJCommittee leadership were obliged to walk a more delicate line when it came to balancing the various internal interests at work within their respective agencies whenever controversial issues presented themselves. In several cases, the national and local leadership bodies of both the ADL and the AJ-Committee found themselves in conflict over whether to involve themselves in the Bible reading and school prayer litigation. Each knew, as did the AJCongress, that amici support for such litigation would probably not extend beyond the Jewish organizations. Fear that they would find their reputation as good, nonquarrelsome citizens compromised was quite common among Jews in the southern states, where opposition to such decisions would run highest, and in the more conservative midwestern towns and cities. Said one lawyer who worked for the AJCommittee and the ADL during this time:

> In the South, many Jews had been accepted as honorary Protestants and did not want to do anything to jeopardize their status. In addressing the concerns of Jews from Atlanta or Birmingham, you have to think like the Jews from Atlanta or Birmingham, not like Jews from New York, something it [New York] was not always too good at doing. Trying to find some common ground among the regional offices was damn difficult. On several occasions, agency politics held up a decision to get involved in some of those cases. It acted as a real constraint and often led to some pretty good screaming matches between us and New York.[44]

But the AJCongress was not above concern over public perception on controversial questions either. In October 1958 an ACLU lawyer named John Babigan informed Pfeffer that a group of Herrick, Long Island, parents had hired an attorney to challenge the decision of the public schools in their communities to adopt the prayer composed by the Board of Regents. Babigan told Pfeffer that in the ACLU's own view, which was based on the information the organization had, the best course of action would be to file a formal complaint with the state commissioner of education rather than pursue litigation. Pfeffer wanted the AJCongress to be involved in a substantial, if not lead, role when a worthy test case was found to challenge sectarian religious practices in the public schools, but he agreed with Babigan that litigation was not yet appropriate. He also recommended, however, that the ACLU should not file a formal complaint with the state Board of Education until a complete investigation of law and fact on the issue had been completed. Pfeffer was especially concerned with two related issues: whether school authorities were coercing students into reciting the regents' prayer, and whether other, more sectarian, prayers were being offered or required.[45] As for the AJCommittee and the ADL, neither was made aware of or demonstrated an independent interest in the Long Island case while it was in its infant stages.

To Pfeffer's disappointment, the ACLU elected not to follow his advice and thus embarked independently on what would come to be known as *Engel v. Vitale*. Moreover, the ACLU was able to persuade the Long Island plaintiffs to allow it to sponsor the case and thus relieve the plaintiffs of whatever financial burden they would have incurred. A month after their initial discussion, Babigan sent Pfeffer a draft petition of the ACLU's complaint attacking the Regents' prayer. In Pfeffer's opinion, the lawsuit was a loser and would give whatever court heard it "another opportunity . . . to become religious and patriotic." Pfeffer was not afraid of involving the AJCongress in litigation on the issue of prayer in the public schools; he just did not believe that the Regents' prayer, by itself, was sufficiently sectarian to warrant the objections of a court on constitutional grounds. Just the year before, the AJCongress had come close to, but decided against, pursuing lawsuits on similar grounds in Baltimore and in Montgomery County, Maryland, the same Washington suburb in which *Torcaso* originated. Pfeffer wanted to initiate a lawsuit in a jurisdiction in which the Lord's Prayer or some other specific sectarian exercise was required by statute, and he had ultimately found the Maryland cases wanting.[46] For similar reasons, Pfeffer recommended that the AJCongress attempt to persuade the ACLU to drop the *Engel* case, or if that failed, to watch how the Regents' case developed and, if appropriate, enter into it in an amicus role later. What the AJCongress did rule out, at least for now, was intervention in the litigation, either as a cosponsor or as an amicus curiae, until it had a better idea of what the prospects were for such a case.[47]

Pfeffer continued his efforts to convince the ACLU not to press the Regents' prayer lawsuit on the grounds that it did not involve the public schools in an overtly sectarian exercise. But Pfeffer was unsuccessful. The ACLU thus commenced this historic litigation in the New York state courts sans the AJCongress. Several of the AJCongress affiliates in other cities had been made aware of the ACLU's decision to sponsor this litigation and had communicated to the national office that little opposition existed within their local membership to a more pronounced role in the lawsuit.[48] Such support was important whenever the national office decided to contest a church-state issue or commence legal action, but it did nothing in this instance to diminish Pfeffer's pessimism over the ACLU's chances of prevailing in the Regents' prayer case.

At the same time, while the AJCongress continued to hold out on public endorsement of the ACLU's lawsuit, it was searching for additional plaintiffs to challenge what Pfeffer believed were the more odious examples of state-sponsored sectarian religion in the public schools: Bible reading and recitation of the Lord's Prayer. Possible criticism from the major Protestant and Catholic organizations was not the issue, nor was lack of adequate financial resources; rather, the desire to initiate a lawsuit that would encompass the sweep of religious practices in the public schools was what kept the AJCongress from joining the ACLU in the litigation over the Regents' prayer. Explained Pfeffer in an internal memorandum for distribution to the AJCongress's regional offices: "The reason for our advice [to the ACLU] is that the prayer involved is the 'Regents' Prayer' which is as non-sectarian as a prayer can be and would be considered by the courts to be quite innocuous. We believe that the first prayer case to be brought should be based upon better facts. We are now discussing with some plaintiffs in Long Island the bringing of a suit involving the Lord's Prayer which we consider a sectarian Christian prayer. It is quite likely that such a suit shall be started shortly, unless, as is also possible, the local Board of Education decides to discontinue the recitation."[49]

But rather than implement its own lawsuit to challenge those New York schools that did engage in these more sectarian religious exercises, the AJCongress—and soon the ADL and the AJCommittee, which found themselves drawn back into the arena of church-state litigation—decided to support the Regents' prayer case. After persistent encouragement from the ACLU, Pfeffer agreed to work behind the scenes to help formulate the arguments that the ACLU would incorporate into the lead plaintiffs' principal brief. Indeed, it was in *Engel* and *Schempp* that Pfeffer began to establish the pattern that would come to characterize both his and the AJCongress's behavior in cases in which the initial decision had been not to participate. According to this pattern, Pfeffer would lend his advice and expertise in an informal way to whoever was representing the plaintiffs during the trial or initial appellate stages. But he would not put his name or that of the AJCongress on record as supporting the litigation until a case reached the Supreme Court, as was the circumstance in *Engel,* or when a case had begun to show more promise by the intermediate stages, as happened in *Schempp.*[50] In fact, as the AJCongress was backing off from the Regents' prayer case, it was turning more and more of its attention to Philadelphia, where another landmark case, *Abington v. Schempp,* had commenced under the sponsorship of the ACLU and, in contrast to *Engel,* with the initial support of the AJCongress as an amicus curiae. Here, too, Pfeffer had been involved from the outset in the prospective litigation, first when he discouraged the prosecution of a less promising case from Nashville and later as an informal advisor to the ACLU's lead counsel and influential amicus participant in the Philadelphia case. *Schempp's* evolution from an isolated complaint into a landmark establishment clause test case provides an excellent opportunity to gain insight into complexities and nuance involved in the organizational politics of the constitutional litigation process.

In October 1955 Pfeffer contacted Philip M. Carden, an editor for the Associated Press news service, to learn more about the lawsuit that he had filed to challenge the constitutionality of a Tennessee law requiring Bible reading in the public schools and to enjoin the Nashville school board from permitting devotional services or inquiring about and keeping records of Sunday school attendance by public school students.[51] Carden had not turned to the local ACLU or a similar organization to prosecute his complaint but had instead hired a prominent Nashville attorney, C. Vernon Hines, to handle the case. Hines replied to Pfeffer that he "would be more than pleased to have the cooperation of the American Jewish Congress in this matter, either by way of an Intervening Petition, or by association with me." Hines also wrote that he "was particularly glad to receive this letter, as I have on my desk your book, *Church, State, and Freedom,* and plan to rely upon it greatly in preparing my case."[52]

With an invitation to assume an active role thus in hand, Pfeffer then contacted key members of Nashville's Jewish community to determine whether support existed for a visible AJCongress role in *Carden.* In his communication with local leaders, Pfeffer stressed that no decision would go forward without the Jewish community's support. He further indicated that the AJCongress would be receptive to alternative approaches to halting the religious practices challenged in *Carden*, such as "voluntary action of the public school authorities in Nashville, without the necessity of litigation."[53] But even so, among the more influential local Jewish leaders enthusiasm for AJCongress intervention in *Carden* was tempered. Rather than confront the local leadership, Pfeffer agreed to abide by their misgivings and refrain from involving the AJCongress in *Carden*.[54] Some dissenters in the Nashville leadership, however, attempted to persuade Pfeffer that the local Jewish community was not quite as adverse to AJCongress involvement in *Carden* as he had been led to believe, as long as whatever assistance it provided remain unpublicized. Should the case reach the Supreme Court, moreover, the local leadership would indeed welcome the open assistance of the AJCongress, an arrangement that Carden's lawyer endorsed.[55]

While this back-and-forth negotiation was in process, the Tennessee Supreme Court ruled that state's Bible reading statute was not unconstitutional.[56] At this point, Pfeffer urged Hines not to consider filing a petition for certiorari with the United States Supreme Court until after the two of them, along with the plaintiff and members of Nashville's Jewish community, could arrange for a conference. In January 1956 Pfeffer accordingly traveled to Nashville to consult with the Jewish community leadership in order to better gauge its support for further prosecution of the litigation and to confer with Hines on whether an appeal was desirable. After several private discussions with well-placed Jewish leaders, Pfeffer concluded that "the Nashville Jewish community is the only Jewish community I have ever come across in the country which appears to me to be more conservative than the general non-Jewish community."[57] Despite encouragement from several local leaders whom Pfeffer characterized as more "progressive and courageous" than what the dominant conservative majority, Pfeffer concluded that insufficient broad-based support existed among Nashville Jews to warrant direct AJCongress involvement in the Bible reading case.

Pfeffer told Hines in their conference that, for these reasons, the AJCongress would withdraw its previous offer to assist him in *Carden*, as well as urging him to encourage his client to drop his appeal. Upon his return to New York, Pfeffer wrote Hines to explain further why he believed it was essential to terminate the litigation:

It is improbable that the Supreme Court would today invalidate Bible reading statutes. I would doubt that the Court would invalidate a practice so widespread without a complete record before it. In the second place, when the time is ripe to bring a Bible reading case before the Court, it should be based upon an exhaustive trial record showing a variety of practices such as hymn singing, prayer recitations, etc. I do not think it necessary for me to expand upon this since I expressed our views orally to you in your office. All I want to do is to reemphasize that we think it would be a mistake to apply for certiorari in this case.[58]

Since Hines had indicated to Pfeffer in their February meeting that his client could not afford to finance an appeal to the Supreme Court, the AJCongress's decision against further prosecution of *Carden* ended the case, its name thus becoming but an asterisk in the annals of church-state jurisprudence.[59]

As even the AJCongress was withdrawing from the *Carden* litigation, sixteen-year-old Ellory Schempp, who attended Abington Senior High School in suburban Philadelphia, had begun a peculiar, silent protest—without his parents' knowledge—against the school's practice of having homeroom teachers read Bible verses and lead the class in the recitation of the Lord's Prayer. Schempp did not vocalize his disapproval of these practices but simply sat silently and read the Koran. His quiet defiance first resulted in Schempp being excused to read his materials elsewhere. But under pressure from the school's principal, Schempp was obliged to remain in class for the Bible reading exercise and to stand during the Lord's Prayer, although he was not expected to recite it as his classmates were. Under the Pennsylvania statute, which *required* public schools to engage in these religious exercises, students were permitted to use their own version of the Bible when they were selected to read scripture or could excuse themselves if their parents had provided written permission. In other words, recitation of the Lord's Prayer was not absolutely mandatory under the statute.

But these contingencies failed to satisfy Schempp, who believed that the school's vested authority to conduct Bible reading and, for all practical purposes, to require the recitation of the Lord's Prayer was misplaced. Schempp contacted the local ACLU to inquire about representation in a lawsuit designed to put an end to these practices, and in April 1957 the ACLU agreed to represent Ellory Schempp. It decided, moreover, that it would challenge not just the Abington Senior High School's Bible reading practices but the entire Pennsylvania statute as violative of the establishment clause. None of the major Jewish organizations were approached by the Schempps to handle the case, perhaps because the family was Unitarian, and none lent their formal support for the litigation until after the ACLU had taken the case to trial before a three-judge federal court. But at the invitation of the ACLU's Philadelphia lawyer, Henry Sawyer, Pfeffer was involved from the beginning in an individual capacity in the consultations over litigation strategy in *Schempp*.[60] Sawyer believed that Pfeffer was the "foremost authority" on the law and history of separation of church and state and wanted his counsel as the litigation commenced, even if the AJCongress was not yet prepared to participate as an amicus or a cosponsor.[61]

On the question of intervention during the early stages of *Schempp*, the AJCongress was of two minds. Its Philadelphia office, which represented the broader Delaware Valley region, had voted to support *Schempp* from the outset.[62] Pfeffer, too, very much wanted to pursue a Bible reading case with the AJCongress in a lead role, but for several reasons he had mixed feelings about *Schempp*'s attractiveness. While Pfeffer endorsed the ACLU's decision to attack both the statute that required Bible reading and the school's practice of having teachers lead the students in a recitation of the Lord's Prayer, he was still of the opinion that "it was a serious mistake to (a) bring this suit in the federal courts and (b) to bring it in behalf of a Unitarian." In an internal memorandum explaining the reasoning behind his position that the AJCongress not intervene in *Schempp*, Pfeffer wrote:

> I think it would be highly desirable if a similar suit sponsored by AJCongress in behalf of a Jewish parent and, if possible, also a Catholic parent, could be brought in a Pennsylvania State court. While I am not sanguine about the outcome of a suit limited to Bible reading, I think a good case could be made to invalidate the Lord's Prayer recitation in a state court. However, we could only have a chance of winning if we could establish a record through trial similar to that established in the Gideon Bible case. . . . The complaint in the ACLU's case sets forth no facts requiring a trial and will probably go up on the pleadings. I am certain that we would never have won the Gideon Bible case if

we would have gone up on the pleadings alone. I therefore recommend that the Philadelphia CLSA . . . be urged to sponsor a suit in the Pennsylvania State Court on Lord's Prayer recitation with which a count of Bible reading could be combined.[63]

On the basis of this analysis, Pfeffer persuaded the AJCongress not to intervene in *Schempp* unless the progression of events indicated that the case might take an unexpected and definite turn in its favor. But in November 1958, after the trial in *Schempp* had been completed before a three-judge federal court, Pfeffer and Shad Polier decided to retreat from the national office's earlier position not to intervene and agreed instead to abide by the Philadelphia chapter's wishes to have the AJCongress file an amicus brief in time for oral argument, which had been set for February 1959. The Pennsylvania attorney general had also requested and been given permission to file an amicus brief in support of the plaintiff's claim that the state Bible reading statute was unconstitutional—which the AJCongress believed opened the door for its full participation because *Schempp's* unpopular cause now had a rare endorsement from the state's chief law enforcement officer. Under pressure from its Philadelphia office—whose most active member, Theodore Mann, had been an instrumental behind-the-scenes force in *Schempp* ever since the ACLU had decided to litigate it—and believing that the case had in any event become too important, win or lose, for the organization to remain on the sidelines, the AJCongress decided to submit an amicus brief before the three-judge court.[64]

A similar blend of internal politics and favorable progress in the case's legal fortunes persuaded the AJCommittee and the ADL to enter *Schempp* as amici during this stage as well, a decision that represented a departure from their recent reticence to participate in controversial litigation involving the religion clauses. In contrast to the AJCongress, neither the ADL nor the AJCommittee had worked with the ACLU to mobilize *Schempp* through the litigation process or had been solicited for their input into the substantive doctrinal or strategic issues that had emerged along the way. Thus, although the decision of the AJCommittee and the ADL to participate in *Schempp* was motivated in part by a desire to influence its outcome, both groups were also anxious to reassert their institutional identities as legitimate and respected representatives of American Jewish opinion on matters involving the proper role of religion in American public life. Much of this new commitment to a visible public presence in church-state litigation came from their respective legal staffs. While still unable to compete with the AJCongress in size, staff, and expertise, the AJCommittee and the ADL legal staffs had begun to push their respective internal decision-making committees for the power to exercise greater discretion when it came to the issue of participation in cases of significant interest to the segments of the Jewish community each organization represented. Events had progressed to the point where neither the AJCommittee nor the ADL could afford to place their heads in the sand and assume that others, such as the AJCongress and the ACLU, would fight their battles for them. Explained one AJCommittee lawyer:

> Ed Lukas and Morris Abram worked hard to bring the agency into modern times. Both were activists who believed that litigation was a very important tool to speak for the agency in civil liberties cases. Lukas used to speak at length about going into cases and the need to use legal action, to file *amicus,* and so on. There were plenty of people here who would have been content not to do any more litigation work after some of the early cases. But Lukas pushed and won out because he was a determined lawyer who convinced the conservatives within the agency that litigation was important because the most sweeping changes in society were coming through the courts, and that we needed to be a part of that. We still remained cautious, compared to the AJCongress, but for us, getting involved in the early prayer cases and so on was a big deal.[65]

In February 1962 the three-judge federal court unanimously declared Pennsylvania's Bible reading statute unconstitutional. Later that summer the Supreme Court agreed to set the Abington school district's appeal for argument during the 1962 term—but not with the intent to reverse the lower court's decision, as is often the reason why the Court grants certiorari to hear such cases. Rather, the Court wanted to use *Schempp* to clarify its momentous decision from the 1961 term that held unconstitutional the recitation of state-composed prayers in public schools, even if participation in such prayers was not required. By then, organized Jewish involvement in *Engel v. Vitale*—initially marked merely by the presence of Leo Pfeffer and the AJCongress's collaboration with the ACLU when the complaint first came to their attention in 1958—had expanded enormously.

Moreover, while *Engel* and *Schempp* were each in litigation, in February 1960 the AJCongress—over the vocal opposition of the local offices of the AJCommittee and the ADL—initiated what became a well-publicized lawsuit in Miami to have a comprehensive catalogue of religious practices that took place in the Dade County public schools declared unconstitutional. In fact, Pfeffer believed that the Miami case, *Chamberlin v. Dade County,* provided a much better opportunity to have the practices at issue in *Engel* and *Schempp,* as well as others that had long concerned the AJCongress, terminated on establishment clause grounds.

The issues in *Chamberlin* involved the in-class singing of religious hymns; the display of religious symbols in classrooms; religious holiday observances; a school-based requirement that teachers take a religious oath as a condition of employment; and that teachers conduct a religious census of their students. Pfeffer believed that *Chamberlin* would permit the development of a more extensive trial record, one that would buffer the constitutional arguments and bolster his case through the appellate process, regardless of what happened in the lower courts. An additional strength of *Chamberlin,* in Pfeffer's opinion, was that it involved a challenge to indisputably sectarian religious practices, a condition he believed the prayer composed by the New York Board of Regents failed to meet, which thus made *Engel* a less attractive test case. The nature of the complaint also satisfied Pfeffer's long-held belief that litigation that encompassed multiple complaints against in-school religious practices—rather than involving just an isolated grievance, as was the case in *Schempp*—stood a much greater chance of reaching the Supreme Court, and of succeeding once there.

By then, *Engel* had reached two New York courts and met with adverse decisions each time, although the state supreme court judge who ruled on the prayer later wrote Pfeffer to tell him how "very much indebted to you for the research and the excellent books, articles and oral arguments before the [Board of Education] for which you have been responsible."[66] Despite having submitted an amicus brief and having worked closely with the ACLU in *Schempp,* though, Pfeffer remained ambivalent about the litigation's chances of succeeding, and even if it did, he was not optimistic about the scope of what the case could accomplish. Believing that neither *Engel* nor *Schempp* was sufficient to attack successfully the entire breadth of religious activities in the public schools, Pfeffer decided to plunge the AJCongress wholeheartedly into *Chamberlin.*

This decision was not well received by the ADL and the AJCommittee, which together exerted far more influence than did the AJCongress in the Jewish communities of Miami and Miami Beach. And despite the official acknowledgment in the influential channels of the Florida Jewish press that the AJCongress's decision to intervene in *Chamberlin* was "unquestionably just and responsible in terms of the constitutional principle involved," editorial commentary was overwhelmingly negative. Opposition in the local Jewish media and in the Jewish community at large to the litigation brought by the AJCongress—and its failure to pursue what they believed were workable alternatives—was rooted in the belief that the prosecution of such a controversial lawsuit in a southern city would inevitably yield a backlash, despite the presence of a significant Jewish population. According to the influential *Jewish Floridian,* Jews in such cities would "reap the wild wind of anti-Jewish opinion which perforce becomes the legacy of the total Jewish community and which the other defense agencies foresaw as a natural and unnecessary consequence."[67]

In contrast, the Jewish press praised the ongoing efforts of the ADL and the AJCommittee to work with the Dade County school board to implement a broad-based program, launched several years earlier, of religious and spiritual values in the public schools, one that would respect the interests of the Jewish community as well as those of other religious minorities. In the eyes of the Jewish press, such cooperation constituted an excellent and judicious alternative to litigation. But the AJCommittee and the ADL did more than just disagree with the AJCongress's emphasis on litigation as a solution to the problem of religious practices in Miami's public schools. They also engaged in behind the scenes efforts to discourage the very presence of the AJCongress in the area by encouraging prominent members of the local Jewish community to criticize its "militance" on the matter as ill-advised. Charles Wittenstein, then an AJCommittee lawyer based in Atlanta, said of *Chamberlin:*

> That whole affair was just another case of Leo Pfeffer having to demonstrate that he knew better than anyone what was right for

Jews. He could never resist the chance to stick it to us or [the] ADL, since he also used to make it quite clear that he thought we knew nothing about standing up for the rights of Jews, that we were too fearful, afraid of what the Gentiles would think. Let me avoid all that and just say that much of the tension among the agencies in that case was caused by his insistence in bringing a real unpopular case in a terrible climate. We had begun to turn the corner on the Regents' case and *Schempp,* to realize that we had to be involved there, so the "fear factor" is not something I believe is fair. We just thought Miami was the wrong place to agitate non-Jewish opinion; hell, our people there used to get bad mail for just suggesting that some principal should be more considerate of Jewish kids in the schools. Did we need to worsen it? No. That was our position.

What [the] Congress didn't realize was that you just didn't run down from New York and tell these people what to do. You have to prepare a community for a major change, to talk with them, deal with the issues and say, "At some point the Supreme Court is going to find these practices unconstitutional, and we are going to have to work together to make peace in this community." You don't say, "Do what I say or I'll sue," which was how the Congress did business. We were more sensitive to local considerations. No New York know-it-all Jewish organization could come running down here waving a copy of the First Amendment and say, "Ah ha, we're right, you're wrong." In those days—well, now as well, I suppose—you have to fight your battles carefully. And that was not one where we thought a whole lot could be accomplished that wasn't already going to be accomplished in the other cases. Luckily, the other cases [*Engel* and *Schempp*] were decided before it made it up to the Court, so the Miami case took care of itself. But it was not pleasant. Sometimes Leo, as gifted and talented as he was, could just be so overbearing.[68]

In addition to their general objection to the strategic purpose of organized Jewish involvement in the Miami litigation, the ADL, the AJCommittee, and influential Jewish newspapers refused to accept the AJCongress's explanation that it had no choice but to intervene in *Chamberlin* because such involvement was the only way that Pfeffer's expertise could be brought to bear on the case. As the *Jewish Floridian* pointed out, Pfeffer had already provided counsel and assistance to the ACLU on several occasions in similar cases involving church-state issues—he was, in fact, working with the ACLU in such a capacity in the New York and Pennsylvania prayer and Bible reading cases then still in litigation—and thus the argument that the AJCongress needed to wave its organizational banner in the Miami case as well came across to them as but a transparent excuse to make their presence felt.[69] Unpersuaded by the criticism that greeted its decision to intervene in the litigation, however, the AJCongress prepared for the trial with the intention that *Chamberlin* could overtake the *Engel* and *Schempp* cases still in litigation. Pfeffer was not merely untroubled by this broad sweep of criticism from the pillars of Miami's Jewish establishment: he dismissed it outright. As he later commented to one Miami colleague who had passed along a draft of the AJCommittee's and the ADL's amicus brief in *Engel*, "If you can make any sense out of the action taken by [them] in fighting us like mad in Miami and then filing a brief in the Regents' Prayer case, which is much less objectionable, then you are a good deal wiser than I am, and this I do not concede."[70]

But events never really turned in favor of Pfeffer and the AJCongress in the Miami litigation. Owing in part to logistics, but also to Pfeffer's trademark technique of building an exhaustive trial record that could withstand the appellate process, a practice that tended to drag litigation out over time, *Chamberlin* was the last of the trilogy of landmark cases involving state-sponsored religious exercises in the public schools to reach the Court, and thus a loser in the race against time. In April 1962, just two months before the United States Supreme Court handed down its decision in *Engel*, the Florida Supreme Court ruled on the entire set of religious practices challenged as violative the federal and Florida constitutions. Somewhat paradoxically, the Florida court held that Bible reading and recitation of the Lord's Prayer were permissible, while ruling that the policies of allowing religious clubs after-hours use of public school classrooms, celebrating religious holidays, and showing religious films in school were unconstitutional. On the one hand, the AJCongress could certainly count having these latter practices declared unconstitutional as a partial triumph toward its broader objective. On the other hand, the organization was understandably disappointed that, having poured so much political and institutional capital into *Chamberlin*, it had failed to convince the Florida court to outlaw the complete roster of the state's policies—and the more blatant ones at that—with respect to religious observances in the public schools.

Two months later, the United States Supreme Court handed down its historic and controversial opinion in *Engel*, in which the Court held as unconstitutional the prayer composed by the New York Board of Regents that had been adopted for use in the public schools statewide. Writing for a six-to-one Court, Justice Black held that neither the non-denominational nor the voluntary nature of the prayer could "serve to free it from the limitations of the Establishment Clause."[71] Only Justice Potter Stewart dissented, criticizing the Court for its "uncritical invocation of metaphors like the 'wall of separation,' a phrase found nowhere in the Constitution" and for brushing aside "the religious traditions of our people, reflected in countless practices of the institutions and officials of our government."[72] But with this sole exception, the Court did not succumb to the temptation to ground its opinion in the gratuitous patriotism of *Zorach*, as the AJCongress had feared it would (and which was, of course, why the AJCongress and especially Pfeffer had believed the case had little chance of succeeding). Rather ironically, while Pfeffer was convinced that *Chamberlin* could accomplish alone what *Engel* and *Schempp* even together could not, he retained a close working relationship with the ACLU attorneys throughout each case— so much so that his name in particular and that of the AJCongress in general were condemned by critics of all three decisions with much greater vociferousness than was that of the ACLU, the formal sponsor of the latter cases and a coplaintiff in the former. Nonetheless, when the Court's decision in *Engel* was announced in June 1962, the major Jewish organizations were as ecstatic as their allies in the ACLU to have won, even though the victory meant that much of their immediate energies would have to go toward defending what was a wildly unpopular ruling against persistent and often vitriolic attacks from political leaders, newspaper editorial writers, and prominent Catholic and Protestant spokesmen. To the disappointment of the AJCongress, its investment in *Chamberlin* would go unreturned, since almost one year to the day from its decision in *Engel* and with far less resulting outrage from the forces that were so vocal after that decision, the Court would uphold, again over the single dissent of Justice Stewart, the lower federal court's decision in *Schempp* that state-mandated Bible reading in the public schools was unconstitutional.[73] These two decisions rendered invalid Florida's state-endorsed policies of Bible reading and recitation of the Lord's Prayer in its public schools. The Court would later vacate the state supreme court's earlier decision in *Chamberlin* that upheld these practices, while continuing to find unconstitutional the others challenged in the Miami litigation.

But such was the unpredictable path of the constitutional politics that culminated in the Court's *Engel* and *Schempp* decisions. In both cases, Pfeffer and the AJCongress misread where the Court was prepared to take the establishment clause on the matter of religion in the public schools, an understandable error in light of their earlier experience in *Zorach*. Even so, Pfeffer remained an integral actor throughout the litigation campaign as a counselor and pivotal strategist, as well as enhancing his public stature as a scholar-advocate in the arena of church-state law. As we have seen, though, Pfeffer also bequeathed to the AJCongress a reputation as the organizational force behind the legal reform movement in this area, to the extent that each became the target of attack by critics of *Engel* and the Court's subsequent decision on Bible reading, even though neither, in their individual or organizational capacities, had initiated these litigation campaigns. Thus when the steady storm of criticism settled in over *Engel*, Pfeffer, the AJCongress, and even the AJCommittee and the ADL found themselves caught square at the cross hairs of religious accommodationists, who were stunned and angered by the Court's decision.

To understand just how synonymous the major Jewish organizations, and especially Pfeffer, had become with the revolution taking place in the Court's approach to the separation principle and the corresponding changes this was producing in the relationship between religion and the state, one need only examine the spate of criticism, much of it cast in acerbic and personal terms, that was directed toward them after *Engel*. Gratuitous condemnation of the decision from conservative senators and representatives in Congress was of course expected: rare is the national political figure who wastes a prime-time chance to invoke God and country at the expense of reasonable public discourse.[74] In the minds of organized American Jewry, though, far more serious than this political grandstanding was the stream of critical commentary penned by the editors of *America* after *Engel*. This soon prompted an exchange between Catholic and Jewish leaders, with an occasional interjection from Protestant quarters and such respected secular journals of opinion as the *New Republic* and the *National Review*. This debate lasted throughout the summer and fall of 1962.

Spirited Catholic criticism of the Jewish organizations' commitment to a vigorous campaign of social and legal reform of establishment clause law dated back to the Court's decision in *McCollum*. But while critical of their position on and approach to the resolution of church-state issues, Catholic opinion had never challenged the right of Jewish groups to advance their organizational goals through litigation or through the political process. In the tone of the *America* editorials, how-ever, there began to be hints that Catholic patience was beginning to wear thin, given the spectacular judicial success that the coalition of separationist groups who had supported *Engel* were enjoying and were bound to repeat in *Schempp* the following year. But rather than upbraid all the actors involved in *Engel*'s progression, *America* turned its rhetor-ical fire on the Jewish organizations.

In words that the *Christian Century*, a major voice in mainline Protes-tant circles, would later refer to as a "thinly veiled threat . . . to frighten Jews into . . . silence on issues involving the constitutional liberties of all citizens, including Jews,"[75] *America*'s editors warned all who would listen:

> The well-publicized Jewish spokesman, Leo Pfeffer, and these Jewish agencies make no secret of their view that "a favorable climate of opinion" will help stop legislation providing grants on loans to church-related institutions of higher learning. Thus, we see that intense efforts are being made in some Jewish quarters to close ranks and to exploit all the resources of group awareness, purposefulness and expertise that are to be found in the Jewish community.
>
> It would be most unfortunate if the entire Jewish community were to be blamed for the unrelenting pressure tactics of a small but overly vocal segment within it. In our opinion, therefore, re-sponsible Jewish spokesmen should make known the fact that the all-out campaign to secularize the public schools and public life from top to bottom, as that campaign is conceived and imple-mented by Mr. Pfeffer and a few organizations, does *not* repre-sent the ideas of the whole Jewish community.
>
> We wonder, therefore, whether it is not time for provident leaders of American Judaism to ask their more militant col-leagues whether what is gained through the courts by such victo-ries is worth the breakdown of community relations which will

inevitably follow them. What will have been accomplished if our Jewish friends win all the legal immunities they seek, but thereby paint themselves into a corner of social and cultural alienation?

The time has come for these fellow citizens of ours to decide among themselves precisely what they conceive to be the final objective of the Jewish community in the United States—in a word, what bargain they are willing to strike as one of the minorities in a pluralistic society. When court victories produce only a harvest of fear and distrust, will it all have been worthwhile?[76]

Despite the strident tone of this first post-*Engel* editorial from *America,* the major Jewish organizations did not shrink from their position on religion in the public schools and their vigorous pursuit of remedies through the litigation process. After years of internal struggle over how and when to pursue their campaign to outlaw state-sponsored religious practices in the public schools—practices that often placed Jewish schoolchildren and their parents at the constitutional margins of the right to equal treatment without regard to religious background—the major Jewish agencies were not about to compromise a stance they believed was valid, consistent, and reasonable under the First and Fourteenth Amendments to the Constitution. Even the AJCommittee and the ADL seemed to be liberated, in part, by the Court's clear rejection of constitutionalized Christian hegemony over the nation's public schools, with each group taking visible roles to defend and later implement the *Engel* and *Schempp* decisions. It was, in fact, the AJCommittee, which so often in the past had served as the apologist for the absolutist philosophy of the AJCongress and other constituent groups of the NCRAC on the separation principle, that issued the first public response from the Jewish organizations involved in *Engel* to the *America* editorial.

In a departure from its traditional restrained approach to such matters, the AJCommittee admonished *America* for suggesting that Jews did not have the same rights as Catholics to pursue their interests "through the impartial judicial process which our democratic state has established for such purposes." Noting that Catholics have never "allowed their minority status to determine their positions on what they have considered crucial issues of principle," it pointed to their successful judicial campaigns to ban the reading of the King James version of the Bible in the public schools in the late nineteenth and early twentieth centuries and to strike down state laws that required children to attend public schools. The AJCommittee reminded *America* that in the latter case, *Pierce v. Society of Sisters,* it had submitted an amicus brief on behalf of the Catholic position, "without regard for whether the victory would produce a 'harvest of fear and distrust,'" as the magazine's editors cautioned the Jews' success in *Engel* just might lead to.[77] But *America* continued its editorials, and the Jewish agencies—along with those Protestant groups drawn into the fray—continued to respond to them, leading to a bitter exchange that went on for weeks, until both sides realized that the other was not about to budge. One might even argue that over the course of this debate each became the other's greatest ally in rallying their supporters to the cause.[78]

In the South, where outrage over *Engel* and later *Schempp* was particularly visible, ADL and AJCommittee community relations and legal personnel began an active campaign to educate school boards, principals and teachers, and parent groups, on whose shoulders would fall the obligation to implement the Court's decisions in the public schools. Here, as an ADL community relations staff professional explained, Catholics were not the problem; Southern Baptists were. In the northern states, the alliances were reversed, with the Jewish organizations receiving greater support from leaders in the mainline Protestant communities. Thus, for example, even C. Emanuel Carlson, the executive director of the Baptist Joint Committee on Public Affairs and hardly a liberal firebrand, said that "he was not disturbed by the elimination of 'required prayers' from schools because he had never felt that recital of such prayers had any real religious value for children."[79]

In a similarly tolerant spirit, Dean Kelley, who would later become an esteemed voice on church-state politics and relations, said that "many Christians will welcome the decision [because] it protects the rights of minorities and guards against the development of public school religion which is neither Christianity nor Judaism but something less than either."[80] Even before the decision in *Engel* was formally announced, Kelley had signaled that the Protestant leadership was prepared to work with the Jewish and secular civil liberties organizations to educate public opinion as to the litigation's true meaning, saying that "neither the church nor the state should use the public school to compel acceptance of any creed or conformity to any specific religious practice."[81] Commented an ADL community relations staff professional on these interfaith tensions:

You wouldn't know from reading *America,* but in the South, we felt that Catholics were our allies. We were both small minorities and we both found religious practices in the public schools offensive, since they were straight Protestant Christianity. To Jews in the South, there was little worry about Catholics—they had no chance to get public money for their schools given who controlled the politics down here. Far from viewing the Catholics as an adversarial group, we view[ed] them as our national allies on church-state issues. In the South, we did not get caught up in that *America* vs. the Jews debate. We sat down with Catholics and asked them to work with us to prepare for the changes that were coming. After the prayer case, everyone knew that Bible reading did not have a chance. Catholics were our friends; they sat next to us while we had meetings with the Protestants and said, "This is what's going to happen, so let's work together to prepare for it." Catholics had struggled for acceptance in the South, and they could see where we were coming from and tried to help us, not fight us. It was very different up North, where those cases originated, and where tensions between Catholics and Jews were far worse.[82]

Pfeffer was content to let the AJCommittee and the ADL handle the public education campaign and work with local community groups to encourage compliance with the Court's decisions, while he turned his attention to other prospective cases that would extend the principles articulated in *Engel* and *Schempp.* The Court's decisions had rendered moot an earlier announcement by the AJCongress that it was considering pursuing a lawsuit against Nassau and Suffolk counties on Long Island, New York, to force an end to Bible reading practices there, since such issues could now be settled without the force of litigation.[83] But before the AJCongress could decide what should come next in its campaign to transform the establishment clause, it recognized that it could not expect the AJCommittee and the ADL to lead the effort at the national level to coordinate support for the Court's decisions in *Engel* and *Schempp.*

Between the Court's rulings in *Engel* and *Schempp,* several conferences were set up that called together the major Jewish organizations, secular civil liberties groups, and the representative bodies of American Protestantism. The purpose of these conferences was to coordinate an education campaign that would prepare the public for the Court's pending decision regarding Bible reading in the schools. Afterward, the same organizations came together to dissuade Congress from ratifying the Becker Amendment, a constitutional amendment introduced after *Schempp* that, if adopted, would have overruled *Engel* as well.[84] Enlisting the Protestant groups in opposition to the Becker Amendment enabled the AJCongress, the AJCommittee, and the ADL to present an interfaith coalition on behalf of an important civil liberties principle that helped to disabuse the perception that vigorous advocacy for a robust interpretation of the separation principle was a cause backed solely by Jews. Here the Jewish organizations took a page from the NAACP's strategy of assembling amicus briefs and other external support in its litigation campaign against racial discrimination, the better to demonstrate that a constitutional commitment to equal protection and nondiscrimination would be to the advantage of all citizens, not just African Americans.

So it was on this—the promise of constitutional equality through the legal reform model—that the AJCongress, the AJCommittee, and the ADL built for the future. For the AJCommittee and the ADL, the progression of *Torcaso, Engel,* and finally *Schempp* had taught them that political jurisprudence was a powerful instrument of constitutional reform, a premise they had been somewhat skeptical of ever since the fallout from *Zorach.* Whereas litigation would never become their preferred tactic in the church-state arena, the AJCommittee and the ADL were no longer allergic to its aggressive use. Each now understood that the legal and social relations models were not mutually exclusive, but complementary.

A number of important internal changes within the ADL and the AJCommittee had conditioned their newfound aggression. First, a generational turnover in staff had occurred, whereby the old guard had given way to more youthful members, who were less inclined to bow to traditional accommodationist approaches to reaching accord with non-Jewish bodies at the expense of their own constitutional rights. This turnover was accompanied by a corresponding increase in the role of legal staff, who generally viewed litigation as a necessary component in any effort to pursue constitutional change. In addition, the Court's triple play in *Torcaso, Engel,* and *Schempp* had made the prospects of constitutional reform through litigation even more attractive. Doctrinal progression in the law, coupled with the defensive position that religious and political conservatives now found themselves in as the tide of constitutional change swept forward, made the external environment more hospitable as well. These internal and external considerations interacted to encourage greater use of the legal reform model on the part of these groups, who were once so shy of litigation.

As for the AJCongress, the Court's decisions in *Torcaso, Engel,* and *Schempp* vindicated its decade-long organizational commitment to constitutional reform through litigation. These decisions were especially gratifying to Pfeffer, since they crystallized the vision of the establishment clause that he had articulated through his scholarship and legal pleadings since he first persuaded the AJCongress, along with the other major Jewish organizations, to file its first amicus brief in this area, in *McCollum.* Although Pfeffer had made his share of strategic mistakes in some cases (notably *Zorach*) and had at times underestimated the Court's readiness to engage in major doctrinal innovation of the establishment clause (*Engel* and *Schempp*), he stood as the uncontested leader of the church-state reform movement. He had established—and would go on to refine, much in the way that Thurgood Marshall did in his work with the NAACP—a rapport with the bench and the bar through his work as a "one-man 'repeat player,' albeit one rooted in a organizational pattern that helped and sustained his efforts," as one scholar later characterized it.[85] As did all the organized interests that collaborated in these historic cases, Pfeffer also discovered that even the most careful efforts to conceive and manage a planned campaign could not always overcome the random twists of fate and unpredictable reversals of opinion that were intertwined with the litigation process. Control over the various forces, whether internal or external, at play in a litigation campaign was much more elusive than Pfeffer had perhaps thought—all of which is indicative of the ad hoc, episodic nature of constitutional litigation in general.

But these were lessons that Pfeffer could absorb for the next phase of the litigation campaign. In the pivotal period from *Zorach* to *Schempp,* Pfeffer had done much to bring the other Jewish organizations around on the advantages of the legal reform model, so much so that another prominent leader from organized American Jewry would write to him that, "for the Jewish community," *Engel* and *Schempp* were "equal in importance to the desegregation decision [*Brown v. Board of Education*] of 1954. I believe that we now have the most potent weapon which have ever possessed to really clean up the religion in the public schools problem. You have indeed become a great hero."[86]

Such praise could offer some comfort to Pfeffer in the face of the vile hate mail he also received after *Engel*, a considerable amount of which was from other Jews. "I feel that because of you and your ilk," wrote one irate Los Angeles Jewish resident, "in all the civilized nations of the world the most despised, spat upon, hated and shunned person is the Jew."[87] An Arlington, Massachusetts, couple accused Pfeffer of having "created more hardship among the Jews than any man since the period of Biblical times. My advice to you is leave the Catholics and Protestants alone. Our struggle is severe enough. Forget about legal or fishy explanations, we have a lot to live down. You are getting *we* the Jews in a terrible mess, keep it up and we shall all again be persecuted."[88] Another self-described "well-meaning Christian" wrote to Pfeffer, "Having a number of good Jewish friends, I was shocked to find where you—one of their leaders, took a stand against the Lord's Prayer used in our schools. I was under the impression that you believed in God like the rest of us. It seems to me the moral standards of our country have sunk to such a low level encouragement should be given to anything that might train our young folks to a reverence for a Supreme God. Your motives seem small, petty and personal."[89]

In another time, such harsh criticism might have mattered a great deal. But, for a mature and more confident Jewish community, too much had changed. It was now time to move on.

5

Litigation Politics and
the Public Purse

The Parochial School Aid Cases

In *Torcaso*, *Engel*, and *Schempp*, the Supreme Court redefined the traditional relationship between the Christian heritage of mainstream American religion and civil society. No longer did government possess the constitutional authority to promote the religious values of political majorities through its public school systems or require that citizens profess adherence to those values in order to participate in public life. In just over a decade, the Court—fueled by the egalitarian impulses that characterized the sixteen-year tenure of Chief Justice Earl Warren—outlawed racial segregation in public education, required state legislatures to guarantee equal representation in the apportionment of their legislative districts, began a radical reform of the rules of criminal procedure, and expanded the free speech rights of political dissenters and advocates of other unpopular positions to near-absolute levels.[1]

The church-state jurisprudence of the Warren Court was no exception to its general tendency toward a dramatic reconfiguration of the American constitutional scheme. Reflective of the emphasis placed on fundamental values by Chief Justice Warren, the Court ruled that the establishment clause made religious faith irrelevant to one's constitutional right to hold public office; prohibited public schools from functioning as instruments for state religious instruction; and held that the rights of conscientious objectors to military service should be expanded to include exemption on nondenominational religious grounds.[2] It would later rule that public schools could not teach Biblical creationism to explain the origin of human existence.[3] In each case, the Court ruled that government could not use religious affiliation to elevate or diminish the status of individual citizens under the Constitution. But while the Warren Court expunged the constitutional inequities that had long existed with respect to the preferred position awarded Christian religious values in American public life, it declined to confront the other, equally divisive issue involving religion and education that had long simmered beneath such inequities: the use of public funds to subsidize private religious schools.

That tax-funded assistance to parochial schools never assumed a dominant place on the establishment clause agenda of the Warren Court is ironic, since this was the very constitutional question that had first pulled the Court into the maelstrom of church-state politics back in 1947, when it decided *Everson v. Board of Education.* While the Warren Court handed down innovative decisions that diminished the power of government to promote or prefer religion and brought about a quantum reformation in the modern definition of the separation principle, it never quite decided how tax subsidies for religious schools fit into the new contours it had created for the establishment clause. Whether parochial schools had a legitimate claim to the public purse and to what extent Congress and state legislatures could include them in the comprehensive educational reform initiatives enacted in the mid-1960s were matters that Warren would leave to his successor as chief justice, Warren Earl Burger, to resolve. Just as the new constitutional limitations on the place of religion in the public schools symbolized establishment clause reform during the 1960s, the question of whether government could channel public funds to parochial schools would dominate the next phase of the Court's drive to reshape the law of church and state, a process that would last well into the 1980s. Religious schools soon replaced public schools as the microcosm for the fundamental debate over the relationship between civil and religious institutions. And the major American Jewish organizations again found themselves in the center, if not in the lead, of the group-driven politics that directed this contentious—and very public—new phase. This still uncertain post-*Engel* period was one in which the core understanding of the relationship between religion and the state awaited further elucidation.

Commenting on the Warren Court era, constitutional scholar and former Solicitor General Archibald Cox has written that "at the same time the . . . responsibility [of the Court] for individuals and minorities was growing, losers in the political process were becoming more conscious of the potentials of constitutional adjudication for achieving goals not attainable through the political process." Concomitant to this development, Cox noted, was "that constitutional litigation came to be conducted more and more by civil rights and civil liberties organizations" rather than by aggrieved individuals.[4] Having been unable to achieve their policy objectives through the legislative and executive branches—and encouraged by the liberal impulses visible in the reform jurisprudence of the Warren Court—the AJCongress, the AJCommittee, and the ADL emerged as classic examples of organized interest groups who turned to litigation to pursue constitutional change. This unprecedented synergism of group-driven litigation and liberal judicial activism had the cumulative effect of making constitutional jurisprudence a newly powerful instrument for social reform.

As twilight began to fall over the Warren Court era, the AJCommittee, the AJCongress, and the ADL—like other liberal, cause-oriented organized interests such as the NAACP and the ACLU that emphasized the power of litigation to effect constitutional reform— found themselves in a much different position than had been the case a generation before. Gone from the public sphere were the pervasive, state-sanctioned and implemented Christian values, symbols, and rhetoric that had stood in the path of society's recognition that religious pluralism had arrived in America. Jews, like members of other unfavored religious faiths before them, were now entitled to acceptance as full and equal members in the American cultural and religious milieu, which now counted pluralism as one of its defining characteristics. Over the previous several decades, the corporate structure that had formed to represent American Jews had modified its response to the frequent assaults on the dual guarantees of separation of church and state and religious free exercise with strategies in order to match the political and constitutional moment. Silence and indifference were thus rejected in favor of assimilation, which was later discarded out of preference for a bolder, more experimental approach. This new approach placed law and litigation at the center of a more cohesive, systematic campaign on the part of these organizations to assert without apology their constitutional rights. As Morton Borden has commented, though, the litigation campaign pursued by this small nucleus of Jewish organizations—a campaign that resulted in the epochal decisions of the 1960s—did more than simply grant Jews their constitutional right to religious equality. It forced mainstream America not only to think about the core principles of the First Amendment but to debate more seriously the issue of how they should blend into the larger constitutional culture that counted liberty and equality among its highest values.[5]

For the major American Jewish organizations, the landmark decisions of the Warren Court took from parchment promise to genuine performance Leo Pfeffer's now well-articulated vision of the First Amendment: that "Caesar was not to meddle in the affairs of God, either to hurt him or to help him."[6] But the AJCommittee, the AJCongress, and the ADL also understood that the Court's decisions were double-edged. Rather than follow the constitutional guidelines the Court had laid down, Congress and several state legislatures, under intense political pressure from constituencies that viewed *Engel, Schempp,* and *Torcaso* as unwelcome breaches of constitutional faith, instead decided to test the reaches of this new church-state jurisprudence. Predictable but unsuccessful efforts were accordingly made to overturn the Court's school prayer and Bible reading decisions through constitutional amendment and later, in a real flight of fantasy, through the introduction of federal statutes designed to remove the Court's jurisdiction to hear cases involving religion and public schools.[7] Although conservative organized interests generated one political firestorm after another on the school prayer issue they were eventually forced to abandon any serious hopes of succeeding.

But while unsuccessful in reinstating religion in public schools, religious conservatives were much more effective in lobbying elected officials at the federal and state levels to include parochial schools in their public expenditures on elementary and secondary education. What complicated the parochial aid issue even further was that some organized interests that had supported *Engel* and *Schempp* drew constitutional distinctions when it came to public support for religious education. Whether the legislative allocation of public funds to assist parochial educators raised constitutional defects that paralleled state sponsorship of religious practices in public schools consequently emerged as the central issue that commanded the litigation politics of establishment clause jurisprudence in the post-*Engel* era.

Well before the major Jewish organizations began to plan their direct attack on parochial school aid, however, Leo Pfeffer had held that it was imperative to force the Court to revisit an old procedural rule limiting the scope of the taxpayer's standing to sue. For forty years this rule had served as a formidable obstacle to taxpayer lawsuits that aimed to challenge federal expenditures alleged to be unconstitutional. The constitutional rule was rooted in a 1923 decision, *Frothingham v. Mellon*,[8] which several current justices had expressed a desire to revisit, although they had not been able to find an appropriate vehicle with which to do so. Pfeffer recognized that the current rules on standing to sue made it all but impossible to initiate taxpayer suits that would challenge federal expenditures, even if such expenditures promoted policies that the plaintiffs believed were unconstitutional. He also saw that, without modification of the standing to sue requirement, there could be no systematic litigation on the parochial aid issue. Pfeffer understood this perhaps better than anyone involved in public interest litigation and was thus determined to reform the *Frothingham* rule. Before all else, this became his—and the Jewish organizations'— first order of business.

Prying Open the Courthouse Door: *Flast v. Cohen*

For decades the Court's position on lawsuits challenging public expenditures was defined by the narrow scope of the standing requirement that it had articulated in *Frothingham v. Mellon*. There, the Court rejected the argument that an individual citizen possessed standing to sue the government when a general public expenditure allegedly violated a constitutional right, absent proof that such an expenditure caused actual harm. *Frothingham* centered on the complaint of a Massachusetts resident who argued that the Maternity Act of 1921, which authorized the federal government to make conditional grants to states that wished to supplement their prenatal and infant care programs, violated her constitutional rights as a taxpayer because it increased her tax burden without due process of law. Without dissent, the Court dismissed Frothingham's claim on the grounds that the plaintiff had failed to demonstrate either that the federal statute in question was invalid or that its administration had resulted in an injury or affliction sufficient to sustain her claim.

Federal courts had, ever since, followed the principle established in *Frothingham*, even though several judges had expressed concern over what they believed was the excessively narrow scope of the ruling. Since 1923 the administrative welfare state had grown in exponential terms. As a result, individuals could now often assert legitimate grievances that in certain cases public expenditures on programs funded by their tax dollars violated their constitutional rights. But the problem was how to demonstrate that such expenditures caused the type of harm that fell within the definition of *Frothingham*—and if one could not demonstrate such harm within the scope of *Frothingham's* holding, then it became pointless to argue that the challenged statute was unconstitutional. How then to proceed with an attack on what seemed like such a well-embedded rule? In the Elementary and Secondary Education Act of 1965 (ESEA), Pfeffer believed that he had found the perfect federal statute on which to litigate these critical procedural issues.

Congress had passed the ESEA in 1965, as of then the most comprehensive federal legislation ever conceived to bolster the financial resources of state and local schools. The general purpose of the ESEA was to supplement lower-income public school districts whose resources were inferior to those of their more affluent neighbors. What distinguished the ESEA from previous federal programs designed to assist state and local educational institutions was more than just its massive scale. For the first time, the federal government made private schools eligible for public funds—indeed, in certain cases the legislation required them to receive such assistance—and in so doing it did not exempt religious schools from receiving these benefits. Congress passed the ESEA and President Johnson signed it during the same legislative session that the major Jewish organizations, with Pfeffer in the lead role, had assembled a broad-based and ecumenical coalition of religious and secular organizations to defeat the Becker Amendment, a constitutional amendment named for Congressman Frank Becker (D–N.Y.) and intended to overturn *Engel* and *Schempp*. But when it came to the ESEA, the Jewish organizations were not able to hold together their traditional alliance with the major public education and teachers lobbies—such as the National Education Association and the United Parents Association, and the mainline Protestant bodies, such as the National Council of Churches—all of which had played a crucial role in defeating the Becker Amendment. Apart from a sole companion, the ACLU, the major American Jewish organizations stood alone. In fact, even Orthodox Jewish agencies, heretofore an unspoken voice in church-state politics and litigation, emerged as enthusiastic supporters of the ESEA, since their own fragile network of religious day schools stood to benefit from the act. As these battles over parochial school aid moved from the legislatures to the courts, the Orthodox Jewish agencies remained consistent advocates of such assistance, opposing their liberal, separationist counterparts at almost every turn.[9] Rather, Orthodox Jewish agencies became important allies of Catholic and other conservative organized interests that supported parochial school assistance, a development whose significance will be discussed later in this chapter.[10]

How does one explain the coalescence of these staunch supporters of the separation principle in American public education with such powerful advocates of public assistance for parochial schools as the National Catholic Welfare Conference (later the United States Catholic Conference), Citizens for Educational Freedom, and other nonchurch bodies representing Catholic and other conservative religious interests? On its face, the acquiescence of the public education lobbies and Protestant agencies in the ESEA negotiations appeared to signal a retreat from the absolute no-aid position these organizations had espoused in *Everson*. After all, it was a well-organized coalition of Protestant and public education organizations that had sponsored Arch Everson's landmark lawsuit that challenged the expenditure of public funds to subsidize the transportation of parochial students to and from school. But the complexities of the ESEA rendered problematic the charge that these crucial allies of the organized Jewish community had abandoned their commitment to strict separationism, a conclusion that the constituent organizations of the NCRAC indeed admitted had no real basis in fact.

Foremost in the decision of the public school and Protestant bodies to support the ESEA was the fear that unless they agreed to a provision that made all private schools eligible for assistance they would lose President Johnson's commitment to the legislation. Rather than oppose the inclusion of religious and secular private schools in the ESEA, the National Council of Churches, the Baptist Joint Committee, and the teachers' groups, in tandem with the constituent bodies of the NCRAC and the ACLU, instead argued for regulations that would require complete public control over all funds expended in connection with the legislation's programs. In exchange for this guarantee, the Protestant and public education lobbies agreed to endorse the legislation. Behind the scenes, however, they worked with the Jewish organizations and the ACLU to craft the best possible safeguards to ensure that religious schools had no control over the distribution of public funds.

Thus the final version of the ESEA of 1965 as written—as even Pfeffer acknowledged in a position paper he prepared for the NCRAC soon after the legislation's enactment—did not violate the establishment clause. But Pfeffer was not convinced that the church-state provisions for which the separationist organizations had fought were strong enough to prevent what he believed were serious constitutional problems pertaining to the administration of the legislation. "Sooner or later," wrote Pfeffer, "the issue of constitutionality will one way or another reach the Supreme Court, *notwithstanding absence of a provision for judicial review.* When that occurs, it will be, I believe, the administration of the act, and not the act itself, that will be declared unconstitutional." [11] For Pfeffer, moreover, the perceived constitutional defects in the ESEA's administrative program served as the theoretical cornerstone on which to challenge *Frothingham's* restrictions. Whether a statute was violative of the First Amendment on its face or as applied should not matter, reasoned Pfeffer.

But before Pfeffer could challenge the ESEA on constitutional grounds, it was first necessary to persuade the Court to modify or overturn its current rules on the taxpayer standing requirement. Pfeffer believed that supporters of parochial school aid well knew that the ESEA's administration would transgress constitutional limitations on government financial assistance to religion, which is why they insisted that the final legislation contain no provision for judicial review. Once this procedural obstacle was eliminated, however, litigation that would challenge the substantive church-state violations in the ESEA's administration could commence.

In pursuit of this objective the AJCongress had by November 1966 persuaded the United Parents Association, the New York Civil Liberties Union, and the United Federation of Teachers to serve as coplaintiffs in the *Flast v. Cohen* litigation, so named for Florence Flast, president of the aforementioned parents' organization. It was agreed that Pfeffer would serve as lead counsel in *Flast*, as well as in the companion case, *Board of Education v. Allen*.[12] The coalition had decided to litigate this second case in state court in an effort to challenge, on substantive criteria, the provisions in Title I of the ESEA that required states to loan textbooks to parochial schools. On this latter point, Pfeffer wanted to test whether the Court's current attitude toward the "child-benefit" theory (first created in *Cochran* and later affirmed in *Everson*), which was intended to rationalize "indirect" forms of assistance to children in parochial schools, had changed in wake of the Court's move toward a more absolutist construction of the establishment clause.

According to the child-benefit theory, so long as the primary beneficiary of the government aid involved was the child and not the church, the Court had indicated, it would not consider such assistance unconstitutional. This doctrine provided the rationale that the public education lobbies and the mainline Protestant groups needed to break the legislative stalemate over the ESEA and accept it as written. It was even easier for them to accept since they knew that litigation to challenge the provisions not only of Title I but of Title II as well was bound to follow. (In addition to books, Title I made general education materials, transportation, and various auxiliary services available to all children in private as well as public schools, while Title II required that public schools allow deprived children in all private schools access to such assistance.) The ESEA was also a compromise with which the Catholic Church, which had profited from the Court's earlier use of the child-benefit rationale in litigation involving public assistance to parochial schools, could live. Thus the parallel state lawsuit in *Allen* was a first effort to find out where the Court stood on the child-benefit theory—which was, Pfeffer alleged, reflecting the position of the AJ-Congress, the AJCommittee, the ADL, and the constituent organizations of the NCRAC, a "legal fiction."[13] Pfeffer was not sure whether the Court was prepared to depart from the child-benefit doctrine. But whether it did or not, Pfeffer did not believe that recent developments in establishment clause law would suffer such an irrevocable setback that future litigation on the standing requirement would be ruled out.

In *Flast* and *Allen*, the major Jewish organizations worked together with their traditional public education and Protestant allies to assemble amicus support for the plaintiffs. In the opinion of these groups, the submission of amicus briefs in each case by several of the groups that had originally supported the passage of the ESEA as written would allow them to explain to explain in a constitutional context the difference between their conception of the law's primary purpose (to assist public education and nonsectarian private schools) and the manner in which it had been or stood to be applied (to subsidize parochial education). Such organizations as Americans United, the National Council of Churches, United Americans for Public Schools, and a coalition of public education and teachers lobbies agreed to participate as amici in *Flast*, although they declined to do so in *Allen*. These same organizations believed that their limited financial and legal resources would be better spent on attacking the *Frothingham* rule rather than in participating in the substantive challenge to Title I of the ESEA. There was, moreover, no doubt in their minds that the questions at issue in *Allen* would end up before the Court sooner rather than later anyway, and they so sought to channel their available litigation resources in the most efficient manner. The major Jewish organizations had no fundamental problem with the position the public education and Protestant groups took in *Allen*. But since the AJCongress was a sponsoring organization in *Flast* and a pivotal actor in *Allen*, they felt that it was in their best interests to participate as amici in both cases.

Flast and *Allen* thus served to thaw the previously chilly relationship of the AJCommittee, the AJCongress, and the ADL to one another. While, to the parties involved, Pfeffer would clearly function as the lead counsel in *Allen*, he did not appear on the plaintiff's principal brief as the attorney of record. This tactic, one that Pfeffer had used before in *Zorach*, enabled him to have substantive input into the amicus briefs that were filed on behalf of the NCRAC, as well as other organized interests that solicited his assistance. In contrast, Pfeffer does appear as the plaintiff's attorney of record in *Flast*. Credit for the amicus brief submitted by the coalition of major Jewish organizations is thus attributed to the legal directors of the AJCommittee, the AJCongress, and the ADL. Other Jewish organizations were, however, eligible to sign on in return for their assistance with costs, even though Pfeffer was still the AJCongress' chief counsel on these matters.[14]

But Pfeffer was not listed as the plaintiff's attorney in *Allen*. Rather, he appears as the lead counsel on the amicus brief jointly submitted by the AJCommittee, the AJCongress, the ADL, and several other national Jewish agencies and rabbinical bodies.[15] That such an approach would be adopted not only offers further evidence for the almost complete dominance that Pfeffer exercised over the legal and political strategy of the major Jewish organizations in church-state affairs but attests to the pervasiveness of the belief that his expertise was so superior to that of any other lawyer involved in church-state issues that the mere presence of his name on an amicus brief was enough to give it the air of authority that few other such participants could claim.

Meanwhile, another change in the organizational relationship between the AJCongress and, together, the AJCommittee and the ADL came about. By the late 1960s the AJCommittee and the ADL had been able to reconcile their once-pronounced strategic and philosophical differences with the AJCongress and rejoin the NCRAC. One immediate result of this decision was the dissipation of the long-standing amicus partnership between the AJCommittee and the ADL in church-state litigation. Although it was never planned as such, *Schempp* marked the last case in which the AJCommittee and the ADL would submit an amicus brief on behalf of themselves independently, a development that broke with a pattern that had been in place since *Zorach*. From *Flast* through the early 1980s, a period when cases involving public funds for parochial schools dominated the Court's church-state agenda, the AJCommittee and the ADL, along with the AJCongress, remained the most activist amici in the litigation underway. But the coalition politics characteristic of the major Jewish organizations' amicus participation in this phase would be much different than it had during the formative period of their involvement in church-state politics and litigation. In some cases, the AJCommittee, the AJCongress, and the ADL would prepare and submit amicus briefs on behalf both of themselves and of other Jewish organizations that wished to join them; in other cases, the AJCommittee would file as part of a larger interfaith coalition, while the ADL or the AJCongress submitted amicus briefs in tandem or alone; and at times or one or more might agree to sign an amicus brief prepared on behalf of a larger coalition of organizations, some of which had no ties to the Jewish or religious network of organized interests.

Internal forces and organizational reaction to new external demands on their resources accounted for much of this alteration in the behavior of the major Jewish organizations in church-state litigation. An effort to explain how these considerations affected the organizational behavior of the AJCommittee, the AJCongress, and the ADL will be made later. For now, we need only to note that *Flast* did more than revolutionize the practice of public interest law over the next generation by making it easier for individuals to initiate lawsuits in their capacity as taxpayers. It also marked the beginning of another critical period of realignment in the organizational politics of Jewish involvement in church-state litigation.

The *Flast* litigation itself commenced when, in 1967, a three-judge federal court rebuked Pfeffer's argument on taxpayer standing, holding that individuals were not entitled to stand in their capacity as taxpayers in order to initiate legal action to restrain the use of public funds for allegedly unconstitutional purposes.[16] Given the *Frothingham* rule, this decision was hardly unexpected. The Supreme Court agreed to hear the plaintiff's appeal, but announced that it would limit oral argument to the question of taxpayer suits and not consider whether the ESEA of 1965 violated the establishment clause. Should the Court decide to relax the *Frothingham* rule so as to permit taxpayer suits, it would then remand the case to federal district court, where the establishment clause issues would be briefed and argued in full. When *Flast* reached the Court, the AJCongress agreed to prepare the amicus brief that would be submitted on behalf of the NCRAC.

An AJCongress-prepared brief on behalf of the major Jewish organizations for submission in *Flast* had been anticipated since the litigation commenced. For the first time since *Zorach*, however, the AJCommittee and the ADL were included among the constituent bodies represented by the NCRAC's brief. But in contrast to the bitter internal strife in *Zorach* that threatened at various times to dissolve that litigation, preparation for the amicus effort in *Flast* proceeded with little fanfare. This absence of discord was due in large part to the simple fact that there were no fundamental disagreements over the arguments that the brief should set forth: ever since the passage of the ESEA, the NCRAC had taken the position that taxpayer suits should be permitted under the Constitution. But to avoid the problems that had plagued the effort of the three major agencies in *Zorach*—including charges that the AJCongress had acted without consulting the AJCommittee or the ADL—the AJCongress formally canvassed the opinion of the constituent bodies of the NCRAC before recommending that a brief should be filed in *Flast*. The AJCongress also said that, although it would prepare the initial draft, it would remain open to suggestions from the other Jewish organizations that wished to join in signing the brief before submitting the final version.[17]

As it turned out, the brief drafted by the AJCongress on behalf of the NCRAC's constituent bodies—which, quite apart from the AJCommittee and the ADL, now totaled over thirty—changed little from its initial outline to the completed document. It followed the arguments set forth in Pfeffer's brief for the plaintiffs and centered on three major points to avoid boxing in the Court's options on *Frothingham*. Each point offered a plausible argument on the basis of which the scope of taxpayer lawsuits could be widened. First, the Court could overrule *Frothingham* altogether and articulate new rules from scratch, a scenario that even Pfeffer believed to be the least plausible option. Second, the Court could rule that *Frothingham* was not applicable in cases where the plaintiff was asserting a First Amendment claim, such as freedom of speech, religion, or association, because individuals should have greater latitude to contest governmental actions that violate fundamental civil liberties. In the AJCongress's opinion, this second argument offered the Court the most feasible route to modifying *Frothingham*. The final argument presented the Court with the narrowest, most conservative alternative: it could hold that the *Frothingham* rule was inapplicable only when a plaintiff asserted an establishment clause claim.

More generally, the *Flast* brief sought to stress that judicial review was a crucial mechanism by which to ensure that the political branches of government were indeed constrained in their power to abridge individual rights and liberties. Furthermore, the law should guarantee access to the federal courts when historically disadvantaged minority groups asserted constitutional claims involving the alleged deprivation of individual rights. As the Court itself had noted on numerous occasions, judicial action is often the only recourse that minority groups have in order to obtain full enforcement of their constitutional rights (a fact the Court had recently affirmed, if under somewhat different circumstances, in *NAACP v. Button*).[18] The *Flast* brief concluded that public expenditures alleged to be unconstitutional should not be an exception to the rule permitting organized interests to litigate on behalf of public interest claims, especially when it meant that religious minorities would have to support the legislative objectives of more powerful religious groups with their tax dollars.[19]

Within the AJCommittee, the ADL, and the NCRAC constituent bodies in general, almost no internal disagreement was expressed over whether to accept the invitation of the AJCongress to participate in *Flast*. What dissent did emerge centered not on the AJCongress's substantive attack on the *Frothingham* rule but rather on the need for an amicus brief from parties other than the plaintiffs. Moreover, in an unusual twist, it was limited to the ADL: it did not even involve its traditional partner in such matters, the AJCommittee. The complaint stemmed from an objection by one the members of the ADL's appointed lay committee charged with policy recommendations in such cases, Gus J. Solomon. Solomon, who also happened to be a federal district judge in Portland, Oregon, voted against the ADL's formal request for permission to participate as an amicus curiae in *Flast*. His opposition was not, however, rooted in the ADL's historical aversion to public involvement in controversial litigation. Nor was it motivated by a fear of possible anti-Semitism triggered by concerted Jewish participation in litigation that, despite the emphasis on the procedural issue at hand, might offend Christians who viewed public support for parochial education as a test of ecumenical cooperation. In his letter to Sol Rabkin, the legal director of the ADL, Judge Solomon did not in fact question the worthiness of the Pfeffer-led challenge to the *Frothingham* rule. He instead argued that the ADL's participation in an amicus coalition was a "useless" expenditure of organizational resources. Wrote Solomon:

> Dear Sol:
>
> I have been troubled by the *Frothingham* decision. Some years ago I followed it, and recently I almost had to decide whether I had jurisdiction to hear a case to enjoin the transfer of government land to a Lutheran school. Fortunately, the government withdrew its offer and rendered the case moot.
>
> I am happy that the Supreme Court has accepted *Flast* for review. Both the ACLU and the AJCongress have mailed bulletins about this appeal. It appears that Leo Pfeffer as well as a number of other able lawyers are already preparing a brief on appeal. I think that they will adequately present the views which the ADL espouses and that any brief which the ADL or the AJCommittee might file will be merely repetitious. It will neither help the Court nor influence its decision. Where a case is being adequately handled, I believe it is folly for a similar organization to file a brief amicus curiae. I have told the same thing to Leo Pfeffer and Will Maslow as well as friends in the AJCommittee. I am sure

that you have plenty of things to do without performing useless work and without spending money that is desperately needed in other areas.

I vote "No" on your request to file a brief amicus curiae in this case.

Sincerely yours,
Gus J. Solomon[20]

Solomon's letter provides an instructive example of the complex and varied internal forces that can influence the decision-making process of organized interests. In this case, the question centered on whether to expend collective resources on behalf of a public cause that bears on the constituency the organization professes to represent. The leadership of the major American Jewish organizations believed that the representation of their interests on the important constitutional issue to be addressed in *Flast*—the right of taxpayers to challenge the administration of laws alleged to have unconstitutional effects—through their joint participation as an amicus curiae was essential. They held this opinion for reasons that were more abstract than the elusive empirical issue of the extent to which the Court might be dependent on such a brief to guide its jurisprudential moorings.

Whether organizations can indeed influence the doctrinal development of the law by submitting such briefs is a question that has drawn much attention from students of the use made of the courts by interest groups. It is one, however, that has not been answered with much success. Judge Solomon's letter predates the work of scholarship that has accused the Court's liberal rules governing the submission of amicus briefs of "encourag[ing], for the most part, a waste of time, effort, and money in a useless function [that] . . . results in a 'cruel hoax' on the parties submitting them."[21] At the same time, neither have the Court's rules on amicus participation, then and now, discouraged the active involvement of interested third parties.[22] Moreover, political scientists and other students of interest groups' use of the courts have also argued that amicus participation, in some cases, does have substantive influence on the litigation process. This latter point raises the question of why the Court would continue to make access to litigation easy for third parties unless it was of some benefit to them. Here, too, one must ask why organized interests would continue to invest time, financial resources, and staff expertise in the amicus dimension of the litigation process if such efforts resulted in no substantive success. These are questions that will be addressed in the conclusion of this book. For now, though, it is enough merely to observe that the presence of such forces helps to illustrate the multivariate internal calculus that conditions the decision process whereby organized interests determine whether and how to utilize their resources in litigation.

One might argue that, in *Flast,* the joint amicus brief filed on behalf of over thirty major Jewish organizations, along with the additional amici support from the National Council of Churches, Americans United, and several public school lobbies, was more important as a collective endorsement of Pfeffer's argument—that taxpayer access to the federal courts was a constitutional question that transcended the special interests of specific communities—than it was in educating the Court on critical matters of law and fact left unaddressed by the plaintiffs. This notion is further buttressed when one examines the Court's opinion in *Flast.* Writing for an eight-to-one Court, Chief Justice Warren held that the *Frothingham* barrier should be lowered when a taxpayer attacks a federal statute on the grounds that it violates the establishment and free exercise clauses of the First Amendment. Chief Justice Warren did acknowledge that it was not altogether clear whether the *Frothingham* precedent itself required a constitutional ban on all taxpayer suits or whether it should simply encourage, but not command, the courts to approach such suits with self-restraint. Lacking a clear legal precedent that established the scope of *Frothingham,* Chief Justice Warren turned to the law reviews for guidance. Having done so, the chief justice concluded that the prevailing view in the law literature was that *Frothingham* did not impose a barrier to such litigation but "announced only a nonconstitutional rule of self-restraint."[23] There was thus no need to overrule *Frothingham* entirely, but the plaintiffs had successfully demonstrated that alternative rules were needed to increase the access to the courts of individuals and of the "private attorneys general" representing them.

The Court's reference to "private attorneys general" was a direct acknowledgement of the value that cause-oriented organized interests attached to litigation as an instrument for redress of their constitutional grievances. Precisely where the Court's desire to further democratize access to federal courts for litigation-oriented constituencies merged with the arguments set forth by Pfeffer and the supporting amici was evident in the new standard it created to govern taxpayer suits. Rather than simply uphold *Frothingham's* rule that took only the litigant's direct financial interests into consideration or to assume the courts were being used as a forum in which to "air . . . generalized grievances about the conduct of the government," the Court developed a two-pronged test to assess the merits of taxpayer challenges. First, the plaintiff was required to demonstrate a logical nexus between his or her status as a taxpayer and the challenged legislation. Second, the taxpayer had to demonstrate how this status related to the constitutional harm alleged. In this case, said the Court, "the taxpayer must show that the challenged enactment exceeds specific constitutional limitations imposed upon the exercise of the congressional taxing and spending power and not simply that the enactment is generally beyond the powers delegated to Congress by Art. I, Sec. 8. When both nexuses are established, the litigant will have shown a taxpayer's stake in the outcome of the controversy and will be a proper and appropriate party to invoke a federal court's jurisdiction."[24] While Pfeffer and the supporting amici cannot claim sole credit for the Court's new "double nexus" rule announced in *Flast*, one must ask whether it is more than coincidence that Chief Justice Warren's opinion follows the arguments set forth in their briefs.

Over time, *Flast* became an invitation to all litigation-oriented organized interests to vindicate their constitutional grievances in the courts without first having to demonstrate personal harm or injury. But for now, the Court confined the scope of redress to the establishment clause, in accordance with the third option presented by Pfeffer in the amicus brief submitted on behalf of the major Jewish organizations. Justice Douglas, concurring, suggested that *Flast* could not be reconciled with *Frothingham* and that the latter should be overruled.[25] In dissent, Justice John Harlan admitted that *Frothingham* acted as an unnecessary obstacle to legitimate taxpayer lawsuits and should be modified but found *Flast* far too permissive in the latitude it granted to "private attorneys general" to pursue public interest litigation. Justice Harlan, echoing the complaint of the Warren Court's posthumous critics, believed that *Flast* would result in a distortion of the judicial function. Justice Harlan warned that *Flast* could lead organized interests to view the litigation process as a means to enshrine policy preferences rather than a venue for the nonpolitical adjudication of law-based claims. Minorities unable to achieve their social and political objectives via the elected branches of government would turn to the courts for resolution, even if the laws presently in place required no such outcome. For the federal courts to become another political branch of government would impair the traditional separation of powers and encourage a view of the law as contingent on the policy preferences of the judges in power.[26]

But in *Board of Education v. Allen*, the major Jewish organizations met with defeat, inasmuch as they were unsuccessful in persuading the Court to find unconstitutional New York state's program of providing state-approved textbooks to private schools, including parochial ones, at no cost. Writing for a six-to-three Court, Justice Byron White held that the textbook program fell within the "child-benefit" standard created in *Everson;* it did not originate in an unconstitutional purpose nor did it promote a similar effect. Interestingly, however, Justice Black, who had authored the Court's *Everson* opinion and formulated the child-benefit rule, dissented in *Allen,* on the grounds that direct assistance to the educational function of religious schools raised far different questions than nondiscriminatory transportation programs. "Upholding a State's power to pay bus or streetcar fares for school children," wrote Justice Black, "cannot provide support for the validity of a state law using tax-raised funds to buy school books for a religious school," whereas Justice White found no such corrosive relationship between church and state in the textbook program.[27] Analyzing the program under the Court's two-pronged purpose-and-effect test created in *Schempp,* Justice White concluded that the New York law was conceived with a secular legislative design in mind and administered in a fashion that neither advanced nor inhibited religion. The plaintiffs, Justice White wrote, had presented but a "meager record" that offered no credible challenge to the state's contention that the use of secular textbooks in parochial schools was unrelated to the propagation of religious beliefs. Thus the Court was unable to hold, "based solely on judicial notice," that the New York program violated the establishment clause.[28]

The decision in *Allen* of course disappointed the major Jewish agencies. They had been hopeful that the Court would rule such textbook programs unconstitutional, which would have allowed them to claim a substantive victory on the issue of aid to parochial schools, one that would match their great triumph in *Flast.* Even so, the success of the

Jewish organizations in *Flast*, for which Pfeffer could take the lion's share of credit, far outweighed their temporary setback in *Allen*. After all, the courthouse doors had now been opened to taxpayers who believed that federal expenditures on religious education violated their constitutional rights—and the major Jewish organizations knew full well that no shortage of potential cases existed with which to revisit the Court's holding in *Allen*. One possible avenue of attack on the Court's establishment clause jurisprudence was in fact suggested by a passage in Justice Black's dissent. In an ominous vein, Justice Black wrote that

> to authorize a State to tax its residents for such church purposes is to put the State squarely in the religious activities of certain religious groups that happen to be strong enough politically to write their own religious preferences and prejudices into the laws. This links state and churches together in controlling the lives and destinies of our citizenship—a citizenship composed of people of myriad religious faiths, some of them bitterly hostile to and completely intolerant of the others.[29]

It was this latter point, regarding the linkage between religious and state institutions, that offered the major Jewish organizations the crucial third piece of the puzzle, the piece needed to complement the purpose-and-effect test that the Court had developed in *Schempp* and used ever since in establishment clause cases. Most of those cases, however, had involved issues that originated outside the arena of public funding. What was needed was an analytical device that could point to the constitutional unwholesomeness of any fiscal interdependence between the public purse and religious institutions. Justice Black referred to a linking of church and state, but he offered no suggestions as to how this concept could be incorporated into the Court's establishment clause jurisprudence to complement the purpose-and-effect test in place since *Schempp*. Pfeffer would later call such linkage "excessive entanglement." Indeed, he and the organizations that supported his work made the insertion of the "excessive entanglement" rule into the *Schempp* purpose-and-effect test the focal point of the next round in the litigation campaign to restrict the flow of public funds to parochial schools.

The Search for New Standards

In effect, the Court had sent mixed messages in *Flast* and *Allen*. The once-firm barrier against taxpayer lawsuits that sought to challenge public expenditures had been lowered so that such litigation could now go forward with relative ease. But the odds that such a challenge could succeed in restricting the use of federal funds to subsidize secular instruction in parochial schools, as well as funds to supplement the "auxiliary services" that Title II of the ESEA of 1965 also permitted, appeared less certain. Coupled with the announcement of Chief Justice Earl Warren's retirement after the Court's 1968 term and President Nixon's choice of Warren Burger, a conservative federal appeals court judge for the D. C. circuit, to succeed him, the near future suggested that separationist groups would confront a litigation environment less hospitable to their interests. As Archibald Cox has pointed out, the transition from Earl Warren to Warren Burger signified the end of an era in which the Court had come "to be influenced by a conscious sense of judicial responsibility for the open and egalitarian operation of the political system . . . [with] constitutional adjudication" as a fundamental tool to achieve that end.[30] But before the Court would return to confront the parochial school aid issues that were being prepared for litigation to test the reaches of *Flast* and *Allen*, it first accepted for review a case that touched a sensitive—and ecumenical—nerve among religious organizations and the communities they represented. The Court's decision to hear *Walz v. Tax Commission* (1970) required the nation's religious bodies to defend a principle of church autonomy so well-embedded in tradition that it had never been seriously contested: the exemption from general taxation of religious properties used for worship-related activities. But neither had the Court ever articulated the jurisprudential principle implicit in the Constitution that justified such a tax exemption. *Walz* would now give the Court that chance, as well as providing a possible glimpse into the direction in which it might venture under its new chief justice.

Pfeffer had often toyed with the idea of bringing a lawsuit to contest the principle of tax exemption for religious institutions, but he could not persuade the AJCongress's leadership to take a position against the current rule. In fact, few inside the AJCongress aside from Pfeffer supported the view that religious tax exemptions violated the establishment clause—a head count of which Pfeffer was well aware. But he knew that the AJCongress would suffer great embarrassment if word got out among the church-state bar that the organization was prepared to take a position that meant opposing the recommendation of its renowned church-state counsel.[31] Worse, he thought the AJCongress might feel obligated to follow his recommendation for the wrong reasons—to save face. In the end, Pfeffer decided that pursuing his position was not worth the problems it might well cause. Thus the organization did not participate in *Walz*, even though several officers within the leadership echelon believed that an amicus brief from the AJCongress in support of religious tax exemption would carry great weight with the Court. Internal tension over the organization's position in *Walz* was less the result of sharp disagreement among competing factions than it was of the AJCongress's refusal to accommodate the policy recommendation not only of its dominant figure on church-state matters but of the entire separationist bar. Commented one AJCongress attorney:

> The major issue in *Walz* that divided Leo from everyone else was whether you view a tax exemption [for religion] as a subsidy. I don't think that it is, and I know my predecessors, Leo excepted, thought the same thing. Given the potential bad public relations of that, the [AJ]Congress decided to stay out. A similar, but more complex question, I think, came up in the *Bob Jones* [*University v. U.S.*] case ten or so years later. Sometimes what might be right on the law is all wrong for organizational purposes. Even if you could make a strong argument that a tax exemption is a subsidy, it's not one of those issues that requires that you put the agency's reputation on the line. In some cases you have the save your battles. *Walz* was like that and even Leo recognized it. But he also knew the agency leadership would not overrule him in a million years. So he ghost-wrote the ACLU's *amicus* brief and got it out of his system.[32]

Pfeffer was indeed the author of the ACLU's brief. Although Pfeffer had resigned as a voting board member of the ACLU's church-state committee a decade before because it was not separationist enough for his tastes,[33] a majority of the organization's leaders were now of the opinion that religious tax exemptions violated the Constitution and wanted to express that position publicly. They thus asked Pfeffer to draft an amicus brief voicing their opposition to religious tax exemptions, although the remainder of the ACLU's leadership favored these exemptions. For this reason, the ACLU decided not to sponsor a tax exemption lawsuit but instead to limit its participation to that of an amicus curiae. Pfeffer was happy to oblige, on the condition that his name not appear on the brief so as to honor his agreement with the AJCongress. With regard to this latter request, *Walz* constituted one of the very rare exceptions to Pfeffer's general rule that his name appear first whenever he cooperated with other parties in the preparation of a church-state case, whether the party was the principal litigant or was simply acting as an amicus curiae. Even after the return of the ADL and the AJCommittee to the NCRAC fold, arguments continued to crop up over the allocation of responsibilities in litigation and the related issue of who should claim principal credit. In these debates, Pfeffer always insisted that his name lead the roster of attorneys serving as counsel of record on the principal or amicus brief.[34] Pfeffer's decision not to insist that the ACLU comply with his otherwise firm rule thus illustrates how fine-tuned the requirements of internal diplomacy can be in organizational decision making.

Ultimately, then, the AJCongress decided to watch Kenneth Walz— an antireligious zealot so committed to his cause that he had even purchased a small parcel of land in New York City to satisfy the taxpayer standing requirement—proceed without the direct support of the AJCongress and the ACLU, the two most influential organized interests in the church-state arena. In contrast to the delicate negotiations within the AJCongress over how to handle the religious tax exemption question, the ADL and the AJCommittee were of a single mind as to the relative merits of *Walz*. Each strongly supported religious tax exemptions as resting on a fully valid and necessary constitutional principle intended to secure religious freedom from the often arbitrary power of government to levy taxes.[35] But even though the ADL and the AJCommittee supported tax exemptions for the worship-related activities of religion, neither organization had taken a position on how it viewed a similar exemption for the unrelated business income generated by religious institutions. So while the ADL and the AJCommittee entertained no illusions about how the Court would (or should) decide the religion-based tax exemption question, because of the more complicated issue of unrelated business income each decided against the submission of an amicus brief in *Walz* for fear that it would box them into a corner when it came time to formulate a position on the latter, more complex, concern.[36]

As anticipated, the Court, by an eight-to-one margin, turned back Kenneth Walz's challenge to the New York statute that exempted religious properties used for worship-related activities from general taxation. Writing for the Court, Chief Justice Burger argued that "the exemption creates only a minimal and remote involvement between church and state and far less than the taxation of churches. It restricts the fiscal relationship between church and state, and tends to complement and reinforce the desired separation insulating each from the other."[37] The Court's opinion was, however, somewhat vague when it came to a specific constitutional principle on which to base its *Walz* holding. Indeed, it even appeared, as Justice Douglas pointed out in his sole dissent, that religious tax exemptions flouted *Everson* and the no-aid interpretation the Court had given the establishment clause in its ruling on that case.[38] But the Court admitted that its position was not informed solely by the text of the Constitution. As Justice Douglas himself acknowledged, the historical record favoring religious tax exemptions had, after all, been almost universal and uninterrupted.[39] That position was further affirmed by the ecumenical lineup of religious organizations that appeared as amici in support of tax exemption, several of whom had found themselves opposing one another in other establishment clause litigation.[40] To add further sustenance to the Court's position that religious tax exemptions advanced neither a religious purpose or effect, Chief Justice Burger added a third component to the original two-pronged *Schempp* test: entanglement.

> We must also be sure that the end result—the effect—is not an *excessive government entanglement* with religion. The test is inescapably one of degree. Either course, taxation or churches, occasions some involvement with religion. Elimination of exemption would tend to expand the involvement of government by giving rise to tax valuation of church property, tax liens, tax foreclosures, and the direct confrontations and conflicts that follow in the train of those legal processes.[41]

In "excessive entanglement," the chief justice uttered the words that the AJCongress, the ADL, and the AJCommittee had long wanted to hear. Pfeffer, in particular, believed that the addition of a nonentanglement requirement to the current purpose-and-effect test would prove quite useful in demonstrating how even public assistance to parochial schools for secular instruction created an unwholesome alliance between religious and civil forces. But while the Court recognized that a reasonably aggressive approach to the establishment clause was necessary to guard against religious intrusions into the public purse, even under the pretext of a secular purpose and effect, its pronouncement that there was "room for play" within the separation principle to promote a "benevolent neutrality" between government and religion made the Jewish organizations, as well as other separationist groups, apprehensive about where the Court was prepared to take its church-state jurisprudence. In Chief Justice Burger's definition, the "benevolent neutrality" concept permitted assistance to religion "so long as none was favored over others and none suffered interference."[42] Did this mean that the Court did not consider the flow of public funds to parochial schools on a par with the inculcation of religious doctrine in the public schools as a constitutional problem? Or could the tax exemption issue be distinguished from other church-state concerns on the grounds of special circumstances? Even before *Walz*, the Jewish organizations had begun to explore possibilities for test-case litigation that might answer this question, but now they had the incentive to move forward with a full-blown litigation campaign on the issue of parochial aid.

The Evolution of the *Lemon* Test

While *Flast v. Cohen* was still in litigation, the Connecticut Jewish Community Relations Council (CJCRC) and the Connecticut Civil Liberties Union (CCLU) agreed to cosponsor two lawsuits, one that would attack the ESEA of 1965 as it had been applied to parochial schools in that state and another to challenge the Higher Education Facilities Act (HEFA) of 1963, which provided federal construction grants and similar auxiliary assistance to both public and private colleges and universities. Catholic colleges in Connecticut, like all such institutions nationwide, were thus receiving substantial federal assistance, which the CJCRC and the CCLU believed was as unconstitutional as equivalent aid to parochial elementary and secondary schools.

Pfeffer was asked to serve as lead counsel in both cases, an offer he accepted in the fall of 1967. Even if the Supreme Court refused to accept the AJCongress-backed appeal in *Flast* and instead continued to

adhere strictly to the *Frothingham* rule, Pfeffer believed that the plaintiffs in the Connecticut cases could overcome the problem of taxpayer
standing by alleging discrimination in the administration of both statutes in favor of religious institutions and by providing evidence that
the ESEA put pressure upon public school teachers to move into the
parochial schools.[43] That concern was soon mooted by the Court's June
1968 decision in *Flast*, which widened access to such lawsuits. Enthusiasm for the Connecticut ESEA litigation later diminished in favor of
stronger cases in Rhode Island and Pennsylvania, but support for the
state's challenge to federally funded assistance to private and religious
colleges for facilities maintenance did not. Indeed, the AJCongress and
the ACLU joined forces as the primary organizational backers of what
became *Tilton v. Richardson*.[44]

In September 1968 Pfeffer filed a suit in federal district court on
behalf of fifteen Connecticut taxpayers that requested an injunction
against the use of HEFA funds to subsidize the construction of facilities at religious colleges and universities on the grounds that such assistance violated the establishment clause. The plaintiff's argument
centered on two points. First, it would attempt to prove that state officials had acted improperly when they decided to include religiously
affiliated colleges as beneficiaries of the 1963 act; and second, it would
attack the HEFA itself as a fundamentally unconstitutional abridge-
ment of the principle of church-state separation. Regarding the latter
charge, Pfeffer noted that approximately 10 percent of the $1.6 billion
in federal aid provided to colleges and universities had gone to institutions with religious affiliations.[45]

Although the lower court failed to grant Pfeffer's request for an injunction, it did agree to convene a three-judge trial court that would
hear the plaintiff's case on the merits. The opportunity to argue the
case before a three-judge panel was especially important to Pfeffer,
since appeals from such courts automatically went straight to the Supreme Court.[46] For the AJCongress, *Tilton* represented the first tangible
result of the Court's decision in *Flast* that opened the door to taxpayer
lawsuits. With *Tilton* in progress, the AJCongress hoped that the lower
federal district court to which *Flast* had subsequently been remanded
for a decision on the merits would rule that both Title I and II of the
ESEA of 1965 were invalid. Nor had the AJCongress, along with the
ADL and the AJCommittee, given up hope that the Court would find
invalid the state-level administration of the ESEA in *Allen*, the New

York case that involved textbook loans to religious schools. Such was the core of the AJCongress's litigation strategy, a strategy designed ultimately to terminate the flow of public funds to parochial schools and related institutions.

But, as we have seen, *Allen*'s promise failed the Jewish organizations. And even more problematic for the broader separationist community was the encouragement that the Court's 1968 decision in *Allen* gave to Catholic bodies and other organized interests that advocated such assistance. Surely, these groups would now begin to press state legislatures to authorize statutes that would provide similar, and perhaps in some cases more comprehensive, aid to parochial schools. Even before the Court handed down its decision in *Allen,* the ADL reported, between 1963 and 1968 twenty states had reauthorized or passed statutes that permitted or required transportation at public expense for children who attended private and/or parochial schools, with only three such proposed statutes defeated. Since 1965, when the ESEA was passed, efforts to enact legislation designed to provide much more extensive and direct services to parochial schools had been initiated in Michigan, Ohio, New York, Minnesota, Pennsylvania, and Rhode Island.[47] And between 1968 and 1970 New Jersey, Louisiana, and Connecticut, each of which provided transportation assistance to religious schools, enacted new statutes that permitted such schools to purchase both direct and auxiliary educational services from the state government.[48] Each state would end up having to defend their statutes in the Supreme Court over the next decade—with little success, in most cases. For now, however, Pfeffer, the Jewish organizations, and their allies in the secular and religious separationist circles decided to concentrate their litigative firepower on the statutes enacted by Rhode Island and Pennsylvania, the most ambitious—and in their opponents' view, egregiously offensive—of these legislative programs.

In July 1968 the Pennsylvania Non-Public Elementary and Secondary Education Act went into effect. The statute allowed the state superintendent of public instruction to contract for the direct purchase of so-called secular education services for use in private and parochial schools. Such secular services included teachers' salaries, books and instructional materials, and auxiliary programs, for which these schools would now be reimbursed. Funding for the program was provided by revenues drawn from Pennsylvania's state harness and horse-racing operations. The statute did contain a provision that prohibited reimbursement to parochial schools for courses and materials that included religious content. Nonetheless, over 96 percent of nonpublic reimbursement went to religious schools, most of which were Catholic.

In September 1969, when the state first began to reimburse religious schools for their "secular" purchases, a broad-based coalition of religious, educational, and civil liberties groups organized by Pfeffer and the ACLU's Henry Sawyer, who had worked with Pfeffer over half a decade earlier in the landmark *Schempp* case, filed suit in federal court. The organizational plaintiffs included the Pennsylvania Jewish Community Relations Council, the Protestant State Council of Churches, the NAACP, the Pennsylvania State Education Association, and the Pennsylvania Civil Liberties Union, who were joined by numerous Pennsylvania residents claiming taxpayer status. Together, they requested that a three-judge court declare the act unconstitutional under the establishment and free exercise clauses, as well as the equal protection clause of the Fourteenth Amendment. By a two-to-one vote, however, the lower court dismissed the plaintiffs' case for failure to state a cause of action. In addition, the court unanimously held that the ruling in *Flast* did not extend to organizational plaintiffs, who thus had no standing to sue. But it did rule that one of the private citizens, Alton Lemon—who had purchased a race track admissions ticket after the statute had gone into effect—was entitled to sue on First Amendment grounds, although not under the equal protection clause.

In this new case, *Lemon v. Kurtzman,* the three-judge court, ruling on the merits, divided over the issue of whether the statute violated the establishment clause.[49] Using the *Schempp* standard, two judges held that the Pennsylvania statute did not have as its primary purpose and effect the dispensation of benefits to parochial schools, but to public schools. Whatever benefits accrued to religious schools under the act were incidental in nature and thus failed to infringe on the establishment clause. The dissenting judge, however, argued that the act, notwithstanding its declared intent to promote the general welfare and secular education of children, did in fact have as its primary purpose and effect the desire to subsidize the education provided by nonpublic schools. The plaintiffs, including the organizations denied standing by the lower court, appealed to the Supreme Court, which in April 1970 noted probable jurisdiction. *Lemon v. Kurtzman* was then set for argument for the October 1970 term.

The debate over a similar Rhode Island statute began in late 1968—

a statute that was even more comprehensive than the Pennsylvania one in the public funds it made available to nonpublic schools. The Rhode Island Salary Supplement Act authorized state education officials to offer instructors in nonpublic schools up to 15 percent of their current annual salary in an effort to equalize compensation levels with those of their public school counterparts. The Rhode Island act did stipulate that the salaries, when supplemented, of teachers in private schools could not exceed the salaries of public schoolteachers, and that teachers eligible for public funds could not provide religious instruction— an obligation that eligible teachers were required to consent to in writing. But to opponents of the legislation, this caveat was for effect only; the legislation's true thrust was to offer very real and substantial assistance to the state's parochial schools. Indeed, as the three-judge federal court later discovered when the statute was challenged as violative of the establishment clause, almost 25 percent of the state's elementary school students attended private institutions, of which 95 percent were Catholic.

Pfeffer had testified against the Rhode Island statute while the case, *DiCenso v. Robinson*, was still before the state legislature, but not on behalf of the AJCongress or the NCRAC constituent organizations.[50] Much like its sister chapter in Pennsylvania, the Rhode Island affiliate of the ACLU had expected the legislature, reacting to consistent and well-organized pressure from the state's private and Catholic school lobbies, to move forward on the parochial school aid issue. During the previous legislative session, Pfeffer had submitted testimony in opposition to a state plan that would provide tuition grants and subsidies to parents whose children attended nonpublic schools, including schools with sectarian affiliations. On this occasion, Pfeffer argued that Rhode Island's tuition assistance program had no constitutional basis in the Court's child-benefit theory and consequently would not survive judicial review in state court. Pfeffer also noted that a Rhode Island court had recently struck down as unconstitutional the state's 1963 effort to provide textbook assistance to parochial school students.[51] In Pfeffer's opinion, state-financed supplemental salaries to nonpublic school teachers constituted an even more transparent attempt to aid parochial schools and would also be found unconstitutional, should the state legislature decide to approve the act.[52]

Despite the opposition of the ACLU, several local Jewish community relations councils, Protestant organizations, and teachers' lobbies,

Rhode Island nevertheless enacted the statute in time for the beginning of the 1969 school year. Soon thereafter the Rhode Island chapter of the ACLU instigated a lawsuit in federal court. In March 1970 the trial court ruled that the Rhode Island Salary Supplement Act fostered "excessive entanglement" between church and state and thus struck it down as violative of the establishment clause. The Rhode Island court, which decided *DiCenso* after the Supreme Court's decision in *Walz v. Tax Commission,* became the first to invalidate a parochial assistance plan under the "excessive entanglement" rule that the Court added in *Walz* to the extant *Schempp* purpose-and-effect test. The lower court's use of the embryonic tripartite purpose-effect-entanglement principle conflicted with the 1969 decision of the Pennsylvania court in *Lemon,* which obviously could not incorporate the issue of entanglement in its analysis.

Conflict between the Pennsylvania and Rhode Island federal courts over which analytical framework was appropriate to evaluate claims brought under the establishment clause, as well as the polar outcomes on the constitutionality of the statutes themselves, left the Supreme Court no choice but to confront once again the parochial aid issue. In June 1970 the Court agreed to review *DiCenso* and later decided to consolidate it with *Lemon* for oral argument in March 1971. Moreover, given that in March 1970 a three-judge federal district court in Connecticut had ruled in *Tilton v. Richardson* that the establishment clause did not prohibit sectarian colleges from receiving congressionally mandated grants under the HEFA,[53] the Court also decided to review *Tilton* the day before it heard *DiCenso* and *Lemon.*

Pfeffer had served as the lead counsel in *Tilton* from the moment preparation began for the lawsuit in September 1967, and in September 1968 the AJCongress, with support from the ACLU, became the chief organizational sponsor of the litigation. This decision stemmed not so much from a desire to get the AJCongress imprint on the *Tilton* litigation—after all, Pfeffer's presence alone ensured that by default, even if the organization had no formal role—but from internal considerations. Between September 1967 and September 1968 the attorneys working with the local organizations that had originally approached Pfeffer to represent them in *Tilton,* the CJCRC and the CCLU, decided to distance themselves from the day-to-day publicity of the events surrounding the case. Their decision resulted not from lack of confidence in the case but from a fear of reprisal under a local bar association ethics rule that prohibited their participation in press conferences and other publicity-related events, which were unavoidable—indeed necessary—in cases such as this one. Moreover, the local CJCRC expressed concern over the public relations impact that interviews with the plaintiffs, some of whom the AJCongress acknowledged were "fairly bigoted—with big mouths," would have on the climate of public opinion for the lawsuit. Quite apart from its need for financial assistance with litigation expenses (something the ACLU would provide as well), the local CJCRC believed that Pfeffer, what with his sophistication in these matters, and the experienced public-relations hand of the AJCongress would be better equipped to handle such difficulties as they arose.[54] Thus, in *DiCenso*, Pfeffer ended up collaborating with the local affiliate of the ACLU, which continued to work with the AJCongress during the trial and appellate phases of the litigation. The ACLU's Henry Sawyer handled the appeal in *Lemon* but worked closely with Pfeffer to build arguments that would reinforce the merits of their respective cases.

The ADL and the AJCommittee were content to let Pfeffer and the AJCongress handle the trial phase in each of these cases: neither became involved in *Tilton*, *DiCenso*, or *Lemon* until the Court decided to hear all three during its October 1970 term. But when it became clear that each decision would have a critical effect on the future of parochial school aid legislation, the ADL and the AJCommittee expressed their desire to participate in all three cases as amici curiae, in tandem with the other constituent organizations of the NCRAC. Their opposition to public assistance to parochial schools, like that of the AJCongress, was clear and unequivocal, as it had been ever since *Everson*. Given the harmony of their views, the AJCongress indicated that it would agree to work with the ADL and the AJCommittee to prepare the NCRAC's amicus brief in the Court's joint *Lemon-DiCenso* review and in *Tilton*.[55] In contrast to the most recent effort of the three major agencies to work together as amici in the litigation over New York's textbook loan program, *Board of Education v. Allen*, there was almost no disagreement over how to approach the issues in these cases.

In *Allen*, which marked their first cooperative amicus effort in almost twenty years, the ADL was initially opposed to the AJCongress's recommendation that, because of Pfeffer's reputation, it should assume responsibility for writing the brief that would bear the NCRAC's name. Sol Rabkin, the ADL's legal director, objected to the AJCongress's contention that it possessed a "special competence" in the church-state arena that the other Jewish organizations lacked. While the AJCommittee had no trouble with the argument that Pfeffer's expertise and reputation merited his request to draft the Jewish organizations' amicus brief in *Allen*, it did note it was the AJCongress's arrogance in such matters that had caused it and the ADL to withdraw from the NCRAC after *Zorach*. It was later agreed that Pfeffer and the AJCongress could draft the *Allen* brief, but that it would be subject to review and approval by the ADL and the AJCommittee. Until the early 1980s, when all three organizations began to work more independently, this approach became more or less the standard pattern of internal preparation in church-state litigation whenever the AJCongress, the ADL, and the AJCommittee decided to participate as amici in conjunction with one another or on behalf of the NCRAC.[56]

Happily, then, internal squabbles were absent during the initial preparation of the joint amicus brief in *Lemon*. With the exception of the Orthodox rabbinical bodies, all the constituent organizations within the NCRAC supported the plaintiffs' contention that Pennsylvania's "secular services" purchase plan and Rhode Island's salary supplement program amounted to the subsidization of parochial schools and were thus unconstitutional. The Orthodox bodies, who argued that such assistance was benevolent in nature, did not support the religious enterprise as much as they did general secular education, which parochial schools were required to provide by law. While Orthodox Jewish organizations were not the prime forces that lobbied on behalf of such legislation, they were not about to turn down assistance that they argued was crucial to the survival of their yeshiva.

But the Orthodox agencies found no home for their views in the NCRAC executive committee. They would participate in *Lemon*, but through the fledgling Commission on Law and Public Affairs (COLPA), a national organization formed to represent dissident Orthodox Jewish agencies in such cases. Rabbi Israel Klavan, the NCRAC representative for the Orthodox Rabbinical Council of America (RCA), warned that all the Jewish agencies, whether Reform, Conservative, or secular, would have to search for common ground on the issue of public assistance for religious schools. Otherwise, the Orthodox groups would increasingly find themselves in conflict with the more established Jewish organizations on this and other matters related to the separation principle, as such statutes proliferated. The NCRAC constituent bodies were sympathetic to Rabbi Klavan's concern about the future vitality of Jewish day schools, but they remained emphatic in their opposition to parochial school assistance on constitutional grounds.[57] This schism between the Orthodox and the non-Orthodox agencies became ever deeper throughout the 1970s and has remained so. The AJCongress, the ADL, and the AJCommittee have refused to compromise their absolute opposition to public assistance for religious schools, while Orthodox bodies have continued to support such measures and defend them as amici curiae in court.[58]

The Orthodox opposition to the dominant position of the three major Jewish organizations on government aid to parochial schools prevented the submission of an amicus brief in *Lemon-DiCenso* on behalf of the NCRAC, since its constituent bodies must be unanimous in order for a brief to be filed under its name. Thus the AJCongress, the AJCommittee, and the ADL were left to file an amicus brief on behalf of themselves, although they were joined by the Reform Central Conference of American Rabbis, the Union of American Hebrew Congregations (which represents the interests of Reform congregations in public affairs), the National Council of Jewish Women, as well as several smaller local Jewish agencies. That the AJCongress was no longer the sole Jewish organization willing to assert itself on controversial public issues that had strong potential implications for interfaith relations was not just visible from the eagerness of the ADL and the AJCommittee, as well as other, less public affairs–oriented agencies, to enter the cause. It was also evident from the support of these groups for one of Pfeffer's more controversial assertions in *Lemon-DiCenso*, namely, that Rhode Island's supplemental salaries program also promoted racial segregation in the state's education system. Pfeffer centered his argument in *DiCenso* on the failure of the Rhode Island statute to withstand scrutiny under the *Schempp* purpose-and-effect test and the more recent nonentanglement requirement of *Walz*, calling the supplemental salaries program a "thin disguise, not taken seriously by anyone," to subsidize parochial education.[59] But in *DiCenso*, Pfeffer went an extra step, one he had previously not taken in a parochial aid case. He argued that "nonpublic schools, including parochial schools, are playing a substantial, though unintended role in the preservation of racial segregation." Wrote Pfeffer:

Should the time come when, through increasing government support of non-public schools, it will be economically feasible for
white middle-income parents to send their children to non-public
schools, the public school system will become the modern day
equivalent of the pre-public education charity school—an institution for society's rejects, most of whom will be members of racial
minorities. We will then end up with two school systems, separate and unequal.[60]

Pfeffer was also able to persuade the ACLU to insert a similar reference
into the plaintiffs' brief in *Lemon,* which ultimately contained a provision referring to private and parochial schools as "havens" of prejudice.[61] This allegation had rankled the Orthodox agencies during the
NCRAC's debate over whether to submit an amicus brief in *Lemon-
DiCenso* and contributed to their decision to disassociate themselves
from any such effort.[62]

But Pfeffer's central argument in *DiCenso,* as well as that of the Jewish amici, concentrated on the failure of Rhode Island to meet the
Court's requirements under *Schempp,* according to which the primary
purpose and effect of such statutes must be secular, and now *Walz,*
which had announced a new rule forbidding "excessive entanglement"
between religious and state institutions. Pfeffer stressed that the Court
should not be wooed by the statements of purpose that prefaced these
statutes but by their actual objectives as reflected in their legislative
history. Pfeffer also asserted that it was impossible to separate secular
and religious instruction in parochial schools, an argument he supported by quoting the "mission statements" of several such schools
and presenting evidence that demonstrated how religious themes were
incorporated into regular instruction in mathematics, literature, and
social studies.[63] On the nonentanglement requirement, Pfeffer argued
that the Rhode Island statute had in effect made the state a partner
with the parochial school system because "it requires the State to send
censors into the schoolrooms" to guard against improper instruction.
These were all legal maneuvers that Pfeffer had coordinated with Sawyer, who would offer similar arguments on behalf of the plaintiffs con-
testing the Pennsylvania statute.[64]

Considerable thought and effort had gone into the amicus effort as
well. In *Lemon* and *DiCenso,* the amicus brief authored jointly by the

AJCongress, the AJCommittee, and the ADL supported the plaintiffs' brief all the way down the line. But it also argued two other crucial points: that Jewish parochial schools were not threatened by the potential loss of public assistance and that other religious schools were more than capable of supporting themselves without state aid.[65] To underscore further the damage that statutes such as those of Rhode Island and Pennsylvania could potentially have on public school resources, Pfeffer assembled a coalition of public education lobbies to participate as amici curiae in *Lemon* and even authored the brief submitted on their behalf.[66] This latter move highlighted one of Pfeffer's favorite techniques of litigation: to conceive the arguments to be set forth in the plaintiff's brief, have someone else represent the plaintiffs, and then coordinate the submission of—or author, as Pfeffer had in several cases—amicus curiae briefs supporting the plaintiff's arguments.

In June 1971 the Court handed down its now historic decision in *Lemon-DiCenso*. Writing for an eight-to-one majority, Chief Justice Burger held that the state assistance contested in both cases did not, by the standards of the *Schempp* purpose-and-effect test, violate the establishment clause. "On the contrary," the chief justice wrote, "the statutes themselves clearly state that they are intended to enhance the quality of the secular education in all schools covered by the compulsory attendance laws, [and] we find nothing here that undermines the state legislative intent; it must therefore be accorded appropriate deference." But these were not the fatal criteria for the Rhode Island and Pennsylvania statutes. Instead, the Court held that both programs were defective because each resulted in "excessive entanglement between government and religion" that placed the institutional separation of church and state at risk. Concluded the Court:

> A comprehensive, discriminating and continuing state surveillance will inevitably be required to ensure that these restrictions are obeyed and the First Amendment otherwise respected. Unlike a book, a teacher cannot be inspected once so as to determine the extent and intent of his or her personal beliefs and subjective acceptance of the limitations imposed by the First Amendment. These prophylactic contacts will involve excessive and enduring entanglement between state and church. . . . We noted "the hazards of government supporting churches" in *Walz*, and we cannot

ignore here the danger that pervasive modern governmental power will ultimately intrude on religion and thus conflict with the Religion Clauses.[67]

The Court's opinion in *Lemon-DiCenso* thus delivered a near-fatal punch to federal and state programs that authorized direct financial aid to religion. Over the next decade the Court administered blow after blow to advocates of government aid to elementary and secondary parochial schools, leaving the defenders of such assistance with nothing but a small amount of pocket change, as opposed to the substantial public funds they had imagined would be forthcoming. Moreover, the Court used the *Lemon-Dicenso* case to weave the purpose-and-effect standard from *Schempp* and the more recent nonentanglement requirement developed in *Walz* into an establishment clause jurisprudence that frowned more sternly than ever before on government financial assistance to religious schools. Excessive entanglement came to constitute an inseparable component in the Court's analysis of statutes that provided financial assistance to religious schools and other church-related institutions. Over time, the Court's insistence on nonentanglement between state and religious institutions, more so than the secular purpose-and-effect test used prior to *Lemon,* became the constitutional threshold that parochial aid statutes modeled on those of Rhode Island and Pennsylvania were unable to overcome. The Court's adaptation of the *Lemon* test and its subsequent use in almost all establishment clause litigation were achievements for which, Pfeffer, through his skill, foresight, and persistence, could claim substantial credit.

As for *Tilton,* however, to the disappointment of Pfeffer and the major Jewish organizations, the Court rejected the plaintiffs' argument that the inclusion of religious colleges and universities in the Higher Education Facilities Act of 1963 violated the establishment clause. But absent in *Tilton* was the near-unanimous consensus that characterized the Court's decision in *Lemon-DiCenso.* For a five-to-four Court, Chief Justice Burger not only dismissed the claim that the HEFA violated the Court's secular purpose-and-effect requirement but held that the "entanglement between church and state is . . . lessened here by the nonideological character of the aid that the Government provides." In contrast with *Lemon-DiCenso,* Chief Justice Burger found that the "potential for divisiveness inherent in the essentially local problems of primary and secondary schools is significantly less with respect to a

college or university whose student constituency is not local but diverse and widely dispersed."[68] Pfeffer had argued that the HEFA was
unconstitutional under the Court's purpose-and-effect test because it
provided public funds to sectarian institutions whose mission was to
propagate the tenets of their respective faiths, offering evidence to support his contention. In addition, Pfeffer argued in *Tilton* that to admin-
ister the HEFA, the "government must police the operations of sectarian educational institutions to make sure that the governmentally
financed facilities are not used for sectarian instruction or religious
worship."[69] On the strength of this latter charge, Pfeffer was at least
able to persuade the Court to invalidate the provision in the HEFA
permitting sectarian recipients to use buildings constructed with federal aid for religious purposes once twenty years had elapsed; but otherwise, the *Tilton* majority, slim though it was, rejected Pfeffer's arguments across the board.

On a personal level, *Tilton's* outcome also gave Pfeffer a split in his
dramatic confrontation with the legendary Washington attorney, Edward Bennett Williams, who often made his services available to Catholic institutions that found themselves engaged in litigation over public assistance and other such related matters, although rarely for free.
Pfeffer knew, in fact, that he had struck a nerve within the community
of parochial aid advocates by challenging the HEFA, confiding to Will
Maslow after the federal trial court had agreed to hear *Tilton* that "the
Catholic Colleges involved . . . are taking this suit seriously. They have
retained as their lawyer Edward Bennett Williams to defend their
case."[70] Williams also handled the Supreme Court appeal in *Earley v.
DiCenso*. While Pfeffer prevailed over Williams in *DiCenso*, he was unable to clear that same hurdle again in *Tilton*. Moreover, Williams was
able to block the effort of the ADL, the AJCommittee, and the AJCongress to enter *Tilton* as amici curiae. The ADL's Sol Rabkin had written
Williams to obtain his consent to submit an amicus brief in *Tilton* on
behalf of his organization, the AJCommittee, and the AJCongress. But
Williams refused. In his reply to Rabkin, he wrote:

> As I am sure you know, Mr. Leo Pfeffer is the principal attorney
> for the appellants in the *Tilton* case, and the publicity generated
> by the appellants in connection with the *Tilton* case has indicated
> quite clearly to me that the American Jewish Congress, along
> with the American Civil Liberties Union, is the moving force and

indeed the sponsor of this litigation. Since I feel that Mr. Pfeffer is adequately presenting the views of and representing the interest of the American Jewish Congress in this litigation, I feel that it is wholly improper and inappropriate for the American Jewish Congress also to be in the position of an *amicus* party before the Supreme Court. Therefore, I do not believe that the American Jewish Congress can properly represent itself to the Supreme Court as nothing more than a "friend of the court" in this case. For that reason I refuse to consent . . . to the *amicus* brief that you propose to prepare.[71]

In contrast to *Lemon-DiCenso,* the amicus effort in *Tilton* was not very well coordinated. In addition to Williams's refusal to allow the Jewish organizations permission to participate as amici, the pettiness absent from their well-orchestrated effort in *Lemon-DiCenso* returned to compromise their involvement in the HEFA case. In describing to Williams the Jewish organizations' preparation of their amicus effort in *Tilton,* Rabkin deliberately painted an image of the AJCongress as a reluctant participant in a brief that was essentially the work of the ADL and the AJCommittee. Unfortunately, this approach did not sit well with the AJCongress itself, since it guarded rather jealously its reputation as the preeminent Jewish organization in church-state law and litigation. In the words of its new CLSA director, Joseph B. Robison, Rabkin's entrepreneurial correspondence with Williams made the AJCongress appear to be *"noch shleppers"* (laggards), an impression that conveyed "a seriously distorted picture." Rabkin defended himself by saying he was trying to get the AJCongress "two bites of the apple" and "avoid the kind of questions that apparently nevertheless did occur to Edward Bennett Williams."[72] Rabkin and Robison soon ended their testy correspondence, the final result being that neither the AJCongress, the AJCommittee, nor the ADL would participate in *Tilton.* Ultimately, in fact, *Tilton* attracted little amicus support. Just two briefs were filed, one by Americans United and the other by the Connecticut chapter of the NAACP, the Connecticut Council of Churches, the CCLU, and the CJCRC, both on behalf of the plaintiffs. *Lemon-DiCenso,* in contrast, attracted nineteen amicus briefs that represented the opinion of over forty separate organizations. From *Lemon* onward, the involvement of organized interests in church-state litigation as amici curiae would continue to grow in popularity. Nonetheless, barely a handful of church-state cases since have attracted the number and range of amicus participants that *Lemon* did.[73]

Law and Litigation after *Lemon*

For well over the next decade, the *Lemon* test stonewalled almost without fail legislative efforts to allocate public funds to parochial schools. Even though Congress and state legislatures were persistent in their attempts to escape the constitutional noose that *Lemon* had placed around the government's discretion to provide aid to elementary and secondary parochial schools, they met with little success. From 1973 to 1980 the Supreme Court decided nine cases that involved either the ESEA of 1965 or state statutes that offered assistance to religious schools beyond textbook loans; seven of those decisions went against the government. Even the two cases in which the government prevailed, the victories were modest, involving no public assistance for the direct or indirect purchase of state-provided educational services, but rather compliance with state administrative requirements.[74]

What makes this line of decisions even more remarkable is that Chief Justice Burger, who had authored the Court's opinion in *Lemon-DiCenso*, soon switched allegiances on the parochial aid issue and sided with the supporters of such assistance for the remainder of his tenure. After *Lemon*, the chief justice authored just one other majority opinion in this area, *Levitt v. PEARL* (1973), in which the Court held unconstitutional a New York statute that authorized public reimbursement to religious schools for costs incurred in the administration of state-mandated student achievement tests. The occasional victories came when moderate justices such as Lewis Powell or Potter Stewart crossed over to support the troika of Chief Justice Burger, Justice Byron White, and Justice William H. Rehnquist, who consistently favored assistance to parochial schools. But Chief Justice Burger most commonly found himself in dissent on the parochial assistance issue, unable to undo what he had created in *Lemon*. Meanwhile, the Court over which he presided for seventeen years proceeded to all but disable the power of government to provide financial aid to parochial schools.

From 1969 to 1980 litigation over public assistance to sectarian schools dominated the Court's church-state docket. During this period the Court decided twenty-seven cases brought under the religion clauses, fourteen (51.8 percent) of which involved financial aid to such institutions. In addition to the cases focusing on parochial school aid, there were four cases involving exemptions from the Selective Service Act, four cases involving church autonomy, three involving a free exercise claim, one involving religious doctrine, and one involving employment discrimination under Title VII of the Civil Rights Act of 1964. Some scholars have argued that the Burger Court's preoccupation with financial aid was a natural evolution from the Warren Court's attention to religious influence in public schools and public life. But there is also little doubt that Pfeffer's determination to litigate the parochial school issue until all the possibilities had been exhausted was pivotal in pushing and keeping the matter before the Court over such an extended period. Nor is it unreasonable to argue that, by this time, Pfeffer's personal force had outdistanced the influence of the various organizational structures that provided the institutional support for his litigation work. This included even the AJCongress, whose relationship with Pfeffer changed dramatically during the 1970s and early 1980s.[75]

Of the nine cases the Court decided between 1973 and 1980 involving financial aid to elementary and secondary religious schools, Pfeffer served as lead counsel in six. In one other, Pfeffer was credited with authorship or coauthorship of the amicus brief submitted on behalf of the Committee for Public Education and Religious Liberty (PEARL), which included among its constituent members the AJCongress, the AJCommittee, and the ADL.[76] (The two cases in which Pfeffer did not participate attracted no amicus briefs from organized interests.) From the early 1970s forward it was PEARL, not the AJCongress, that began to command the majority of Pfeffer's time and attention; and it was PEARL that most often served as the organizational support structure behind the Pfeffer-directed litigation campaign against federal and state parochial aid.

But PEARL's entrance into the litigation arena did not happen overnight. PEARL had formed in March 1967 in response to an intensive statewide campaign by supporters of parochial school aid who were working to repeal the provision in the New York state constitution that banned the use of public funds for such purposes. Consisting of twenty-two New York–based professional, civic, educational, religious, and civil liberties organizations, including the AJCommittee, the AJCongress, and the ADL, PEARL was the brainchild of Pfeffer, who believed that such an organization was required to stave off the inevitable demands from influential pro–parochial aid forces that the government provide subsidies for their educational and social institutions. Given the orientation of its constituent organizations, Pfeffer also believed that PEARL could provide a centralizing mechanism capable of coordinating the inevitable spate of litigation involving parochial aid that would follow the Court's decisions in *Flast* and *Allen*, regardless of the outcome of these cases. Rather than waste valuable financial resources and staff expertise on "turf" battles between like-minded agencies over who was best qualified to conduct such litigation, Pfeffer argued, it was better to consolidate their interests under a single organization. PEARL accordingly took on a federal structure, spinning off into several state affiliates whose activities were coordinated by a national office, for which Pfeffer served as PEARL's general counsel and litigation chief.[77]

For the remainder of the 1970s PEARL succeeded as the centralizing force in church-state litigation, a role that Pfeffer had envisioned for it. In July 1971, just one week after the Court's decision in *Lemon-DiCenso*, the AJCongress and the ACLU announced that together they would soon initiate lawsuits nationwide intended to terminate state aid to parochial schools.[78] While the AJCongress and the ACLU did proceed as planned, over time PEARL assumed control of the bulk of this litigation, with Pfeffer situated at the strategic helm. And Pfeffer's success during the period from 1973 to 1980 was nothing short of spectacular. In 1973 alone Pfeffer was responsible for the litigation that resulted in the Court's decisions in *Sloan v. Lemon*, *PEARL v. Nyquist*, and *Levitt v. PEARL*, which together struck down laws allowing direct reimbursement from the state for expenses incurred by parents whose children attended religious schools. Shortly thereafter, Pfeffer argued two more successful cases before the Court, *Wheeler v. Barerra* and *Meek v. Pettinger*, which invalidated two separate state statutes authorizing supplementary funds for parochial schools to help cover the cost of their special and auxiliary education programs. By 1980, backed by a committed organizational structure, Pfeffer had succeeded in building a corpus of case law that made it almost impossible for religious schools and parents whose children attended them to secure public financial assistance.

It would be Pfeffer's success with PEARL and his now-transcendent status within the separationist church-state bar that would lead to a reconfiguration of the organizational politics among the major Jewish organizations and of Pfeffer's individual relationship with the AJCongress and, to a lesser extent, the AJCommittee and the ADL. By 1980, when Pfeffer argued his last parochial aid case before the Court, PEARL had evolved from a consortium of like-minded groups into an organizational mechanism that enabled him to carry out his personal agenda. Granted, Pfeffer's personal agenda and PEARL's litigation agenda were often identical, but even so other organizations found it difficult to assert themselves in a legal environment that for so long had been dominated by such a strong individual. In the middle 1960s Pfeffer had assumed the title of "special counsel" to the AJCongress. This enabled him to pursue other opportunities, which, in addition to his litigation work, included a long tenure at Long Island University as a professor of political science.

While Pfeffer would continue to work on occasion with the AJCongress until 1985, their relationship became less intimate as new and in some cases quite different opportunities for Pfeffer to utilize his individual expertise continued to manifest themselves. But Pfeffer's departure from active involvement with the AJCongress left it in the unfamiliar situation of being without a dominant individual figure in the church-state arena. The time had long since passed when potential "clients" came to the AJCongress for assistance; instead, potential test cases and important litigation were referred to Pfeffer, who, as the central figure in church-state law and litigation, simply needed an organizational structure to carry out his judicial agenda. So when Pfeffer resigned as chief counsel from PEARL in the early 1980s because of illness, an institutional and personal leadership void was created within the separationist community. For the first time in over thirty years, Leo Pfeffer was not there to serve as the guiding force in church-state law and litigation. Fortunately, the AJCongress experienced a turnover in personnel that resulted in an influx of talented young attorneys. The organization was thus given a golden opportunity to reassert its institutional leverage in church-state law and politics, a leverage it had lacked since Pfeffer's departure.

Critical changes were taking place with the AJCommittee and the ADL as well. Neither organization had much involvement with PEARL, preferring instead to carry out their litigation work through the NCRAC. But, although old animosities had surfaced briefly during the preparation of their joint amicus brief in *Tilton*, the AJCommittee and the ADL worked fairly harmoniously with the AJCongress for the remainder of the 1970s. In one case, *Wheeler v. Barerra* (1974), the AJ-

Congress and the ADL coauthored an amicus brief on behalf of several smaller Jewish organizations without the AJCommittee's involvement; in *Wolman v. Walter* (1977), the ADL filed its first-ever solo amicus brief in Supreme Court church-state litigation—a departure from tradition that, by the early 1980s, would evolve into an organizational norm. In another case, the AJCommittee joined in signing the amicus brief prepared by an interfaith coalition of religious organizations, a decision that also pointed to its future pattern of involvement in church-state litigation. For the most part, though, attention to church-state issues within the AJCommittee after *Lemon* took a backseat to other matters that were of greater immediate concern to their members. As the legal director of the AJCommittee explained:

> After *Lemon* and some of the other early religious school cases, church-state was an important, but no longer burning issue to our members. So many other things were happening that affected the Jewish community that were more immediate. Civil rights, the school problems here in New York, and above all the concern over Israel's security—especially Israel.
>
> You see, Leo so dominated that area in the 70s, more so than even before because he had become bigger than the AJCongress, which gave him his start. We supported these efforts through our *amicus* work; and we even did some community relations to assist religious schools with fundraising, budgeting and things like that. We even outlined a program that called for "shared time" between public and religious schools, on the *Zorach* model, to ease the burden that some parents felt after *Lemon*. Yes, we believed strongly that tax money for parochial schools was unconstitutional and we opposed it without qualification. But we believed, as we always have, that these issues have a life beyond litigation and you have to pursue that.
>
> But as the single biggest concern to our membership, Israel, far surpassed church-state. American Jews simply feared a world with Christmas trees and the like far less than a world without Israel.[79]

Even so, the major Jewish organizations continued to dominate the legal and organizational environment of church-state litigation in the period from *Flast* (1968) to *PEARL v. Regan* (1980). No other religious or secular organizations, save the ACLU, participated in this litigation to the extent that the three major Jewish agencies did, which continued a pattern that had been in place since the 1950s. Consistent with the line of separationist decisions on parochial school assistance handed down by the Burger Court during the 1970s, the environment of church-state litigation was dominated by religious and secular organizations whose ideological tendencies were supportive of these outcomes. But the major Jewish organizations were mistaken if they believed that they could now relax after their hard-fought effort over two generations to construct a favorable core of establishment clause law. After 1980 the entrance of powerful and ideologically conservative evangelical and fundamentalist Christian organizations, coupled with significant changes in the Court's personnel, would alter the legal and political environment of church-state law and litigation, tipping the balance of power in an unexpected and unimagined way.

6

Defending the Status Quo

Litigation in a Changed Environment

Starting in 1980, the environment in which federal church-state litigation was conducted underwent a dramatic transformation. Organized religious interests, long active and effective advocates in public affairs and politics, became even more visible and influential in the litigation process over the course of the decade. Recent scholarship has produced several fine accounts documenting the rise of a strong network of Christian evangelical and fundamentalist groups to positions of power in the political and electoral processes.[1] The conservative religious movement, which historically had rarely been able to generate much enthusiasm for its social agenda in the political mainstream, suddenly found its views on issues ranging from abortion rights to foreign policy commanding attention in state legislatures, Congress, and the White House. In addition to finding the channels of political influence now more open and hospitable to their interests than in recent memory, conservative religious organizations also discovered that the federal courts were no longer allied with the once-powerful constitutional reform movement initiated by liberal litigation-oriented organizations. In a manner unparalleled since Franklin D. Roosevelt had reshaped the ideological cast of the federal

judiciary almost half a century before, from the inception of his successful 1980 presidential campaign Ronald Reagan was determined to
mold the courts into an extension of presidential power and policy.
Accordingly, President Reagan encouraged his administration to engage in a systematic effort to appoint judges to the federal courts who
would bolster his own conservative social agenda. Included in this program of conservative constitutional and judicial reform was the loosen-
ing of the restraints that a generation of the Court's decisions had imposed on the government's power to accommodate, much less favor,
religion in the conduct of American public life.[2]

In order for the Reagan administration to advance these objectives
in the church-state arena, the appointment of judges to all levels of the
federal judiciary who did not consider the establishment clause a barrier to government support for private religious claims became imperative. Over time, the Supreme Court, as well as the lower federal courts,
did depart from the separationist impulses that had guided church-
state jurisprudence for over a generation in favor of a less absolute,
more accommodationist approach to the establishment clause. This
more favorable political and legal climate encouraged numerous well-
established conservative religious groups to expand their organizational capacities so that they could include litigation as an instrument
of policy advocacy. This more aggressive use of judicially based advocacy mirrored the growing emphasis that secular conservative organizations in general were placing on litigation as an instrument of collective action. In recognizing the potential power to effect constitutional
change through litigation, the conservative public interest movement
simply took a page from the book of its liberal nemeses and began to
use it to its advantage.[3]

The fusion of religious and secular conservative interests into a
powerful public interest law movement in its own right created a much
more complicated and confrontational environment in the federal
courts—and nowhere was this reconfiguration more evident than in
establishment clause litigation. Ever since the Court's decision in *Everson v. Board of Education* (1947), church-state litigation had been dominated by a powerful nucleus of liberal, separationist civil liberties and
religious organizations, as we have seen. But with the advent of the
Reagan administration, this ceased to be the case.

For example, prior to the Court's 1979 term, no self-identified conservative evangelical or fundamentalist religious organization had ever

participated in establishment clause litigation, either as an amicus curiae or as the primary sponsor. After 1980, however, these organizations began to enter church-state litigation as often as their liberal
counterparts, and, almost without fail, always on behalf of the accommodationist claim. This development startled the traditional coalition
of mainline religious bodies, education lobbies, and civil liberties organizations, which until this time had exercised firm control over the
alignment of organized interests active in church-state litigation before
the Court. With the litigation environment transformed into one more
complex and ideologically confrontational, no one organization or concentrated alliance of organized interests was able to control the litigation process in the manner that the AJCongress, the ACLU, and, later,
PEARL had once done. Combined with a sometimes idiosyncratic but
generally more conservative Court, separationist organizations that
had once used the litigation process with great success to pursue constitutional reform now found themselves forced to engage in a more
reactive, less aggressive approach to litigation just to preserve the victories for which they had fought so hard for three decades.[4]

Another important component in this new, more complex litigation
environment was the lack of any single recurring church-state issue to
come before the Court. In contrast to the period from *Flast v. Cohen*
(1968) through *PEARL v. Regan* (1980)—when organized interests so
pushed the parochial aid issue that it dominated the Court's church-
state agenda for over a decade—or from *McCollum v. Board of Education*
(1948) through *Abington v. Schempp* (1963)—when the relationship between private religion and public education underwent a constitutional redefinition—since 1980 no one issue has defined the litigation
that has arisen under the religion clauses. From its 1980 through to its
1992 term, the Court decided more cases focusing on the free exercise
clause than it did claims brought under the establishment clause. In
fact, the most frequently argued issue before the Court during the
1980s was that of the extent to which religious individuals or organizations are entitled to exemptions from compliance with criminal and
civil laws when the conduct prescribed by their religion conflicts with
these laws. Such claims constituted 41.4 percent of the Court's religion
clause decisions. Cases involving conflict between public institutions
and religious doctrine or preference accounted for 24.3 percent; claims
regarding tax assistance to parochial institutions for 17 percent; employment discrimination claims brought under Title VII for 7 percent;

and cases centering on the commercial regulation of religious properties for 9.7 percent. Compare this with the range of the Court's church-
state docket in the decade between *Walz v. Tax Commission* (1970) and
PEARL v. Regan. During this period, over half of the Court's decisions
involved parochial assistance alone, compared to less than 5 percent
that focused on state support for religious doctrine or preference.[5]
Thus cases clustering around the broader issue of the free exercise of
religion, which had hitherto received minuscule attention in the
Court's larger frame of religion clause reform, increasingly commanded the moment, although with less sweep and specificity as litigation over parochial assistance had during the 1970s.

But environmental factors alone do not condition the behavior of
organized interests. For the AJCommittee, the AJCongress, and the
ADL, the reconfiguration of the litigation environment—from one that
favored their doctrinal objectives and offered little political or ideological competition from conservative organized interests to the reverse—
led to a reconsideration of both their individual and collective behavior in this process. After 1980 the AJCommittee, the AJCongress, and
the ADL each underwent internal changes that resulted in new approaches to their choice and use of litigation in the church-state arena.
What these internal changes were and how they interacted with the
new litigation environment in which the major Jewish organizations
now found themselves are the questions now to be addressed.

Transition in the Major
Jewish Organizations

From the late 1940s through the mid-1970s the AJCongress had earned
a reputation as the dominant organizational force in church-state litigation, an achievement that can be attributed in large part to the presence
of Leo Pfeffer as its lead counsel. While Pfeffer's relationship with the
other major Jewish organizations was characterized by alternating periods of friction, rejection, and grudging cooperation, these organizations also acknowledged that their own staff was incapable of match-
ing his legal and academic expertise in church-state matters. Political
scientist Samuel Krislov has commented that Pfeffer, over the course
of his career, was able to establish himself as a one-man "repeat
player," albeit one rooted in an organizational support structure, as a
result of his steadfast commitment to incremental law building

through careful, concerted test-case litigation.⁶ Moreover, as previous chapters have described, Pfeffer's expertise and dominance over establishment clause litigation ultimately evolved to the point where he transcended organizational boundaries and himself became the integrative figure in the litigation process on behalf of the larger separationist bar. Organizations that enlisted or benefited from Pfeffer's services ranged from numerous local Jewish community relations and rabbinical bodies to major civil liberties organizations, such as the ACLU, to more specialized and secular church-state advocacy groups, such as Americans United and, later, PEARL.

As we have also seen, by the late 1970s Pfeffer was no longer a real factor in the day-to-day litigation activities of the AJCongress, either in terms of whether or how it chose to intervene in particular cases or what position it should take in its briefs. Pfeffer's more entrepreneurial approach to advancing his legal agenda and his ability to litigate as an independent contractor reduced his need for the AJCongress as his primary organizational anchor. This development had the effect of diminishing the AJCongress's once unquestioned position as the preeminent representative among the major national Jewish organizations active in church-state law and politics and, more generally, the larger separationist community. For the AJCongress, the loss of Pfeffer—who was beyond doubt the most dominant and influential advocate of his generation (and quite possibly of all time) in the field of church-state law—meant that it was no longer able to exercise the control over the litigation process it once had, since its organizational reputation in this arena had been largely due to Pfeffer's twenty-five-year association with the AJCongress. Coupled with Pfeffer's semiretirement, in the early 1980s, from active participation in church-state law and litigation, for the first time in over thirty years both the organized Jewish and separationist communities were left without a central figure to coordinate their involvement in the litigation process. Nonetheless, one important consequence of Pfeffer's departure from the scene, according to Marc D. Stern, who joined the legal staff of the CLSA in 1981, was a "greater feeling of independence among all the groups, Jewish and otherwise, in how we go about our business." Expanding on this point, Stern remarked:

> Leo used to be *the* person for the Jewish community. When this all began, [the] ADL and the [AJ]Committee had relatively little

interest in it, compared to us. He was the great guru of all this and brought all the other groups along, including the ACLU, which was then still oriented to other civil liberties issues. And that's the way things were for years and years. Leo ran the show.

That's not true anymore and hasn't been for sometime. There isn't any dominant personality to direct litigation now—the volume and complexity of litigation makes that impossible. Also— this is important—there are several groups now that have the capacity to litigate in some way, including [the] ADL and [AJ]-Committee, plus at least half a dozen other groups outside the Jewish community that I consider competent. We all feel free to disagree with each other because we all think we're right, something that was not the case in Leo's day. People in the other agencies might have felt that way, but that was kept from Leo. Even if it wasn't, he wouldn't hear of it. No one who claimed to be on the same side as Leo Pfeffer dared to tell him that he was wrong in public. Organizational differences that were once hushed out of deference to Leo or because of him are now out in the open. And they're legitimate and cannot be denied. There is much more competition now among the Jewish organizations to be the true guardian of the church-state principle, or [the interest of Jews] in general for that matter.[7]

While Pfeffer's departure reduced the control that the AJCongress had over the broader litigation process after 1980, staff expertise, as well as the organization's commitment to church-state matters, remained high. For reasons involving other internal factors such as financial resources and external factors such as a less receptive judicial environment, however, the AJCongress was generally forced to limit itself to participation as an amicus curiae when it came to articulating its organizational interests in current church-state litigation. With the AJCongress now more dependent on amicus participation than on direct sponsorship, expertise became even more important because it enabled the organization to continue to command influence over the litigation process, given the prestige it had built up as an organizational litigant over its an extended period of involvement in church-state law and litigation. Staff expertise enabled the AJCongress to prepare its legal work in house, without having to resort to outside counsel or participation in a multigroup coalition in order to ease the burden on its resources. As Stern put it:

> It is always an advantage if agencies possess the capacities to control their own work product. You can tell instantly the difference between a brief that's been written by someone who knows an area of law and someone who doesn't. It is just a fact of life that experienced lawyers write better briefs. If there is expertise in antitrust law and tax law, why shouldn't there be expertise in church-state law?
>
> When you are dependent on amicus work to make your voice heard, as we are more or less now, all this doubles in importance. When you're talking about the Supreme Court, you are talking about nine very gifted individuals that don't necessarily need your help. It is the only court in this country that specializes in the First Amendment. But when they are busy, or faced with a new development that we are already aware of because we began dealing with the issue in a state legislature or lower court, then a brief with the name "American Jewish Congress" on it probably gets read and maybe even pulls some weight. And that is not because we are a reputable public interest law firm, so to speak, but because of our reputation on church-state. If you are pressed for time, whose brief do you read? You read ours because someone of our stature has chosen to address the issues in a given case, and not just in a way that repeats what the principal [litigant] said. If that's not how it works, then I have no idea why I do this.[8]

Perhaps the most important internal factor to account for the gradual movement of the AJCongress away from a preference for direct control over lawsuits to its almost complete reliance on an amicus strategy after 1980 was the extent of the financial resources available for its litigation program. From a budget of less than $1 million in 1945, when the AJCongress created the CLSA to initiate its program of law and litigation designed to attack discrimination and fight for the expansion of civil liberties, through the late 1980s, when its budget amounted to over $7 million, financial resources kept steady pace, but only with inflation.[9] Furthermore, a more diversified and expansive domestic and international agenda, combined with an exorbitant increase in the

cost of litigation, made it almost impossible for the AJCongress to continue to engage in the direct sponsorship of legal cases. One general
consequence of the financial crunch, said Stern, was to force the AJ-
Congress to reevaluate how it structured its litigation program:

> Money is the big factor. Most of the time if you catch somebody
> with their pants down on a church-state violation, they'll stop it.
> If you win the smaller cases—the "sure things"—you get attor-
> neys fees back, so it turns into a minor profit center. But you have
> to bear that cost until you win, and with the courts full of Reagan
> appointees there is no guarantee of winning anything nowadays.
> And the lawsuits that we are interested in can be very expensive.
>
> So you raise $500,000? So what. We began a drive several years
> ago, after some bad Supreme Court decisions, to raise money for
> this very purpose. But how many cases do you think that can
> spin off? Not a whole lot. What happens when you lose? That's
> money gone. How many cases can you afford to bring at any-
> where from $100,000 to $250,000 a shot? The cost of litigation is
> so much, and the risk is so much higher than fifteen or twenty-
> five years ago, that I do not know how we will be able to continue
> to bring church-state lawsuits. We have been really been forced
> into an amicus strategy.[10]

Limited financial resources for litigation had an additional effect on
the organizational goals of the AJCongress. Whereas in a more prosperous time, as well as in a more favorable litigation environment, Pfeffer and the AJCongress would more readily sue in the lower courts to
enforce settled or recently pronounced legal precedents, rising costs
associated with even simple litigation made such action less feasible.
Commented Stern:

> Litigation to enforce existing precedent has become prohibitively
> expensive. This gives the people at the local level, who are re-
> sponsible for the violation, an advantage because they have to
> know there is a real threat of enforcement to change their ways.
> If there's not, then they have no incentive. So what do you do?
> Enter a case to force a school principal to stop praying with his
> students, or save your resources for a major constitutional chal-
> lenge down the road? Our hands are tied on money. We operate
> on limited resources. I don't know what the solution is—it's a
> real, real problem.

One potential solution is to work with other groups, but then everyone wants to run the show. A case is no longer your case because everyone wants to claim credit. There's also the problem of compromise. If compromises get to the point where the lawsuit becomes tentative enforcement, you have to ask yourself what's the whole point of getting involved. That's another spin-off of life after Leo—there's no one person whose reputation can get the money or support to do it one way. Everyone can now say, "We don't like what's going on in the schools. Give us a contribution so we can stop it." Who's to say anyone has a special claim on the establishment clause anymore?[11]

In sum, internal changes in financial resources, staff expertise, and organizational commitment to church-state issues have been among the important forces responsible for the different approach the AJCongress has taken to litigation since 1980. But an examination of how these internal factors have influenced the organizational behavior of the ADL in the litigation process will show that such changes do not always affect the behavior of organized interests in similar fashion.

In contrast to the stagnant litigation budget of the AJCongress, which did not allow it to pursue the more aggressive legal strategies it would have liked, the financial commitment of the ADL to its legal program increased substantially during this same period. But greater financial resources did not prompt the ADL to reevaluate its long-standing organizational commitment to confine its involvement in major church-state litigation to participation as an amicus curiae. The overall budget of the ADL increased from $5.5 million in 1971 to over $28 million by the early 1990s. And included among the internal beneficiaries of this dramatic upswing in financial resources was the agency's legal program. But rather than encourage the ADL to consider direct sponsorship of litigation, more substantial financial resources allowed the ADL to create a separate Legal Affairs Division. The Legal Affairs Division has since operated as a far more autonomous and influential force within the ADL than did its previous two-person legal department. Moreover, since 1968 the ADL has increased the size of its national legal staff and the number of full-time attorneys assigned to regional offices fourfold.[12]

For the ADL, greater affluence translated into growth in the size of its legal staff and greater expertise in the church-state field, since it was now positioned to hire lawyers whose training and skills were rooted in public interest law. Interviews with members of the ADL's legal staff suggest that two major shifts in its organizational behavior with regard to the litigation process can be linked to these changes: more control and independence in the preparation of its amicus briefs and the ability to participate in litigation more frequently and without the need for coalitional partners. This more aggressive and independent attitude toward litigation has been reflected in the ADL's approach to its amicus participation. From the 1980 to the 1992 terms of the Supreme Court, eleven of the sixteen amicus briefs filed by the ADL in church-state cases have been solo filings, an almost complete turnaround from the organization's prior behavior.[13] Commented Steven Freeman, legal affairs director of the ADL:

> Our resources are such now that we don't have to depend on other groups anymore, or ask someone outside the agency who may be well-intentioned but unlearned to prepare a brief. We can now file our own briefs if we feel the importance of the cases merits it, or because the arguments are not being made in someone else's brief. It's also important for our own credibility and prestige. Plus the agency, having put all this money into our law program, expects us to do it. If a some other group wants to sign our brief, that's fine, but not at the expense of changing something it might not like and we do. We are not dependent on other groups, or in need of a partner, like the AJCommittee in the old days, to get something out. We will still form coalitions, but not for those reasons.
>
> Money will never determine whether we would ever decide to sponsor a case or not. That's just not what the agency seeks in litigation. We want to represent the agency, represent the Jewish community that looks to us for leadership and do so in our own voice. That's what money means to us. We could have all the money in the world and it would not mean that we would start running around the country filing lawsuits.[14]

The ADL's organizational commitment to an active presence in church-state litigation has increased over time, but even with its additional financial resources, legal expertise, and willingness to intervene in such matters, church versus state has not become the issue with which the ADL, while well respected, has become synonymous. This is by design. Whereas the AJCongress, as still the most litigation-oriented of the major Jewish organizations, continues to honor as best it can the desire of CLSA's founders to act as the "private attorney general" for American Jews, especially on matters related to religious freedom and the separation of church and state, the ADL views such concerns as one of several major civil rights and liberties issues on its organizational palette. As a general rule, questions of church versus state do not necessarily carry more weight within the Legal Affairs Division of the ADL than do legal actions to attack racial supremacist organizations, efforts to prohibit invidious discrimination and harassment in the workplace, or the pursuit of legislative and judicial remedies for "hate crimes." Emphasis on a given issue will change from year to year, depending on how critical the issue may be in the panorama of the ADL's broader organizational goals. And litigation is not always the ADL's first response when it is confronted with a church-state problem. This, of course, marks the continuation of a policy that has remained consistent throughout the ADL's historical involvement in this arena. Commented an ADL community relations professional:

> Church-state issues are an important concern—one of *the* most important—of this agency, but not its overriding concern. It is an aspect of our total work, but not the central issue. But it is necessary to show our involvement in things that are not related to Israel, because so much of our work in recent years has had to do with Israel. It's important that we show [that] our interests are diversified and [that we] involve ourselves in the many issues of concern to Jews. But we don't put the same emphasis on church-state as the AJCongress. That is its main thing.
>
> There have been cases where we have gotten a call from an ADL person in smaller towns about a problem and been asked if we should get involved. One I remember involved a city seal on a garbage truck that had "Christianity" in it. We decided, in consultation with New York, that it was *de minimus* and let it go. I don't know how much pain it would cause Jews the world over if there is a garbage truck with "Christianity" painted in small letters on its seal. But the AJCongress got involved, I remember, because it thought it was a major constitutional issue. To me, it's not. But that's their specialty, so that's what they do. On another issue that we feel we're more suited to take the lead on, it might

be the other way around, with AJCongress wondering why anyone would get involved in something. If we all worried about the
same things all the time, then someone would go out of
business.[15]

In contrast to the ADL, the AJCommittee has not experienced any
great upsurge in the quantity of financial resources it can devote to
its litigation program, its ability to increase staff size, or its litigation
capacity. Even so, the AJCommittee has maintained the vibrant organizational commitment to an active and visible presence in church-state
litigation that it began in earnest during the early 1960s, although it
did not become as independent and aggressive in this arena as its former civic defense partner, the ADL.

In the late 1980s the AJCommittee's yearly budget stood at close to
$20 million, an increase of over $10 million from 1971.[16] But as with the
ADL, finances have never been a defining factor in the AJCommittee's
approach to litigation; its roots in community relations and noncon-
frontational approaches to conflict resolution are too deep, according
to Samuel Rabinove, who has served as its legal director since 1967,
for the organization to consider becoming a "plaintiff's counsel." Commented Rabinove:

> We have never been a litigation-happy group. That is not to say
> we don't view litigation as important. We do. Edwin Lukas, the
> first legal director here, had to fight like hell for a budget with
> our board to get this thing started back in the late 1940s. Al-
> though what we did and wanted to do was really nothing com-
> pared to the [AJ]Congress, it still shook up some of our more
> conservative members, who still like the idea of "working behind
> the scenes." But it would not have mattered how much money
> the leadership raised; it was not going to become another [AJ]-
> Congress. Money did not affect our decisions then and doesn't
> really affect them now, in that way.[17]

Financial resources have thus never really had any serious impact
on how the AJCommittee chooses to conduct litigation—that is, on its
choice to limit its involvement to participation as an amicus curiae. But
such resources have had a demonstrable impact on the AJCommittee's
ability to hire specialized counsel, as well as to expand its organizational commitment to church-state issues as a proportion of its total
civil rights and liberties agenda. Since the late 1940s, when the AJCom-

mittee first created a legal department, the number of full-time staff has never exceeded more than two. Because of the small size of its legal staff, the AJCommittee's options in litigation, even as an amicus curiae, were much more constrained than those of either the AJCongress or the ADL. Moreover, the AJCommittee continued to remain more dependent on outside counsel or allied organized interests to assist in the preparation of its briefs than either the AJCongress or the ADL. Rabinove explained how staff constraints affected the amicus participation of the AJCommittee:

> What we do in many instances is this: we will write a piece of the brief here. If there are two major points on a brief, then we will do one here and have a group we may be working with do another, or perhaps one of our volunteer lawyers will do it. In some situations we will allow a volunteer lawyer to do the entire brief. In *Lynch v. Donnelly*, for example, we did that. One of our volunteer lawyers had an associate in his firm do the basic brief and then we selectively edited it. I signed and listed the volunteer lawyer's name as "Of Counsel." The National Council of Churches joined us and provided the other parts of the legal analysis.[18]

From 1980 to 1992, the AJCommittee has participated as an amicus curiae in almost one third of the establishment and free exercise clause cases decided by the Supreme Court, a rate surpassed only by the AJCongress, the ADL, and the ACLU. But in contrast to its historic pattern of amicus participation, which involved different degrees of coalitional involvement with the other major Jewish organizations, the AJCommittee has, since 1980, conducted most of its church-state litigation in close cooperation with non-Jewish religious organizations. Indeed, during the more recent period close to three-fourths of the AJ-Committee's amicus participation in church-state litigation before the Court has been as a member of an interfaith coalition, whereas before participation in such an arrangement was nonexistent.[19] Just as internal forces account for the major changes in how the AJCongress and the ADL have conducted litigation since 1980, similar, but less clear-cut, forces have been at work behind the AJCommittee's decision to use litigation to promote the more general objective of improving interfaith relations.

Just as financial resources, staff expertise, and issue-focus are all relevant to the post-1980 approaches of the AJCongress and the ADL to litigation, so they are to understanding how the AJCommittee conducts its litigation work. The AJCommittee's decision to work with such diverse non-Jewish organizations as the Baptist Joint Committee, the National Council of Churches, the Christian Legal Society, and the Lutheran Council USA in litigation clearly reflects the organization's more general concern to promote interfaith relations, through both the legal process and social relations channels. Beyond that, however, one cannot point to a more specific internal factor, such as money or staff expertise, or external concerns, such as the relative receptivity or hostility of the federal courts, to account for this strategic choice. Rabinove commented in 1990 that the AJCommittee's recent move toward an interfaith approach to litigation is simply an extension of the organization's long-standing commitment to the reduction of prejudice through dialogue and education, albeit with an increasingly use of the language of law, rather than efforts to foster better community relations:

> We have always done a lot of interfaith work. In recent years we have stressed interfaith dialogue even more. That resulted from the rise of the religious right in the eighties, and the need for Jews to educate Christians about our religion and our concerns as a religious minority. The Court was faced with a number of sensitive issues that mobilized the religious community—*Lynch* and then *[County of] Allegheny v. ACLU*, *[Wallace v.] Jaffree*, *Edwards v. Aguillard*, and then equal access. Part of our endeavor is to acquaint people with the reality that Jews are not antireligion or anti-Christianity. Working with Christians in church-state cases helps us towards that end.
>
> But a lot of credit for that goes to Marc Tannenbaum, our [former] director of interfaith relations. He [was] the Jewish leader in this field. This was essentially his idea, and I have tried to pull our thrust in that direction wherever it is possible. Our membership has been very receptive to that, but the decision to do this was decided among the leadership and the community relations professionals. It blends together.[20]

Since their decision to enter the arena of public interest law in the late 1940s, one factor that has remained constant in the internal calculus of the AJCommittee, the AJCongress, and the ADL has been the need for congruence between their national offices, which in most cases are responsible for the work connected to a case, and the local communities in which these cases originate. Here is where Mark Tushnet's observations on litigation as a social process that operates on both general and specific levels becomes especially relevant. If an organization is to claim that it represents the public interest of particular constituencies, that organization's decision to enter litigation on behalf of these constituencies, whether as plaintiffs's counsel or as an amicus curiae, must reflect their prevailing social objectives. In other words, one would assume that the decision of the AJCongress, the AJCommittee, or the ADL to engage in litigation in order to prevent, for example, the specific problem of the use of a religious symbol on municipal property or to pursue aggressively the general principle of religious freedom represents the wishes of the local residents who belong to or identify with the organization in question. Failure to achieve such social and political congruence raises ethical questions about the practice of public interest law, as Tushnet also notes. Lawyers working for such groups who pursue personal goals at the expense of their clients—namely, the organization's members, or, in the case of non-membership groups such as the ADL, their financial contributors and lay leadership—are generally held to have violated legal ethics.[21]

In chapter 5 I described how the efforts of Leo Pfeffer and the AJCongress to develop test-case litigation on the issue of religious practices in public schools in two Southern communities, Nashville and Miami, were either abandoned or seriously compromised by conflicts between national and local objectives. But in these instances the conflicts did not result from disagreement between the leadership and membership of the AJCongress itself, but from serious organizational friction between the AJCongress and the leadership and membership of the AJCommittee and the ADL. Somewhat along the same lines, Tushnet observes how the NAACP legal staff often had to overcome opposition in local communities, which, because of their experience with and proximity to hostile white communities, were less optimistic about the efficacy of legal remedies than was the national office. Indeed, in some cases, the NAACP was unable to generate sufficient local support for lawsuits—when the constituencies in question felt that other, more accommodationist approaches offered the best chance for social change—and thus was forced to abandon litigation.[22]

Appropriate parallels, as well as important differences, can be drawn between the experience of the major Jewish organizations in

Nashville and Miami and the circumstances about which Tushnet writes. In contrast to the NAACP, which was the sole legal representative of the African American community in the judicial struggle to overcome segregation, the AJCommittee, the AJCongress, and the ADL were created to represent the diverse ethnic, economic, social, and political subcommunities within American Jewry. Membership in a public interest group is self-selected and thus minimizes potential leadership-membership conflict. When an organization fails to represent the interests of its members or supporters, those members are free to transfer their loyalties to another organization—assuming, of course, that another, more compatible organization exists to represent their interests. Because the AJCommittee, the AJCongress, and the ADL have traditionally represented different constituencies within the American Jewish community, the potential for conflict has remained highest among the three groups rather than within any one of them. This lack of serious policy conflict within each organization has in turn enabled them to avoid the ethical dilemma to which Tushnet refers and by extension the practical difficulties that the NAACP encountered as the sole representative of the law-based civil rights grievances of the African American community. Jill Kahn, the ADL's assistant legal director, commented in 1989 about leadership-membership conflict and congruence:

> New York will not take a case and rush into court if it's not what our local office wants us to do. In the Pawtucket case [*Lynch v. Donnelly*], ADL people there did not want us to file a brief and had their reasons. For those reasons, we did not file when it was in the First Circuit. When it got to the Supreme Court, we felt we had to be in on it and told our local people so. There was a little more distance from the local scene. We were convinced of the national importance of the case and there was agreement on that point. It is rarely the case that we would file over the objection of our regional offices. But sometimes we are in a better position than our local offices to see a case that has national implications and for us to be in on it outweighs community concerns, especially at the Supreme Court level.[23]

Membership constraints were also a minor (or, more often, a nonexistent) factor in the decisions of the AJCongress and the AJCommittee to enter litigation. Like that of the ADL, the leadership of each group had substantial latitude to develop and carry out legal policy, although it remained sensitive to the concerns of its local members when conflicts arose. The membership is not actively canvassed when the national office debates whether to pursue litigation, even when, as in the case of the AJCongress, it may decide to represent the plaintiff as lead counsel. Since American Jews have multiple choices for organizational representation in law and public affairs, leadership-membership conflicts are minimized. Thus, to borrow a typology from the congressional scholar Richard Fenno, the leaders of the AJCongress, the AJCommittee, and even those of the ADL (which does not officially recognize membership) act as trustees, rather than as delegates or politicos, on behalf of their constituents.[24] As the AJCongress's Marc Stern remarked:

> In most cases we do not actively solicit the opinion of our membership. Sure, there is an organizational structure, but here the tradition has been to let the lawyers do the work and that those decisions are for lawyers. We are most knowledgeable about church-state of anyone involved [with the agency] so there is no real formal need to go to our membership. And I don't think it is even interested in the day-to-day of those kinds of questions. If I was to say I was in favor of aid to parochial schools then our membership would rise up and revolt. That's an extreme example. One of the reasons that people join the [AJ]Congress is because of our position on church-state, not in spite of it.[25]

One example that Stern cited in which leadership-membership differences did manifest themselves concerned the decision of the AJCongress not to participate in *Bob Jones v. U.S.,* which centered on the question of whether the IRS could revoke the tax exemption of private, religious universities that discriminated on the basis of race in their admissions process.[26] The ADL and the AJCommittee viewed *Bob Jones* as an antidiscrimination civil rights case and filed in support of the IRS. But the CLSA of the AJCongress did not:

> Our CLSA thought that *Bob Jones* was right. The first question— and primary question—was whether a tax exemption is a subsidy. I don't think that it is. Our CLSA also believed that the free exercise claim was very strong. It was a very tangential form of race discrimination. But you could not take that position publicly. No way. We would have had some company in that case that

our leadership could not bear to keep. So we stayed out. Those decisions are for the leadership, which generally recognizes our limitations. The irony, if there is any, is this: a year or two later we file an amicus brief on behalf of the Scientologists, who were faced with another tax problem. It's nobody's first choice to rush into court and defend Scientology, but sometimes, when an issue can hit everybody over the head because the government isn't thinking, you have to. Then we send out all kinds of press releases defending ourselves. Sometimes you have hold your nose and dive in and hope you cover yourself well.[27]

But Stern also pointed out that there are cases over the which the leadership can agonize, finally decide to enter, and face the consequences, all without the membership ever having any significant knowledge of how the channels of decision making had worked. Such a case was *Aguilar v. Felton,* in which the Court held parochial schools were ineligible under Title I of the ESEA to receive federal funds to supplement remedial education programs for poor children. Said Stern:

> *Aguilar* gave people fits. It was litigated by PEARL on the theory that any form of government aid to parochial schools is bad. But that's their particular ideology. We agonized over it. Burt Neuborne [of the ACLU] and I would go back and forth on the phone as ask ourselves, "Why are we doing this case? What valuable social purpose does it serve?" But the answer was that you couldn't draw a line between this and something that was really bad. There was no way of knowing that the aid program would have worked out benignly because there would have been a whole new series of programs that chipped away at the edge of church-state separation. It was a rare case where the slippery slope argument made sense because politically that's what would have happened. But it didn't leave anybody with a great feeling afterwards.[28]

The AJCommittee, the AJCongress, and the ADL each experienced little discord between the specific and general objectives of the national leadership. Organizational mode made no difference in whether and how the AJCongress or the AJCommittee, as membership-based agencies, or the ADL, as a nonmembership, contributor-based group, decided to approach their goals through litigation. Each pursued a trustee relationship with their constituents and thereby satisfied the ethical need to represent their fears and hopes when those constituents became clients in church-state litigation.

The New Legal Landscape as an External Constraint

We have seen how internal factors can account for some of the changes in the way the AJCommittee, the AJCongress, and the ADL have conducted themselves in the litigation process. Unfortunately, we cannot ascertain from the available data whether these internal forces in fact outweighed the more complex and confrontational church-state litigation environment that emerged during the 1980s as the primary determinants underlying these changes. But what we do know is that forces internal and external to an organization interact to produce changes in its attitude toward litigation. I will now turn now to the shifts in the litigation environment after 1980 and how, in conjunction with internal factors, they influenced the organizational behavior of the AJCommittee, the AJCongress, and the ADL.

Litigation occurs in an environment surrounded by a phalanx of social, political, and legal forces. An issue or problem is first brought to the attention of the leadership of an interest group, either by its membership or other concerned parties. Discussion and deliberation then take place over what kind of collective action is appropriate, and, if so, whether the pursuit of legal remedies should be included as a one of the fitting methods to redress the grievances in question. The most visible port of entry into litigation can take the form of either direct sponsorship or participation as an amicus curiae, although organizations can take important behind-the-scenes roles as well. Either way, an organization's decision to participate in litigation must indeed represent the interests of its membership or constituents. Otherwise, ethical problems arise over the misrepresentation of clients, the extraneous use of financial resources, and the baseline purpose of collective representation. Issues such as these, as Tushnet has argued, illustrate the social dimension of the litigation process. People initially come together for the purpose of solving a communal problem. They engage in a process of social interaction that reflects both the concerns of the individuals who live in the communities where litigation has been undertaken and the lawyers who must represent the interests of their clients. Public interest lawyers must thus remain sensitive to the balance between the goals of their leadership and their membership if they are to remain faithful to the broader organizational interests they ostensibly wish to advance through litigation.

Scholarship on public interest law has generally argued that if the leadership and membership can agree on the need for litigation, and if the internal capacities of the organization permit it to pursue this recommendation, then external considerations become a significant operative force in whether and how organized interests enter the litigation process. This scholarship posits, although not with universal emphasis, that the most obvious and critical of these external considerations are, first, the doctrinal, or legal, environment in which litigation takes place and second, the political pressure that opposition groups are able to place on their potential organizational rivals in the litigation process.

More recently, political scientists have argued that competition among interest groups for organizational access to the political process in general provides some explanation for the rise and increasing pluralism of interest group participation in Supreme Court litigation. In the opinion of these scholars, one reason the litigation environment has become more densely and diversely populated is that, when a case is of broad potential import to their particular constituencies, organized interests now seek to balance the submission of amicus curiae briefs by their rivals by filing their own. This theoretical assumption is drawn from the premise that the manner in which the Court mediates the demands of rival organized interests is not "significantly different from the legislative and executive processes." Thus, the thesis that organized interests are motivated to enter litigation in an effort to persuade the Court to mediate between competitive forces seems entirely plausible. Nor does the idea seem unreasonable that the courts, like the elected branches of government, have an institutional obligation to accommodate a plural environment of ideologically diverse, multifactional organized interests in order to represent equitably the interests that come before it. Otherwise, why would the Court continue to welcome the voluminous number of amici that it does? Organized interests press their agenda before the Court because they believe it will be sensitive to their group interests, in much the same way that the elected branches of government have an institutional responsibility to consider divergent constituent demands.[29]

Theoretical expectations, then, might lead one to argue that the behavior of the major American Jewish organizations, as a sample in the universe of organized interests that engage in litigation, has been driven in substantial part by the belief that the Court is a responsive, representative, and politically accountable institution. It is also plausible to argue that the desire to offset or counterbalance competing group interests, as much as the doctrinal significance of the case under review, is responsible for shaping organizational behavior in this particular area of Supreme Court litigation. If courts do indeed synthesize the diverse organizational interests that appear before it into a broader public interest—the classic Madisonian role of the legislative process—then such a theoretical expectation seems to appear even more well-founded. Individual organized interests will enter the litigation process to assure not merely that the immediate needs of their constituents are satisfied but to use their leverage as citizen-representatives to influence the development of the Court's jurisprudence.

When analyzed at the aggregate level, patterns of group participation and competition in Supreme Court church-state litigation appear to confirm these theoretical expectations. If one applies the measure of intergroup competition developed by Gregory A. Calderia and John Wright to examine amicus curiae participation to church-state litigation since 1969, one discovers that the qualities that have defined this environment are now far more contentious and confrontational than they were during the heyday of the Warren Court.[30] Prior to 1969 opposition to amici that supported establishment clause claims before the Court was almost nonexistent, instead manifesting itself in aggressive editorial attacks in the mass and specialized media, the manipulation of public opinion, and/or pressuring Congress or state legislatures to rescind the Court's decisions through legislation or constitutional amendment.[31] From the 1969 to the 1979 terms of the Court, however, the submission of amicus briefs in opposition to establishment clause claims increased to almost one in four cases (22.7 percent). Even more striking, between 1980 and 1989, contentiousness in establishment clause litigation doubled to over one in two cases (55.1 percent), a figure directly linked to the entrance of a vibrant network of conservative—predominantly Christian, evangelical, and fundamentalist—organized interests into the arena of church-state litigation.

Has this more confrontational atmosphere been rooted in a desire on the part of litigating groups to balance competing interests in hopes of carving out a piece of an advantageous judicial outcome? Or is the more plural nature of the litigation environment attributable to the newfound desire of conservative organizations to use the language of law to represent their interests before a now more conservative Court and the concomitant desire of their liberal, separationist counterparts to defend a generation of favorable precedent against judicial counterattack? In previous research, I questioned whether the application of the competitive articulation framework to the litigation process is a useful means to in understanding what drives what is quite clearly a far more diverse church-state litigation environment.[32] The interview data presented there suggested that concerns over legal doctrine far outweigh external political forces—to the extent that such forces matter at all—when organized interests decide to enter litigation. In the present, more particular case study of the AJCommittee, the AJCongress, and the ADL no new interview data has emerged that would confound the conclusion reached from that earlier, more representative sample of organized religious interests active in the litigation process. Commented the ADL's Jill Kahn and Steven Freeman:

> In some instances, who is pushing a case might give us some insight into what that case is really about. In *Edwards v. Aguillard,* the presence of several groups that had been involved in *Epperson* made it quite clear to us that the case was about more than equal time for teaching "scientific creationism." A situation like that might shape, in a small way, the arguments you make, such as the true purpose of such a statute. But the public and the press, rightly or wrongly, find that more helpful in figuring out how the politics of a case sort out than to us as lawyers [who are] responsible for making constitutional arguments.
>
> We would have been in *Aguillard* regardless. To make ourselves heard on such an important issue was our reason for getting in. The number of opposing briefs has very little to do with it. We don't feel compelled to balance the number of groups in a case. We don't feel the Court looks at all the organizations involved in a case as entitled to a slice of the opinion. We are there to express the position of our agency. We will do that based on the case, whether none, one, or a hundred groups happen to be there as well.[33]

A similar view was expressed by the AJCommittee's Samuel Rabinove, who suggested that while it

> might appear that several groups lined up in opposition are there to offset the others' presence, I don't consider that to be our real motivation. We certainly will make [other groups] aware that we have an interest in the case, but the big cases are going to attract everyone, not just Jews and Christians, but liberals, conservatives, and points beyond and in between. If you go beyond that, I think you have a tendency to read things into this that aren't really there. What appears to drive this process and the concerns that actually do are not necessarily the same. From the surface, it can be quite deceiving.[34]

The AJCongress's Marc Stern went even further in rejecting the view that the courts perform an inclusive, deliberative function that mediates between the demands of competing organized interests:

> That is absolutely ridiculous. The justices do not assemble amicus briefs, call us into their chambers, and ask us to hammer out a deal that makes everyone happy. That is the function of Congress. The fact that the Court accepts so many amicus briefs is independent of how it uses them, if it uses them at all. I will acknowledge that one of our functions is to counter certain public interest movements. But filing briefs in the Supreme Court is not one of them. We are there to satisfy our own objectives.[35]

Far more important to the decision of the major Jewish organizations to enter the litigation process is their assessment of whether the judicial forum is likely to be receptive to their interests. And from 1980 onward the Court's doctrinal innovations in church-state litigation have not been favorable to the interests of the AJCommittee, the AJCongress, and the ADL. For the AJCongress, the combination of scarcer financial resources and a far more conservative Court than was the case during the Warren and the early Burger eras—a period that coincided with Pfeffer's dominance as the Jewish and larger separationist community's premier advocate—has resulted in a far different approach to its litigation strategy. To understand how the doctrinal environment surrounding the religion clauses has altered since 1980, consider the rate at which separationist and free exercise claims have prevailed before the Court. In the decade from 1969 to 1979, a period concurrent with Pfeffer's major victories on parochial school aid and an expansive interpretation of religion-based claims for exemption from generally applicable laws, the Court decided *in favor* of the establishment or free exercise claim in almost 70 percent of the cases it reviewed. Since its 1980 term, however, the Court has ruled *against* such claims 68 percent of the time.[36] Stern commented on how the Court's doctrinal evolution has affected the AJCongress's attitude toward litigation:

> No one has any idea what this Court is going to do. It's impossible to get a handle on it. Just when you think the Court is going to junk the establishment clause, it throws you a little bone that gives you some hope. Then the next term is does something completely contradictory. There was a time in which there was a far-reaching strategy to advance the religious liberty principle, broadly defined. Now we just react to different events and different cases. The decisions of this Court just have no consistency: school prayer is still unconstitutional, but legislative prayers are not; crêches are constitutional if they're religious, but not too religious. These are just some examples. The Court's decisions do not make us feel comfortable to invest in a major test case. I've already talked about the money problems. So not only are we poor, but we've lost our best friend. Not a good situation.

But an adverse legal atmosphere does not absolve the obligation of organized interests with stated and demonstrated concerns in a particular field to represent organizational needs and thus satisfy the maintenance function necessary to sustain the life of any organization. Rabinove commented that the AJCommittee's move toward interfaith amicus participation in church-state litigation actually reinforces its organizational commitment to promoting Jewish-Christian dialogue as part of its more general framework. Even if its arguments do not win acceptance in the Court, the AJCommittee has still satisfied an internal need, a function that the AJCongress and the ADL acknowledged that litigation serves for them as well.

Whether an organization's success before the Court is on the rise or the downturn, doctrinal evolution influences how organizational lawyers structure their arguments, especially in their role as amici curiae. Commented Stern:

Whereas years ago the question was *how* to move the Court further in our direction, the issue now is really how to preserve what we have left. If I assume that the Court respects our record and expertise on church-state—and I think it does—then we still have to think strategically, actually more tactically. Twenty years ago the feeling in the Jewish organizations was, "The Court going to strike this down or that down. How do we want them to do it?" Now the question is, "How do we cover ourselves if the Court suggests it might just go ahead and abolish the establishment clause?" Do I say, "This is a Court that doesn't care about law and the Court as legal institutions and will do anything?" Or do I say, "If you want to do this, you are going to have to overrule all these cases. Are you as an institution prepared to do that?" Because I still have a notion of law that is not as political as some others, I will still try to make arguments that emphasize stare decisis and other institutional elements.

Now to do that, I may shape a brief for a particular justice, but it depends on the case. If a particular justice has expressed concern over and over about a particular problem, then you might want to remind that justice—without saying, "This brief is for Mr. or Ms. Justice X only"—that you understand that problem too and here is why you should remain concerned. If this is the case, you always aim it at a particular justice.

But a justice's concerns expressed in words are frequently not a precise reflection of his or her beliefs. Thoughts at a particular moment in time are not necessarily static—and you have to be careful not to get caught up in a fact that may only control one opinion. You can be misled by a statement or even a majority opinion. You have to sense that the Court is moving in a particular direction or towards a new idea. The trick is to catch [it] at that point in time. That, I think, is a little different than saying, "I'm only writing this brief for Mr. Justice X."[37]

In short, the fundamentally changed environment of church-state law and litigation in which the major Jewish organizations found themselves after 1980 required that they reconsider their respective approaches to the practice of public interest law, at least insofar as the representation of organizational interests before the Supreme Court was concerned. In the case of the AJCongress, the less predictable, more conservative nature of the Court, combined with the organization's own limited financial resources, required it to reevaluate the feasibility of sponsoring test-case litigation. While direct sponsorship of test-case litigation had never been a component of the litigation strategies of the AJCommittee and the ADL, this new environment had a demonstrable influence on both the motivation and ultimate objectives of their traditional participation as amici curiae. But as I have also described, the amicus strategies of the AJCongress were also not immune to the reconfiguration of the social and legal forces that comprise the litigation environment. While internal considerations thus weighed heavily on the choices and uses of litigation available to all three organizations, so did the principal external factor: the Court's legal posture and its compatibility with their respective agendas. I believe this latter conclusion is worth some additional discussion, since it differs somewhat from the argument recently advanced by Epstein and Kobylka in their provocative book, *The Supreme Court and Legal Change,* on the extent to which organized interests exert control over the Court's doctrinal innovations.

In their book, which examines the constitutional development of abortion and death penalty law, Epstein and Kobylka suggest that the organized interests responsible for litigation in those areas bear the ultimate responsibility for the success or failure of their arguments with the Court. Thus the NAACP Legal Defense and Educational Fund is entitled to claim credit for the Court's 1972 decision in *Furman v. Georgia* that invalidated the death penalty in Georgia and most all other states as it was currently being applied. But by the same token the NAACP LDF must also shoulder the blame for the Court's decision four years later in *Gregg v. Georgia* to uphold new death penalty statutes that were void of the constitutional defects described in *Furman.* The LDF clung to the unworkable strategy that the imposition of death, regardless of the circumstances, was a unique form of punishment and should be struck down as unconstitutional per se, whereas, the authors suggest, the LDF should have prepared a more flexible response.

A similar fate befell the pro-choice organized interests that failed to retain their initial victories in *Roe v. Wade* and *Doe v. Bolton,* the Court's landmark decisions that constitutionalized the right to abortion. Here again, organizational litigants must bear the blame for the "judicial retreat" in the line of cases that led to the Court's 1989 decision in *Webster v. Reproductive Health Services,* which granted states greater power to place restrictions on abortion services—a case that has proven over time to have generated more bluster than actual bite. Still, according to Epstein and Kobylka, the manner in which Planned Parenthood, the ACLU, and other organizational advocates framed their arguments in the post-*Roe* era of abortion litigation accounts for the Court's failure to adhere to its original conceptualization of the right to abortion. Epstein and Kobylka do examine alternative explanations to account for legal change, such as personnel changes in the Court and shifts in public opinion as reflected in legislative enactments. But while acknowledging that these factors are not irrelevant to understanding legal change, Epstein and Kobylka ultimately stand firmly by their argument that, more than any other factor, litigants and the arguments they make before the Court determine doctrinal outcomes.[38]

In contrast, the evidence I have marshaled here from personal interviews and other original source documents suggests that such an explanation is weightless as far as the issues presently under discussion are concerned. I would argue instead that few individual or organizational litigants, no matter how experienced, skilled, and accomplished as practitioners of public interest law, possess the power to overcome the hostile reception their views may command in the Court during a particular moment. I have found little data to support the conclusion that the AJCommittee, the AJCongress, and the ADL, as well as the greater separationist church-state bar, are somehow responsible for the Court's retreat from the broad separationist impulses that guided its church-state jurisprudence from the late 1940s until the early 1980s. Nor does the data suggest that these organizations are less competent advocates in the current moment because they no longer command the kind of success they once did. Rather, all three organizations possess keen legal expertise and have assiduously attempted to couch their arguments within a legal structure the Court would find persuasive, even if this meant writing entire briefs to capture the votes of just one or two justices. In fact, given the nuances of the organizational dynamics that lie behind the choice and execution of a litigation strategy, it is difficult (if not impossible) to determine with any kind of empirical rigor whether group litigants possess the influence to shape the doctrinal innovation of an indifferent or hostile Court. But I would also argue that such a determination remains equally difficult when amicus litigants find themselves within friendly judicial confines.

Lee v. Weisman (1992) provides a recent and useful example to illustrate this point. *Weisman* centered on a challenge brought by the ACLU on behalf of high school student Deborah Weisman, who argued that the introduction of a state-directed prayer at her commencement exercise violated the establishment clause. Two federal courts agreed with her and struck down such religious exercises with little fanfare. But what eventually made *Weisman* such an epicenter of political controversy was not the constitutional question. After all, the Court had consistently blocked state-supported attempts to introduce prayer in public schools in the years subsequent to *Engel* and *Schempp*.[39]

Notice that *Weisman* would prove to be more than just another doomed effort to return state-supported religion to the public schools was first served when the solicitor general filed an amicus brief with the Court during the certiorari stage. The solicitor general asked the Court to use *Weisman* as a vehicle to consider replacing the *Lemon* test with the less restrictive framework that Justice Anthony Kennedy had set forth in his opinion in *County of Allegheny v. American Civil Liberties Union,* a case that involved the constitutionality of religious symbols displayed on public land. In *County of Allegheny,* Justice Kennedy wrote that *Lemon* as applied bordered on "latent hostility towards religion" inasmuch as it "require[d] government in all its multifaceted roles to acknowledge only the secular, to the exclusion and so to the detriment of the religious." In place of the *Lemon* test, Justice Kennedy suggested that the Court adopt a "noncoercion" rule with which to analyze establishment clause cases. Such a framework would allow "noncoercive government action within the realm of flexible accommodation or passive acknowledgment of existing symbols does not violate the Establishment Clause unless it benefits religion in a way more direct and more substantial than practices that are accepted in our national heritage."[40] Government could not formally establish a religion, nor explicitly prefer one over another, nor coerce individuals into accepting or practicing religious beliefs against their will. But government could permit several other forms of religious inclusion in the culture, including nondiscriminatory participation in public programs and the right of schools to permit "noncoercive" religious practices.

So when *Lee v. Weisman* was scheduled for oral argument in October 1991, the consensus among many commentators was that the Court had granted certiorari to reverse on the merits and then set *Lemon* for the judicial guillotine.[41] Why else then would the Court agree to hear a case on a constitutional matter it had decided decades ago? Concern was manifest among the principal litigants and their respective amici that Justice Kennedy held the fate of *Lemon* and thus the future of the Court's establishment clause jurisprudence in his hands—so much so that the thrust of most of their arguments centered on his proposed noncoercion standard, with far less attention given to the prayer issue.[42] It is no stretch to argue that the last scenario in anyone's mind when Justice Kennedy began to read the Court's opinion from the bench on the morning of June 24, 1992 was that state-sponsored school prayer would remain unconstitutional, that *Lemon* would emerge none the worse for wear, and that Justice Kennedy would be the author of the Court's majority opinion holding such. But that is exactly what happened.

We are less concerned, though, with what happened: that we know. The more interesting question is why *Weisman* ended as it did—and the answer to that, I would argue, cannot be found within the analytical framework offered by Epstein and Kobylka. After all, the solicitor general, the conservative organized interests present as amici, and the lead counsel for the school board in *Weisman*, Chuck Cooper (himself a former high-ranking Department of Justice official in the Reagan Administration who was well-versed in Supreme Court litigation)—built their legal rationale on the language and logic offered by Justice Kennedy in *County of Allegheny*. In addition, the plaintiffs did not neglect to address other pertinent arguments that members of the Court's conservative wing had developed in a line of anti-*Lemon* dissents that dated back for several years.[43] Did Justice Kennedy's and subsequently the Court's apparent reversal in *Weisman* thus occur because of some major strategic error on the part of the school board's attorneys and their amici supporters in the presentation of their arguments? Did Justice Kennedy's dicta in *County of Allegheny* simply represent some thinking out loud on his part, as opposed to his true beliefs on the establishment clause and the use of the *Lemon* test to analyze it? Or, despite the hyperbole generated by the parties involved and their allies in the broader community, did Justice Kennedy view *Weisman* as a school prayer case, plain and simple, covered by the Court's precedents in *Engel* and *Schempp* and thus unconstitutional?

There is some evidence to support an argument that Justice Kennedy had simply failed to think through precisely where he wanted the Court to take the establishment clause. Quite explicitly, Justice Kennedy argued that:

> This case does not require us to revisit the difficult questions dividing us in recent cases, questions of the definition and full scope of the principles governing the extent of permitted accommodation by the State for the religious beliefs and practices of many of its citizens. For without reference to those principles [citing *Allegheny, Wallace* and *Lynch*] in other contexts, the controlling precedents as they relate to prayer and religious exercise in primary and secondary public schools compel the holding here that the policy of the city of Providence is unconstitutional. We can decide the case without reconsidering the general constitutional framework by which public schools' efforts to accommodate religion are measured. Thus we do not accept the invitation of the petitioners and *amicus* the United States to reconsider our decision in *Lemon v. Kurtzman.*

Justice Kennedy then confined the remainder of his opinion to the facts, holding that *Weisman* fell squarely within the Court's line of post-*Engel* school prayer precedents.[44]

So what happened? In my view, it is finally not possible to answer with empirical certainty any of the above questions, absent data drawn from interviews with the justices themselves (or perhaps their clerks), who are by no means easy of access, and/or permission to examine their memoranda and private papers.[45] Nor do I see how it is possible to argue, on the basis of secondary data, that a causal relationship exists between the quality of the arguments that organized interests advance in litigation and the likelihood of doctrinal innovation in the Court. I believe similar problems beset the conclusion that the plurality of voices currently making themselves heard in church-state litigation reflects a new need of organized interests to offset the policy demands of one another. Ideological confrontation is a well-documented feature of the modern Supreme Court litigation. But why organizational representation in the litigation process has become more complex and confrontational over time has almost everything to do with the recent alteration in the Court's doctrinal direction and its impact on affected constituencies—and virtually nothing to do with a general desire to mitigate the demands of competing interests.

We can continue to learn more about the social forces that condition the behavior of organized interests in the litigation process because, through empirical observation of the latter, we can deduce the former. But on the strength of these same observations, we cannot expect the same progress on what we know about the Court's obligation—perceived, real, or nonexistent—to respond to and ultimately resolve the competing interests that come before it based simply on aggregate-level patterns of organizational conflict. Until scholars have full access to original source data from within the Court of the sort mentioned above, speculation on the responsiveness of the Court to organized social pressure as represented through the litigation process will remain just that. At the same time, while I recognize the dangers of generalizing from specific case analyses, the data presented and analyzed in this book do provide some evidence that group advocacy might be conditioned by a much more subtle and complex mosaic of social forces than several previous studies have concluded. In other words, we can at least draw instructive lessons about the manner in which public interest litigation is practiced by examining the activities of the AJCommittee, the AJCongress, and the ADL over the course of their forty-five years of participation in church-state litigation. And it is to those lessons that we now turn.

Conclusion

In 1945 the AJCongress decided to merge what were then its two separate internal commissions on economic discrimination and law and legislation into a single committee, the Commission on Law and Social Action. The CLSA was created for the purpose of engaging in direct-action strategies that would encompass legislative and judicial measures to redress what it believed were the legitimate constitutional grievances of American Jews. This decision created shock waves that reverberated throughout the other major American Jewish organizations that also claimed to represent these same interests, the AJCommittee and the ADL, both of which were committed to education and goodwill campaigns as the best means of educating America about Jewish concerns and interests. The AJCommittee and the ADL responded to the external challenge of their rival by forming litigation capacities of their own, although with nowhere near the same scope and sophistication. Nor did either organization share the AJCongress's degree of commitment to the efficacy of litigation as an instrument with which to achieve social and constitutional change. In the nascent stages of the development of the three organizations, some initial effort was expended to establish a constructive, coordinate structure through which to share resources, skills, and ideas. But this effort lacked a serious and comprehensive design. Moreover, it soon fizzled as organizational differences, rooted in the divergent concerns of the segments of American Jewry that each group had formed to represent, crystallized with greater clarity.

But it takes more than demographic, economic, political, and policy disagreements to sow the seeds of organizational dissolution. If it was that simple, then one would have to struggle to explain the success of the NAACP during the period leading up to and shortly after *Brown v. Board of Education*, given that the NAACP was essentially the sole representative of the civil rights grievances of African Americans in the courts. Mark Tushnet and Stephen Wasby have both provided persuasive documentation to support their assertions that, as skilled and refined as its litigation campaign to attack segregation became, the NAACP was never without its difficulties in terms of policy coherence, internal organization, and the execution of its legal strategies. As Tushnet notes, there were occasional problems with some African American communities in the South who feared the consequences that litigation would have for the local population. After all, legal victories might well result in the promised abolition of legal discrimination. But in the South no small number of African Americans feared that forcing whites to implement such radical legal doctrines would intensify their resentment toward blacks, which might in turn actually retard the social acceptance of African Americans into southern culture. In some cases, the conflict between the wishes of lawyers and their potential clients reached a point where such differences became irreconcilable and hope for litigation had to be abandoned. But in numerous instances similar conflicts were smoothed over. Tushnet attributes much of the NAACP's success to the venerable reputation it had built up throughout African American communities across the nation as the most powerful vehicle through which the repulsive state-imposed legal discrimination to which blacks had been formally subjected could finally be abolished. Although the NAACP developed its justified reputation as a premiere organizational advocate in the courts for several reasons, none was more crucial than the political and legal brilliance of the lawyers—such as Thurgood Marshall, Charles Hamilton Houston, Oliver Hill, Constance Baker Motley, Robert Carter, and Jack Greenberg—who crafted and implemented its strategy of social change through constitutional litigation.

When an organization is blessed with a charismatic leader who possesses the political and legal skills necessary to formulate and realize a vision and the force of personality to carry it out, such a leader can serve to centralize a cause within the organization. This in turn gives an organized interest, as it did the NAACP, the chance to leave both an organizational and individual imprint on legal development. No one can seriously question the legacy that the NAACP bequeathed to the practice of public interest law as it demolished, step-by-step, the Jim Crow laws of the American South, nor the personal impact of the lawyer who led that effort, Thurgood Marshall. From the late 1930s through the late 1950s, Marshall and the NAACP so thoroughly controlled the ebb and flow of equal protection litigation through the courts that the two became more or less synonymous with each other. Students of the NAACP's involvement in the litigation process do not exaggerate when they argue that the organizational greatness it developed throughout its formative years was due in large part to Marshall's presence. As talented as the NAACP's administrative and legal staff was, it was Marshall who gave the movement so much of its energy and vitality.

While I do not wish to draw a direct comparison between the brilliance of Marshall and anyone else as practitioners of public interest law, the evidence marshalled in this study leads one to the inescapable conclusion that is likewise impossible to overestimate the impact that Leo Pfeffer, as an individual and as a public interest lawyer, had on the constitutional development of church-state law during the latter half of this century. Samuel Krislov has commented that Pfeffer is sui generis in the annals of modern constitutional litigation, for no lawyer has exercised such complete intellectual dominance over a chosen area of law for so extensive a period—as an author, scholar, public citizen, and, above all, legal advocate who harnessed his multiple and formidable talents into a single force capable of satisfying all that an institution needs for a successful constitutional reform movement.[1] If the imprint that Pfeffer left on establishment clause law and church-state scholarship were not clear enough, the examination undertaken here of his personal papers—together with those of the AJCongress, as well as related memoranda and documents, and interviews with lawyers and other professionals who worked with him—produces incontrovertible evidence to support such a conclusion. This evidence not only affirms without question but elucidates in further detail and richness just how responsible Pfeffer was for the intellectual transformation of modern establishment clause law and the litigation strategies that were required to implement these innovations in constitutional theory over time.

But Pfeffer's emergence as such a singular force in the modern constitutional reform movement would not have been possible without the commitment of his first and longest employer, the AJCongress, to his vision of legal change. No lawyer dedicated to an agenda of constitutional reform as sweeping as Pfeffer's eventually became can succeed over such an extended period of time without an institutional locus and organizational structure to support that agenda. When Pfeffer began work with the AJCongress as a junior staff lawyer in 1945, the organization's leadership had already decided to turn to litigation as a means to confront legal discrimination against American Jews, rather than relying solely on the traditional techniques of reducing prejudice through improved community relations, techniques it believed could no longer effectively eliminate such practices on their own. Thus an organizational model built around a broad agenda of law-based constitutional reform was in place when Pfeffer arrived, one that had already won praise from academic commentators as both visionary and promising. But it was Pfeffer, more so than any other lawyer among an extraordinarily talented staff, who pushed the CLSA of the AJCongress into the arena of church-state law and politics.

In contrast to the NAACP, which was created to attack the legal shackles that excluded African Americans from virtually all aspects of American life, the CLSA's policy was never intended to center specifically on church-state grievances but to pursue a much broader constitutional rights agenda. That Pfeffer, through an enviable combination of skill, sheer determination, and persistence, was able in such a short period of time to make church-state reform the foremost cause with which rival organizations associated the AJCongress illustrates well the impact that individual lawyers endowed with exceptional skills can have on the character and life of the organizations for which they work. Even though Pfeffer came into an organization that was already committed to the legal reform model as an instrument to effect social and legal change, that he was able, like Marshall, to leave a personal as well as organizational imprint on the evolution of modern church-state law and doctrine places him in the rarified company of the figures crucial to the modern constitutional reform movement. As if to confirm the extent to which Pfeffer is associated with post-*Everson* constitutional development, even the major critics of the Court's church-state jurisprudence during this period and the modern doctrine of separationism rarely fail to make reference to Pfeffer as the central force responsible for what they lament as the lost meaning of the establishment clause.[2]

What also is evident from this study is just how complex and in many instances ad hoc even the most well-conceived efforts to conduct a rational, planned litigation campaign designed to achieve some constitutional end really are. In contrast with some of the earlier literature on interest group use of the courts, which stressed the rational and predictable nature of reform-based constitutional litigation, recent studies have argued that this process is much more vulnerable to demands for major tactical and strategic adjustments brought on by internal organizational forces and the need to adapt to the environment in which litigation takes place. The evidence presented here confirms this latter conclusion. Organized interests can and do decide to challenge extant constitutional doctrine and thus shape the legal dynamics of the litigation process, but it is far more difficult to argue that organizations can exert full control over the internal and external considerations they must confront in order to achieve their objectives.

This was certainly true of the litigation in which the major Jewish organizations became involved. The AJCongress (especially), the AJCommittee, and the ADL were pivotal actors in the carefully planned campaigns to initiate litigation on released-time, school prayer, taxpayer standing, and parochial school aid. But once the decision had been made, rival organizational needs began to manifest themselves, arguments ensued over control and credit, and disagreements surfaced on such extralitigation concerns as public relations or policy implementation. In some cases, unforeseen circumstances, such as dissatisfied clients or the reversal of public opinion in the community where litigation had begun, necessitated the revision of once firm litigation strategies. At the same time, external factors, such as the ideological transformation of the federal courts in a direction hostile to their efforts, can leave the most sophisticated organizational litigants helpless to advance even the narrowest objectives through litigation. Organized interests experienced and active in the litigation process are, at heart, legal realists. They believe that law matters; but they know that politics does as well.

In the case of the AJCommittee, the AJCongress, and the ADL, litigation continues to be an efficacious instrument with which to articulate their interests in church-state issues that come before the Supreme Court. But expectations are far different now than during the salad days of the Warren and early Burger Courts. The Court's evolution over the last decade or so has produced a litigation environment very different from the one that produced such glorious victories on school prayer and parochial school aid. These changes in the atmosphere of the Court have required the major Jewish organizations to adapt their litigation strategies and reevaluate what such participation can realistically hope to accomplish. Even if organizations are possessed of sufficient financial resources, abundant skill, and the experience that comes from forty years as skilled organizational litigants, certain forces cannot be overcome, absent of a fundamental shift in the ideological and political tenor of the Court. Sometimes the Court simply does what it wants. The evidence, too, is persuasive on this last point.

Even so, the transformation of the major representative agencies of American Jewry from social service agencies and civic institutions into full-service organized interests continues to unfold. It is crucial to remember that differences in ethnic origin, economic class, and religious faith once led to heated debates within the Jewish community over assimilation versus emancipation in American life. These conflicts were significant enough to mandate the formation of multiple agencies to represent the plural interests of American Jewry—and an awareness of the social forces that account for the dynamic pluralism within ethnic communities is certainly fundamental if one wishes to understand better this one small but important component of the Jewish experience in America. What is remarkable about the journey of the AJCongress, the AJCommittee, and the ADL is that, after over three generations of involvement in the mainstream of American politics, litigation, and public affairs, their organizational philosophies and approaches to public life remain guided in significant part by the social forces that originally defined their separate identities.

NOTES

BIBLIOGRAPHY

INDEX

Introduction

1. Walz v. Tax Commission, 397 U.S. 664 at 676 (1970).

2. See Gregg Ivers, "Religious Organizations as Constitutional Litigants"; James E. Wood, Jr., "Church Lobbying and Public Policy."

3. See, for example, Ivers, "Religious Organizations as Constitutional Litigants"; Naomi Cohen, *The Struggle for Religious Equality: Jews in Christian America*; Gregg Ivers, "Organized Religion and the Supreme Court"; Frank Sorauf, *The Wall of Separation: The Constitutional Politics of Church and State*; Richard E. Morgan, *The Politics of Religious Conflict*; Yale Comment, "Private Attorneys-General: Action in the Fight for Civil Liberties."

4. Theodore Mann, "The Courts," p. 27. For further discussion, see Arthur Hertzberg, *The Jews in America: Four Centuries of Uneasy Encounter*, pp. 301–15; Deborah Dash Moore, *B'nai B'rith and the Challenge of Ethnic Leadership*; Naomi Cohen, *Not Free to Desist: The American Jewish Committee, 1906–1966*.

5. Will Maslow, "The Use of Law in the Struggle for Equality," p. 298.

6. Yale Comment, "Private Attorneys-General," p. 594.

7. McCollum v. Board of Education, 333 U.S. 203 (1948).

8. See, for example, Allen D. Hertzke, *Representing God in Washington*; A. James Reichley, *Religion in American Public Life*.

9. See, for example, Ivers, "Religious Organizations as Constitutional Litigants"; Leo Pfeffer, "An Autobiographical Sketch" and "Amici in Church-State Litigation"; Eliot Tenofsky, "Interest Groups and Litigation: The Commission on Law and Social Action of the American Jewish Congress" (Ph.D. diss., 1979); Sorauf, *Wall of Separation*; Morgan, *Politics of Religious Conflict*.

Chapter 1. Law, the Courts, and Political Jurisprudence

1. Alexis de Tocqueville, *Democracy in America*, pp. 513–14.

2. Ibid., p. 270.

3. See, for example, Ivers, "Religious Organizations as Constitutional Litigants"; Wayne R. Swanson, *The Christ Child Goes to Court*; Pfeffer, "Amici in Church-State Litigation"; Sorauf, *Wall of Separation*; Morgan, *Politics of Religious Conflict*; Robert F. Drinan, *Religion, the Courts, and Public Policy*; David Manwaring, *Render unto Caesar: The Flag Salute Controversy*.

4. See, for example, Matthew C. Moen, *The Christian Right and Congress*; Her-

tzke, *Representing God in Washington;* Reichley, *Religion in American Public Life;* Paul J. Weber, "Examining the Religious Lobbies."

5. Clement Vose, *Caucasians Only.* Vose also published several articles prior to *Caucasians Only* that examined the NAACP LDF and the NCL as constitutional litigants. See, for example, his "Litigation as a Form of Pressure Group Activity," "National Consumer's League and the Brandeis Brief," and "NAACP Strategy in Restrictive Covenant Cases."

6. Shelley v. Kraemer, 334 U.S. 1 (1948).

7. The literature on the involvement of organized interests in constitutional litigation is extensive. See, for example, Donald R. Songer and Reginald S. Sheehan, "Interest Group Success in the Court: Amicus Participation in the Supreme Court"; Lee Epstein and Joseph F. Kobylka, *The Supreme Court and Legal Change;* Lee Epstein and C. K. Rowland, "Debunking the Myth of Interest Group Invincibility in the Courts"; Gregory A. Calderia and John R. Wright, "Amici Curiae before the Supreme Court: Who Participates, When, and How Much?" and "Organized Interests and Agenda Setting in the U.S. Supreme Court"; Joseph F. Kobylka, "A Court-Created Context for Group Litigation"; Lee Epstein, *Conservatives in Court;* Timothy J. O'Neill, *Bakke and the Politics of Inequality;* Stephen L. Wasby, "How Planned is 'Planned Litigation'?"; Karen O'Connor and Lee Epstein, "Rebalancing the Scales of Justice: An Assessment of Public Interest Law" and "The Rise of Conservative Interest Group Litigation"; Karen O'Connor, *Women's Organizations' Use of the Courts;* Ruth B. Cowan, "Women's Rights through Litigation: An Examination of the American Civil Liberties Union Women's Rights Project, 1971–76"; Richard C. Cortner, "Strategies and Tactics of Litigants in Constitutional Cases"; Lucius Barker, "Third Parties in Litigation: A Systematic View of the Judicial Function"; Robert H. Birkby and Walter Murphy, "Interest Group Conflict in the Judicial Arena"; Fowler V. Harper and Edwin Etherington, "Lobbyists before the Court."

8. Cantwell v. Connecticut, 310 U.S. 296 (1940); Everson v. Board of Education, 330 U.S. 1 (1947).

9. E.g., Hamilton v. Board of Regents, 293 U.S. 245 (1934); Pierce v. Society of Sisters, 268 U.S. 510 (1925); Meyer v. Nebraska, 262 U.S. 390 (1923); Watson v. Jones, 13 Wall. 679 (1872).

10. Watson v. Jones, 13 Wall. 679 (1872); Meyer v. Nebraska, 262 U.S. 390 (1923).

11. Gitlow v. New York, 268 U.S. 652 (1925).

12. Everson v. Board of Education, 330 U.S. 1 (1947); Cantwell v. Connecticut, 310 U.S. 296 (1940); DeJonge v. Oregon, 299 U.S. 353 (1937); Near v. Minnesota, 283 U.S. 359 (1931); Stromberg v. California, 283 U.S. 359 (1931). For the most comprehensive discussion of the "incorporation" of the Bill of Rights into the Fourteenth Amendment, see Richard C. Cortner, *The Supreme Court and the Second Bill of Rights.*

13. For the Court's extension of the incorporation doctrine to cover the criminal

due process guarantees, see, for example, Miranda v. Arizona, 384 U.S. 436 (1966); Pointer v. Texas, 380 U.S. 400 (1965); Gideon v. Wainwright, 372 U.S. 335 (1963); Robinson v. California, 370 U.S. 660 (1962); Mapp v. Ohio, 367 U.S. 643 (1961). On the issue of the applicability of the entire Bill of Rights to individual states, see Benton v. Maryland, 395 U.S. 784 (1969).

14. Palko v. Connecticut, 302 U.S. 319 at 324–25 (1937).

15. Cortner, *Supreme Court and the Second Bill of Rights,* pp. 63–98, 124–39.

16. U.S. v. Carolene Products, 304 U.S. 144 at 152–53, n. 4 (1938).

17. Cortner, "Strategies and Tactics of Litigants in Constitutional Cases."

18. Thomas J. Curry, *The First Freedoms: Church and State in America to the Passage of the First Amendment.*

19. Manwaring, *Render unto Caesar.*

20. See U.S. v. Carolene Products, 304 U.S. 144 at 152–53, n. 4 (1938).

21. For a description of hostile action taken against the Witnesses for their refusal to salute the flag, see Peter Irons, *The Courage of Their Convictions,* pp. 3–36.

22. Cortner, *Supreme Court and the Second Bill of Rights,* pp. 100–108, 279–91.

23. Ibid., p. 283. Cortner refers to West Virginia v. Barnette, 319 U.S. 624 (1943).

24. Manwaring, *Render unto Caesar,* p. 58.

25. Ibid., p. 59.

26. Unless otherwise noted, the following description of the legislative and litigation history of *Everson* is taken from Cortner, *Supreme Court and the Second Bill of Rights,* pp. 108–23.

27. Cochran v. Board of Education, 281 U.S. 370 at 374 (1930).

28. In his comprehensive history of the ACLU, *In Defense of American Liberties,* Samuel Walker has written that the ACLU sponsored the *Everson* case. That is not correct. The ACLU did not sponsor the *Everson* case, but worked closely with the JOAUM as an *amicus curiae* throughout the litigation.

29. Transcript, "Sectarianism in the Public Schools," Joint Session of the National Community Relations Advisory Council, New York, June 10–12, 1947, pp. 109–18, Leo Pfeffer papers, box 1, George Arendts Research Library, Syracuse University, Syracuse, N. Y. (hereafter referred to as Leo Pfeffer papers).

30. Ibid.

31. Memorandum, Leo Pfeffer to David W. Petegorsky, Dec. 23, 1946, in which Pfeffer suggests that the AJCongress intervene in a local case involving Bible reading in the public schools, arguing that such action was necessary if "CLSA is to justify what I deem to be its true function—counsel for the American Jewish community" (Leo Pfeffer papers, box 1). The perception that the AJCongress should be the "private attorney general" for the Jewish community was reinforced in an influential law review article on the early efforts of the AJCongress, the ACLU, and the NAACP to affect public policy change through litigation. See Yale Comment, "Private Attorneys-General."

32. Cortner, *Supreme Court and the Second Bill of Rights*, p. 117.

33. Transcript, "Sectarianism in the Public Schools," passim, Leo Pfeffer papers, box 1.

34. Memorandum, Leo Pfeffer to Will Maslow, Oct. 14, 1946, Leo Pfeffer papers, box 19.

35. Author interview with Will Maslow, general counsel of the American Jewish Congress, Aug. 5, 1992, New York.

36. Memorandum, Leo Pfeffer to Will Maslow, Oct. 14, 1946, Leo Pfeffer papers, box 19.

37. Memorandum, Leo Pfeffer to David W. Petegorsky, Dec. 23, 1946, Leo Pfeffer papers, box 22.

38. *New York Times,* May 7, 1946.

39. Everson v. Board of Education, 330 U.S. 1 at 17–18 (1947).

40. Ibid., at 15, citing Cochran v. Board of Education, 281 U.S. 370 at 370, 374 (1930).

41. For criticism of *Everson* on constitutional and historical grounds, see, for example, Daniel L. Dreisbach, *Real Threat and Mere Shadow: Religious Liberty and the First Amendment;* Robert L. Cord, *Separation of Church and State: Historical Fact and Current Fiction.* For support of Justice Black's establishment clause analysis in *Everson* but disagreement with the Court's decision to uphold the bus subsidies for parochial schools, see Pfeffer, *Church, State and Freedom,* but also Leonard Levy, *The Establishment Clause: Religion and the First Amendment.*

42. Everson v. Board of Education, 330 U.S. 1 at 12, 18 (1947).

43. A. E. Dick Howard, "The Wall of Separation: The Supreme Court as Uncertain Stonemason," p. 88; Everson v. Board of Education, 330 U.S. 1 at 15–16 (1947).

44. See, for example, the editorial response in the Jesuit magazine *America,* "Supreme Court Decision on Bus Transportation," Feb. 22, 1947, p. 561. The fear that Justice Black's establishment clause analysis in *Everson* might prove fatal in future cases was realized the following term in McCollum v. Board of Education, 333 U.S. 203 (1948). For *America's* editorial comment on that case, see, "The McCollum Case," April 24, 1948. See also "High Court Backs State Right to Run Parochial Buses," *New York Times,* Feb. 11, 1947.

45. See "High Court Backs State Right to Run Parochial Buses."

46. "Manifesto of Protestants and Other Americans United for the Separation of Church and State," reproduced in a memorandum from Leo Pfeffer to Charles Posner, Jan. 15, 1948, Leo Pfeffer papers, box 14.

47. Of the considerable anti-Catholic literature that emerged in the period immediately after World War II, by far the most influential was *American Freedom and Catholic Power* (Boston: Beacon Press, 1949), written by Paul Blanshard, a founder and until 1951 a staff member of POAU.

48. Memorandum, Leo Pfeffer to Charles Posner, Jan. 15, 1948, Leo Pfeffer papers, box 14.

49. For a more extended treatment of American United's involvement in church-state litigation in the two decades after *Everson*, see Sorauf, *Wall of Separation*.

50. Leo Pfeffer, "The Outlook in Church-State," *Congress Weekly*, April 16, 1956, p. 9, American Jewish Congress Archives, New York.

51. Transcript, "Sectarianism in the Public Schools," pp. 112–14, Leo Pfeffer papers, box 1.

52. Ibid., pp. 114–18.

53. Transcript, "Religious Instruction in the Public Schools," Joint Session of the National Community Relations Advisory Council, New York, Nov. 11–12, 1946, pp. 17–29, 126–32, 135–43, Leo Pfeffer papers, box 1.

54. Transcript, "Sectarianism in the Public Schools," p. 111, Leo Pfeffer papers, box 1.

55. Ibid.

56. Karen O'Connor and Lee Epstein effectively laid to rest over a decade ago the once pervasive "folklore," as Nathan Hakman called it, that organized interests had no systemic presence in Supreme Court litigation. See Karen O'Connor and Lee Epstein, "Amicus Curiae Participation in U.S. Supreme Court Litigation: An Appraisal of Hakman's 'Folklore.'"

57. Mark V. Tushnet, *The NAACP's Legal Strategy against Segregated Education, 1925–1950*, pp. xi–xiv, 138–66.

58. Ibid., pp. 144, 143–66.

59. In addition to Tushnet, Stephen L. Wasby also raises this point: see, for example, "The Multi-Faceted Elephant: Litigator Perspectives on Planned Litigation for Social Change," and "How Planned is 'Planned Litigation'?" In their more recent book, *The Supreme Court and Legal Change*, Lee Epstein and Joseph F. Kobylka contend that organized interests have more control over their fate in the litigation process than Tushnet and Wasby suggest, to the point where failure to achieve their constitutional and policy objectives through litigation can be traced to the weaknesses in their own strategy, advocacy and presentation—regardless of the Court's position on the issues before it or the individual positions of the justices. I find this argument flawed and overstated, for reasons that I shall address later in this book. For effective criticism of the two case studies (on abortion and the death penalty) used to make this argument, see Gerald Rosenberg's review in the *American Political Science Review* 87 (1993): 1024–25; see also "Book Note," *Harvard Law Review*.

60. Drinan, *Religion, the Courts, and Public Policy*, p. 52.

Chapter 2. The Political Organization of American Jewry, 1906–1947

1. Will Herberg, *Protestant, Catholic, and Jew: An Essay in Religious Sociology*, p. 181.

2. Irving Howe, *World of Our Fathers*, p. 26.

3. See Reichley, *Religion in American Public Life*, pp. 229–38, 307–11; Yale Comment, "Private Attorneys-General," pp. 574–98.

4. For further discussion, see Hertzke, *Representing God in Washington*; Reichley, *Religion in American Public Life*; Ivers, "Religious Organizations as Constitutional Litigants"; Sorauf, *Wall of Separation*; Herberg, *Protestant, Catholic, and Jew*; Yale Comment, "Private Attorneys-General."

5. Constitution of the American Jewish Committee, quoted in Cohen, *Not Free to Desist*, p. 19.

6. Judith Goldstein, "The Politics of Ethnic Pressure: The American Jewish Committee as Lobbyist" (Ph.D. diss., 1972).

7. Ibid., p. 9.

8. Cohen, *Not Free to Desist*, p. 29.

9. Ibid., pp. 338–39.

10. For Straus's position, see Goldstein, "Politics of Ethnic Pressure," p. 14; see also Naomi Cohen, *The Public Career of Oscar S. Straus*, pp. 137–46.

11. Louis Marshall, quoted in Goldstein, "Politics of Ethnic Pressure," pp. 338–39; see also Yonathan Shapiro, "Leadership of the American Zionist Organizations, 1897–1930" (Ph.D diss., 1964), p. 26.

12. Reichley, *Religion in American Public Life*, p. 231; on this latter point more generally, see Paul Johnson, *A History of the Jews*.

13. See Daniel J. Elazar, *Community and Polity: The Organizational Dynamics of American Jewry*, p. 195.

14. See Cohen, *Not Free to Desist*, p. 31.

15. Leonard Dinnerstein, *The Leo Frank Case*, p. 63.

16. See Howe, *World of Our Fathers*, pp. 51–53; see also Elazar, *Community and Polity*.

17. The brief in question was submitted in connection with Nixon v. Herndon, 273 U.S. 536 (1927). On Marshall's work for the NAACP, see Vose, *Caucasians Only*, p. 40.

18. Pierce v. Society of Sisters, 268 U.S. 510 (1925); Portersfield v. Webb, 263 U.S. 225 (1923).

19. Frank v. Georgia, 141 Ga. 243 (1914), cert. denied, 237 U.S. 326 (1915).

20. Dinnerstein, *Leo Frank Case*, pp. 74–75.

21. Ibid., pp. 91, 42.

22. See, for example, Howe, *World of Our Fathers*, pp. 409–13, for an excellent account of the anti-Jewish discrimination practiced by private establishments in resort communities around New York. See also Dinnerstein, *Leo Frank Case*, pp. 37–61, for a description of the discrimination that Jews encountered in criminal trials. To take one example, prosecutors would identify defendants or their witnesses as Jewish to any tap possible anti-Semitic prejudice in a jury.

23. Cohen, *Not Free to Desist*, p. 34; see also Moore, *B'nai B'rith and the Challenge*

of Ethnic Leadership, p. 108; Morris Frommer, "The American Jewish Congress: A History, 1914–1950" (Ph.D. diss., 1978), p. 515.

24. Cohen, *Not Free to Desist,* p. 36.

25. See, for example, Alan Brinkley, *Voices of Protest: Huey Long, Father Coughlin, and the Great Depression,* pp. 242–83.

26. Cohen, *Not Free to Desist,* p. 386.

27. Ibid., p. 336.

28. Author interview with AJCommittee legal staff, May 18, 1988, New York.

29. Cohen, *Not Free to Desist,* p. 386.

30. Author interviews with regional AJCommittee professional staff, June 2, 1988, Atlanta.

31. Shelley v. Kraemer, 334 U.S. 1 (1948).

32. See Vose, *Caucasians Only,* pp. 40, 242–43.

33. Cohen, *Not Free to Desist,* p. 409; but see also Yale Comment, "Private Attorneys-General," pp. 574–98.

34. "Spellman Pleads for an End to Bias," *New York Times,* Jan. 13, 1944.

35. Information on organizational expansion and membership growth were obtained through correspondence in 1988 with the Blaustein Library, Institute for Human Relations of the American Jewish Committee, New York.

36. Frommer, "American Jewish Congress," pp. 528–29; Herberg, *Catholic, Protestant, and Jew,* p. 182; Frommer, "American Jewish Congress," p. 202.

37. Phillipa Strum, *Louis Brandeis: A Justice for the People* , p. 267.

38. Elazar, *Community and Polity,* p. 158.

39. Quoted in Frommer, "American Jewish Congress," p. 203.

40. Reichley, *Religion in American Public Life,* p. 233.

41. Cohen, *Not Free to Desist,* p. 220.

42. Stephen S. Wise, "The Case of the Jewish People: Address Delivered before the American Jewish Congress by Dr. Stephen Wise" (1925), p. 2, American Jewish Congress Archives, New York.

43. Frommer, "American Jewish Congress," p. 501.

44. Ibid., pp. 497, 503.

45. For more extensive discussion of the early NAACP litigation campaign to secure the constitutional rights of black Americans, see, for example, Tushnet, *NAACP's Legal Strategy against Segregated Education;* Richard Kluger, *Simple Justice* (New York: Alfred A. Knopf, 1975); Vose, *Caucasians Only.*

46. Frommer, "American Jewish Congress," pp. 513–14.

47. Memorandum, "The Two Commissions and Their Role in the Congress Movement," Aug. 31, 1945, p. 53, American Jewish Congress Archives, New York (hereafter referred to as the "The Two Commissions and Their Role").

48. See Elazar, *Community and Polity,* pp. 168–69.

49. "The Two Commissions and Their Role," p. 53.

50. Memorandum, Henry Siegman to Will Maslow, "Early History of CLSA,"

April 4, 1984, p. 1, American Jewish Congress Archives, New York (hereafter referred to as "Early History of CLSA").

51. "The Two Commissions and Their Role," pp. 64–65.

52. Ibid., p. 13.

53. "A Pioneering Approach," *Congress Weekly*, April 16, 1956, p. 3, American Jewish Congress Archives, New York.

54. "Early History of CLSA," p. 2; Yale Comment, "Private-Attorneys General," pp. 594–98.

55. See Yale Comment, "Private Attorneys-General," pp. 589–90; see also "Organization Gets Aid of Bias Agency," *New York Times*, Oct. 8, 1946; "Job Blank Change Seen at Columbia," *New York Times*, Feb. 25, 1947; "Cites Queries on Religion," *New York Times*, July 3, 1948. Some of the studies published by the CLSA documenting these practices included "The 'Distinctive Name' Method of Determining Jewish Enrollment in Medical School" (1947) and "Surveys of College Application Blanks in New York State" (1948), both of which were obtained from the American Jewish Congress Archives, New York.

56. Yale Comment, "Private Attorneys-General," pp. 591–92.

57. Will Maslow, "Anti-Semitism and the Law," *Congress Weekly*, Nov. 16, 1945, p. 5.

58. Yale Comment, "Private Attorneys-General," p. 590.

59. The NCRAC was formed shortly after World War II as a joint policy-making and coordinating agency of the AJCongress, the AJCommittee, the ADL, and several other Jewish groups. Its major goals were to consolidate the redundant efforts of these different groups in the areas of civil rights and community relations and to iron out policy disagreements. However, the institutional rivalries that have always existed among NCRAC's constituent groups made both these goals rather elusive.

60. Yale Comment, "Private Attorneys-General," p. 590; see also "Impact on the Jewish Community," *Congress Weekly*, April 16, 1956, p. 5, American Jewish Congress Archives, New York; and Vose, *Caucasians Only*, pp. 170–73.

61. Yale Comment, "Private Attorneys-General," p. 595.

62. Leo Pfeffer, "The Outlook in Church and State," *Congress Weekly*, April 16, 1956, p. 8.

63. Moore, *B'nai B'rith and the Challenge of Ethnic Leadership*, pp. 104–15.

64. "To Boycott Stage Jew," *New York Times*, April 25, 1913.

65. John P. Roche, *The Quest for the Dream: The Development of Civil Rights and Liberties*, pp. 23–25; see also Moore, *B'nai B'rith and the Challenge of Ethnic Leadership*, pp. 105–7.

66. Moore, *B'nai B'rith and the Challenge of Ethnic Leadership*, p. 105.

67. Author interviews with regional ADL professional staff and attorneys, June 4, 1988.

68. Moore, *B'nai B'rith and the Challenge of Ethnic Leadership*, p. 105.

69. Ibid., p. 108.

70. "ADL Proclamation," *B'nai B'rith News,* Oct. 1, 1913, Anti-Defamation League Archives, New York.

71. See Moore, *B'nai B'rith and the Challenge of Ethnic Leadership,* pp. 108, 121; see also Cohen, *Not Free to Desist,* p. 226.

72. Moore, *B'nai B'rith and the Challenge of Ethnic Leadership,* p. 109.

73. "Self-Protection or Self-Assertion?" *B'nai B'rith News,* n.d. [1913], Anti-Defamation League Archives, New York.

74. Cohen, *Not Free to Desist,* p. 226; Moore, *B'nai B'rith and the Challenge of Ethnic Leadership,* p. 111.

75. Brinkley, *Voices of Protest,* pp. 266, 269–73; see also Glen Jeansonne, "Combating Anti-Semitism: The Case of Gerald K. Smith"; Richard Hofstadter, *The Paranoid Style in American Politics,* pp. 3–40.

76. For examples of the ADL's work in this area, see "ADL Model Hate Crimes Statute," *ADL Law Report* (Spring 1992); "ADL Paramilitary Statute: A Response to Extremism," *ADL Law Report* (Fall 1986); *Extremism on the Right: A Handbook* (New York: Anti-Defamation League of B'nai B'rith, 1991–92).

77. Moore, *B'nai B'rith and the Challenge of Ethnic Leadership,* p. 114; see also "The Issues Before Us," *National Jewish Monthly,* April 1942, p. 250, Anti-Defamation League Archives, New York.

78. Moore, *B'nai B'rith and the Challenge of Ethnic Leadership,* pp. 123–24.

79. Vose, *Caucasians Only,* p. 242.

80. Elazar, *Community and Polity,* p. 173.

81. Moore, *B'nai B'rith and the Challenge of Ethnic Leadership,* p. 132.

82. See Herberg, *Protestant, Catholic, and Jew,* pp. 182, 198.

83. See "A Pioneering Approach," pp. 4–5.

Chapter 3. Challenging the Public Schools: The Released-Time Cases

1. See, for example, "Supreme Court Decision on Bus Transportation," *America,* Feb. 22, 1947, p. 561.

2. Everson v. Board of Education, 330 U.S. 1 at 18–19 (1947); Justice Jackson, dissenting.

3. Ibid., at 31–32; Justice Rutledge, dissenting.

4. Ibid.

5. Ibid.

6. Ibid., at 63.

7. See "The Two Commissions and Their Role."

8. Pfeffer, "An Autobiographical Sketch," p. 489.

9. Memorandum, Leo Pfeffer to Alexander Pekelis, "Preliminary Report on Released Time," Oct. 31, 1945, Leo Pfeffer papers, box 14.

10. Leo Pfeffer, *Religion and the Public Schools* (American Jewish Congress, 1st ed. 1947; 2d ed. 1948; 3d ed. 1949).

11. Memorandum, Leo Pfeffer to Alexander Pekelis, "Preliminary Report on Released Time," Oct. 31, 1945, pp. 1–2, 3–4, Leo Pfeffer papers, box 14.

12. Draft memorandum, "Office of Jewish Information Pamphlet on Released Time" (revised copy), Leo Pfeffer to C. Chagy, April 29, 1947, p. 34, Leo Pfeffer papers, box 19.

13. Transcript, "Sectarianism in the Public Schools," June 10–12, 1947, p. 111, Leo Pfeffer papers, box 1.

14. Transcript, "Religious Instruction in the Public Schools," Nov. 11–12, 1946, p. 140, Leo Pfeffer papers, box 1.

15. Ibid., p. 141.

16. Ibid., p. 142.

17. Ibid., pp. 129–31.

18. Ibid., p. 131.

19. Ibid., p. 132.

20. Transcript, "Sectarianism in the Public Schools," June 10–12, 1947, p. 117, Leo Pfeffer papers, box 1.

21. Ibid., p. 118 (emphasis in the original).

22. Irving Kane, "Impact on the Jewish Community," *Congress Weekly*, Apr. 16, 1956, p. 5.

23. Pfeffer, *Religion and the Public Schools* (1st ed., 1947), pp. 11–13.

24. Transcript, "Religious Instruction in the Public Schools," Nov. 11–12, 1946, p. 127, Leo Pfeffer papers, box 1.

25. For the AJCommittee's stance on this proposal, see Cohen, *Not Free to Desist*, pp. 440–41.

26. Brief of the National Community Relations Advisory Council and the Synagogue Council of America, amicus curiae, McCollum v. Board of Education, 333 U.S. 203 at 6–7 (1948).

27. Ibid., p. 7.

28. Ibid., p. 3.

29. Ibid., pp. 9–14.

30. McCollum v. Board of Education, 333 U.S. 203 at 210, 210–11 (1948).

31. Ibid., at 227; Justice Frankfurter, concurring.

32. Ibid., at 228.

33. Kane, "Impact on the Jewish Community," *Congress Weekly*, p. 5.

34. McCollum v. Board of Education, 333 U.S. 203 at 228 (1948); Justice Frankfurter, concurring.

35. See Drinan, *Religion, the Courts, and Public Policy*, pp. 62–63; see also Reichley, *Religion in American Public Life*, pp. 146–47.

36. Original manifesto, Protestants and Other Americans United for the Separation of Church and State, May 28, 1947. The original document was made available

to me at my request by Americans United, March 26, 1992, to whom I extend my thanks.

37. "Current Comment: Jewish Congress on Church-State," *America*, Jan. 10, 1953, p. 386.

38. For Catholic and Protestant reaction to *McCollum*, see, for example, "The McCollum Case," *America*, April 24, 1948, p. 49; "McCollum," *Commonweal*, March 26, 1948; "The Champaign Case," *Christian Century*, April 7, 1948.

39. "Memorandum of Understanding between the Committee, Anti-Defamation League and Congress," June 23, 1948, Leo Pfeffer papers, box 14.

40. Transcript of trial record, Zorach v. Clausen, 198 Misc. (N.Y.) 631 (1950).

41. Letter, Frederick C. McLaughlin to Clifford Forster, June 16, 1948, Leo Pfeffer papers, box 14.

42. Ibid.

43. Memorandum, Leo Pfeffer to Shad Polier, Nov. 22, 1948, Leo Pfeffer papers, box 14.

44. Ibid., n. 45.

45. Letter, Theodore Leskes, director of the AJCommittee Civil Rights Division, to Leo Pfeffer, Oct. 27, 1949, Blaustein Library, American Jewish Committee Archives, New York.

46. Zorach v. Clausen, 198 Misc. (N.Y.) 631 at 637–41 (1950).

47. Ibid., at 642.

48. Zorach v. Clausen, 278 App. Div. 573 (1951); Zorach v. Clausen, 303 N. Y. 161 (1951).

49. Letter, Sol Rabkin to Jules Cohen, national director of the National Community Relations Advisory Council, April 6, 1951, Anti-Defamation League Archives, New York.

50. Joint memorandum of the AJCommittee, the AJCongress, and the ADL (written by Leo Pfeffer, Theodore Leskes, and Sol Rabkin) to local chapter offices, March 10, 1952, Leo Pfeffer papers, box 19.

51. Zorach v. Clausen, 343 U.S. 306 at 313–14 (1952).

52. Ibid., at 316.

53. Justice Black later recanted his holding in *Everson* more explicitly in *Board of Education v. Allen*, 392 U.S. 236 at 244–47 (1968).

54. Zorach v. Clausen, 343 U.S. 306 at 317 (1952); Justice Black, dissenting.

55. Ibid., at 318.

56. Ibid., at 324, 325; Justice Jackson, dissenting.

57. Letter, Leo Pfeffer to Jules Cohen, National Community Relations Advisory Council, Aug. 9, 1950, pp. 1–2, Leo Pfeffer papers, box 15.

58. Ibid., p. 4 (my emphasis).

59. Letter, Arnold Forster to Shad Polier, March 8, 1949, Anti-Defamation League Archives, New York.

60. Letter, Leo Pfeffer to Theodore Leskes, of the AJCommittee, Feb. 13, 1952,

p. 1 and attachments, Leo Pfeffer papers, box 15. Changes that Pfeffer demanded included dropping the phrase "the first draft of" from the following sentence: "The American Jewish Congress prepared the first draft of the pleadings and briefs for the petitioners in all courts through which the case passed on its way to the United States Supreme Court." Pfeffer also found unacceptable Lukas's language in the following sentence: "Those drafts were then reviewed and approved by members of the Strategy Committee." He insisted that "drafts" be dropped and replaced by "pleadings and briefs" and "approved" substituted for "edited." Compare this language against the final memorandum, "Argument of *Zorach v. Clausen* (New York released-time) case before the United States Supreme Court," issued collectively by the AJCommittee, the AJCongress, and the Anti-Defamation League, March 10, 1952, Leo Pfeffer papers, box 19.

Chapter 4. Separation to the Fore: *Torcaso, Engel, Schempp,* and Beyond

1. This collaboration occurred in connection with Flast v. Cohen, 392 U.S. 83 (1968).

2. From the 1947 to the 1968 term, the Court decided thirty establishment and free exercise clause cases. The ACLU sponsored or cosponsored eight and submitted amicus briefs in eight; the AJCongress sponsored or cosponsored only four but submitted amicus briefs in eleven; the AJCommittee and the ADL cosponsored one case (*Zorach*) and submitted amicus briefs in eight. Americans United, in contrast, submitted amicus briefs in just two cases and sponsored none.

3. These were Engel v. Vitale, 370 U.S. 421 (1962), and Abington v. Schempp, 374 U.S. 203 (1963), both of which will be discussed in greater detail later in this chapter.

4. Cohen, *Not Free to Desist,* pp. 390–404.

5. Sorauf, *Wall of Separation,* pp. 111–20.

6. "Current Comment: Jewish Congress on Church-State," *America,* Jan. 10, 1953, p. 386 (my emphasis).

7. See, for example, "Blue Laws—A Minority Opinion," *Christian Century,* Nov. 25, 1952, p. 1373.

8. Will Herberg, "The Sectarian Conflict over Church and State," *Commentary,* Nov. 1952, pp. 450–62.

9. The AJCommittee's other magazine, *Moment,* is a liberal monthly that covers a wide range of national and international issues of concern to Jews, but it has a less confrontational style than *Commentary.*

10. Author interview Will Maslow, Aug. 2, 1992 (telephone).

11. Doremus v. Board of Education, 7 N.J. Super. 442, 71 A.2d 732, aff'd without opinion, 342 U.S. 429 (1952).

12. Memorandum, Pfeffer to Shad Polier, Dec. 13, 1950, Leo Pfeffer papers, box 20.

13. Examples include Yates v. U.S., 354 U.S. 298 (1957); Sweezy v. New Hampshire, 354 U.S. 234 (1957); Watkins v. U.S., 354 U.S. 178 (1957); Jencks v. U.S., 353 U.S. 657 (1957).

14. Quoted in Bernard Schwartz, *Super Chief: Earl Warren and His Supreme Court — A Judicial Biography,* p. 280.

15. Memorandum, Leo Pfeffer to Shad Polier, July 30, 1959, Leo Pfeffer papers, box 13.

16. Letter, Leo Pfeffer to Joseph Sickles, Oct. 28, 1959, Leo Pfeffer papers, box 13.

17. Memorandum, Ben Strouse to Regional Board, Anti-Defamation League, Dec. 8, 1959, Leo Pfeffer papers, box 13 (my emphasis).

18. Memorandum, Sandy Bolz to Leo Pfeffer, Dec. 22, 1959, Leo Pfeffer papers, box 13.

19. Letter, Will Maslow to Benjamin R. Epstein, May 3, 1961, Leo Pfeffer papers, box 13.

20. Letter, Lawrence Speiser to Theodore Leskes, Jan. 19, 1961, Leo Pfeffer papers, box 13.

21. Thus, for example, the ADL and the AJCommittee also participated as amici in one of the four Sunday-closing cases decided during the fall 1960 term: Gallagher v. Crown Kosher Market, 366 U.S. 617 (1961).

22. These were, in addition to Gallagher v. Crown Kosher Market, McGowan v. Maryland, 366 U.S. 420 (1961); Two Guys v. McGinley, 366 U.S. 582 (1961); and Braunfeld v. Brown, 366 U.S. 599 (1961).

23. Torcaso v. Watkins, 367 U.S. 488 at 495–96 (1961).

24. On the public reaction to Supreme Court rulings more generally, see Thomas R. Marshall, *Public Opinion and the Supreme Court.*

25. Brown v. Board of Education, 347 U.S. 483 (1954); Yates v. U.S., 354 U.S. 298 (1957); Mapp v. Ohio, 367 U.S. 643 (1961); Miranda v. Arizona, 384 U.S. 436 (1966).

26. Letter, Samuel L. Scheiner to Leo Pfeffer, June 25, 1962, Leo Pfeffer papers, box 23.

27. Doremus v. Board of Education, 342 U.S. 429 (1952); Carden v. Board of Education, 288 S.W.2d 718 (1956).

28. Quoted in a joint memorandum of the AJCommittee and the ADL, Arnold Forster and Edwin J. Lukas to CRC Offices, ADL Regional Offices, and AJC[ommittee] Chapters, Oct. 27, 1950, Blaustein Library, Institute for Human Relations of the American Jewish Committee, New York.

29. Ibid.

30. Memorandum, Albert Vorspan to Leo Pfeffer, Sol Rabkin, Phil Jacobson, Hirsch Freund, May 11, 1950, Leo Pfeffer papers, box 23.

31. Memorandum, Leo Pfeffer to Shad Polier, Dec. 13, 1950, Leo Pfeffer papers, box 20.

32. Ibid.

33. Ibid.

34. Memorandum, Leo Pfeffer to Shad Polier, March 14, 1951, Leo Pfeffer papers, box 20.

35. Memorandum, Leo Pfeffer to Will Maslow, June 6, 1951, Leo Pfeffer papers, box 20.

36. Letter, Herbert Monte Levy, staff counsel to the ACLU, to Leo Pfeffer, July 16, 1951, Leo Pfeffer papers, box 20.

37. Memorandum, Leo Pfeffer to Will Maslow, July 17, 1951, Leo Pfeffer papers, box 20.

38. Later that autumn the ADL and the AJCommittee would again demur on a similar issue that centered on baccalaureate ceremonies during a public school graduation in a New York suburb. They opposed intervention in a matter that each believed was *de minimus*, whereas the AJCongress wanted to encourage some joint, albeit nonconspicuous, NCRAC action. Given this lack of cohesion among the Jewish organizations, nothing happened: letter, Albert Vorspan to Isaac Frank, re: Joint Advisory Committee of the NCRAC, Oct. 31, 1951, Blaustein Library, Institute for Human Relations of the American Jewish Committee, New York.

39. Memorandum, Leo Pfeffer to Will Maslow, June 3, 1952, Leo Pfeffer papers, box 23.

40. "Prayer in School Still a State Issue," *New York Times*, Jan. 3, 1954.

41. This strategy is described further in a white paper prepared by Leo Pfeffer and Jules Cohen, national director of the NCRAC, for a conference held on religion and the public schools after *Engel* and *Schempp* had commenced. See "Religion, the Public Schools, and the Jewish Community: A Thirteen-Year Review, 1946–1959," paper presented at the "Conference for a Reassessment of Strategy and Approaches in Implementing Policies on Religion and the Public Schools," Joint Advisory Committee of the Synagogue Council of America and the National Community Relations Advisory Council, Dec. 13–15, 1959.

42. These problems are described in numerous public sources and private documents. See, for example, Daniel J. Hafrey, "Group Opposes Religion in the Public Schools," *Minneapolis Morning Tribune*, June 6, 1955; memorandum, "Report on Midwest Trip," Leo Pfeffer to Will Maslow, Dec. 27, 1955, Leo Pfeffer papers, box 14; memorandum, "Report on Southern Trip," Leo Pfeffer to Will Maslow, Feb. 16, 1956, Leo Pfeffer papers, box 13.

43. See, for example, Leo Mindlin's chronicle of this intergroup battle between the AJCongress, and the ADL ,and the AJCommittee, in his column "During the Week ... As I See It," in the *Jewish Floridian*, July 29, Aug. 5, Aug. 21, and Oct. 28, 1960.

44. Author interview with Charles Wittenstein, June 2, 1988, who was a staff

attorney for the AJCommittee from 1958 to 1963 and the ADL's legal director for the Southeast from 1963 to 1992.

45. Memorandum, Leo Pfeffer to Shad Polier, Oct. 21, 1958, Leo Pfeffer papers, box 23.

46. Memorandum, Leo Pfeffer to Sandy Bolz, Oct. 15, 1957; see also memorandum, Sandy Bolz to Leo Pfeffer, re: The Lord's Prayer, Oct. 9, 1957; memorandum, Sandy Bolz to Leo Pfeffer, Oct. 16, 1957; all in Leo Pfeffer papers, box 23.

47. Memorandum, Leo Pfeffer to Shad Polier, Nov. 24, 1958, Leo Pfeffer papers, box 23.

48. Memorandum, Samuel L. Gaber, Jan. 27, 1959, Leo Pfeffer papers, box 23.

49. Memorandum, Leo Pfeffer to Sam Gaber, Feb. 2, 1959, Leo Pfeffer papers, box 23.

50. Frank Sorauf made a similar observation about the behavior of Pfeffer and the AJCongress in such cases: see *Wall of Separation*, pp. 95–129.

51. "AP Editor Files Suit Challenging Bible Reading in Schools," *Religious News Service*, Sept. 21, 1955.

52. Letter, C. Vernon Hines to Leo Pfeffer, Oct. 1, 1955, Leo Pfeffer papers, box 23.

53. Letter, Leo Pfeffer to Daniel May and Rabbi Arthur Hertzberg, Oct. 6, 1955, Leo Pfeffer papers, box 23.

54. Letter, Leo Pfeffer to Daniel May, Nov. 8, 1955, Leo Pfeffer papers, box 23.

55. Memorandum, Leo Pfeffer to Will Maslow, Dec. 28, 1955, Leo Pfeffer papers, box 23.

56. Carden v. Bland, 288 S.W.2d (1956).

57. Memorandum, "Report on Southern Trip," Leo Pfeffer to Shad Polier, Feb. 21, 1956, p. 6, Leo Pfeffer papers, box 13.

58. Letter, Leo Pfeffer to C. Vernon Hines, April 5, 1956, Leo Pfeffer papers, box 23.

59. Letter, C. Vernon Hines to Leo Pfeffer, March 13, 1956, Leo Pfeffer papers, box 23.

60. Letter, Theodore R. Mann to Shad Polier, Aug. 1, 1957, Leo Pfeffer papers, box 23.

61. Letter, Theodore R. Mann to Leo Pfeffer, Nov. 21, 1957; letter, Theodore R. Mann to Leo Pfeffer, Dec. 27, 1957; both in Leo Pfeffer papers, box 23.

62. Letter, Theodore R. Mann to Shad Polier, Aug. 1, 1957, Leo Pfeffer papers, box 23.

63. Memorandum, Leo Pfeffer to Shad Polier, April 15, 1958, Leo Pfeffer papers, box 23. In his mention of "the Gideon Bible case," Pfeffer is referring to Tudor v. Board of Education, 100 A.2d 370 (1953), in which the AJCongress successfully argued in state court that distribution of Gideon Bibles in New Jersey public schools was unconstitutional.

64. Memorandum, Leo Pfeffer to Will Maslow, Nov. 26, 1958, Leo Pfeffer papers, box 23.

65. Author interview, Samuel Rabinove, American Jewish Committee Legal Director, March 1, 1990.

66. Letter, Justice Bernard S. Meyer to Leo Pfeffer, Aug. 24, 1959, Leo Pfeffer papers, box 23.

67. Author interview with Charles Wittenstein, June 2, 1988. But see also Leo Mindlin, "During the Week . . . As I See It," *Jewish Floridan,* Aug. 5, 1960.

68. Author interview with Charles Wittenstein, June 2, 1988.

69. Leo Mindlin, "During the Week . . . As I See It," *Jewish Floridian,* Oct. 20, 1960.

70. Letter, Leo Pfeffer to Tobias Simon, April 17, 1962, Leo Pfeffer papers, box 23.

71. Engel v. Vitale, 370 U.S. 421 at 430 (1962). Justices Frankfurter and White did not participate in the decision.

72. Ibid., at 445; Justice Stewart, dissenting.

73. In affirming *Schempp,* the Court—in Murray v. Curlett, 374 U.S. 203 (1963)—also reversed the decision of the Maryland Court of Appeals that had upheld a challenge brought by the soon-to-be famous national atheist spokeswoman, Madalyn Murray, against an almost identical state statute. The two cases were consolidated in oral argument and decided together.

74. Among the more rhetorically flamboyant reactions to *Engel* came from Senator Sam Ervin (D–N.C.), who later rose to fame as one of President Richard Nixon's chief antagonists during the Watergate scandal. Ervin declared that "the Supreme Court has made God unconstitutional" (*Washington Post,* July 7, 1962), while Representative George Andrews (D–Ala.) complained that the Court "put Negroes in the schools and now [it has] taken God out" (*New York Times,* July 1, 1962).

75. "Is *America* Trying to Bully the Jews?" *Christian Century,* Sept. 5, 1962, pp. 1057–58.

76. "To Our Jewish Friends," *America,* Sept. 1, 1962, p. 666.

77. Samuel Rabinove, "To Our Catholic Friends," *America,* Sept. 8, 1962, pp. 679–80.

78. See "The Main Issue," *America,* Sept. 15, 1962; "P.S.—To Our Jewish Friends," *America,* Sept. 22, 1962. At the same time, *Commonweal,* another well-respected Catholic journal of opinion, defended the Jews against *America's* editorial criticism. See, for example, "Religion and Pluralism," *Commonweal,* Sept. 1962, pp. 6–8.

79. C. Emanuel Carlson, quoted in "Prayer Ban Stirs Wide Discussion," *New York Times,* June 27, 1962.

80. Dean Kelley, quoted in "Wide Impact and Many New Court Cases Anticipated from Decision on Prayer," *New York Times,* June 26, 1962.

81. Dean Kelley, quoted in *New York Times,* June 18, 1962.

82. Author interview with Stuart Lewengrub, director of the Anti-Defamation League for the Southeast, June 3, 1988.

83. See "Bible Reading Is Growing L.I. Controversy," *Newsday*, Feb. 26, 1962; "American Jewish Congress Asks Board of Education to Halt Bible Reading in Public Schools," American Jewish Congress press release, Feb. 6, 1962, Leo Pfeffer papers, box 16.

84. On April 11, 1963, a consultation on *Engel v. Vitale* was held at the Statler-Hilton Hotel in New York City that included all the major Jewish organizations, as well as several rabbinical groups; representatives from the National Council of Churches and the Episcopal, Baptist, and Lutheran denominations; and several Protestant theological seminaries. The purpose was to draft a general strategy aimed at lobbying Congress not to pass any constitutional amendments that would restore state-directed religious exercises in the public schools (Leo Pfeffer papers, box 23).

85. Samuel Krislov, "Alternatives to Separation of Church and State in Countries Outside the United States," p. 421.

86. Letter, Samuel L. Scheiner to Leo Pfeffer, June 25, 1962, Leo Pfeffer Papers, box 23.

87. Letter, Paul Miller to Leo Pfeffer, June 25, 1962, Leo Pfeffer papers, box 23.

88. Letter, Mr. and Mrs. Fabian Goldstein to Leo Pfeffer, Sept. 11, 1962, Leo Pfeffer papers, box 23.

89. Letter, Mrs. W. A. Judd to Leo Pfeffer, June 26, 1962, Leo Pfeffer papers, box 23.

Chapter 5. Litigation and the Public Purse: The Parochial School Aid Cases

1. The pivotal cases in these four areas were: Brown v. Board of Education, 347 U.S. 483 (1954); Baker v. Carr, 363 U.S. 186 (1962); Mapp v. Ohio, 367 U.S. 643 (1961); and, among others, Yates v. U.S., 354 U.S. 298 (1954), and Brandenburg v. Ohio, 395 U.S. 444 (1969).

2. U.S. v. Seeger, 380 U.S. 163 (1965).

3. Epperson v. Arkansas, 393 U.S. 97 (1968).

4. Archibald Cox, *The Court and the Constitution*, p. 180.

5. Morton Borden, *Jews, Turks, and Infidels*, p. 128.

6. Leo Pfeffer, *God, Caesar, and the Constitution*, p. 358.

7. For further discussion, see Edward Keynes and Randall K. Miller, *The Court vs. Congress: Prayer, Busing, and Abortion*.

8. Frothingham v. Mellon, 262 U.S. 447 (1923).

9. "Orthodox Rapped for Seeking Federal Funds," *Jewish Ledger*, March 24, 1967.

10. For an empirical description of this point and the formation of other cross-religious coalitions in Supreme Court church-state litigation, see Ivers, "Religious Organizations as Constitutional Litigants," pp. 247–59.

11. Leo Pfeffer, "Is the First Amendment Obsolete?" position paper delivered to the Joint Advisory Committee of the Synagogue Council of America and the National Community Relations Advisory Council, Oct. 16, 1966, p. 8, Leo Pfeffer papers, box 1.

12. Board of Education v. Allen, 392 U.S. 236 (1968).

13. For Pfeffer's complete critique of the child-benefit theory, see his *Child-Benefit Theory: A Legal Fiction,* a pamphlet based on an address delivered on February 18, 1966, to Americans United's Eighteenth National Conference on Church and State, Leo Pfeffer papers, box 1.

14. Memorandum, Joseph B. Robison to Howard Squadron, Feb. 2, 1968, Leo Pfeffer papers, box 16.

15. Memorandum, Leo Pfeffer to Will Maslow, Nov. 14, 1966, Leo Pfeffer papers, box 26.

16. Flast v. Gardner, 271 F. Supp. 1 (1967).

17. Letter, Joseph B. Robison to Philip Jacobson, Oct. 17, 1967, Leo Pfeffer papers, box 20.

18. NAACP v. Button, 371 U.S. 415 (1963).

19. Brief of the American Jewish Congress, the American Jewish Committee, and the Anti-Defamation League of B'nai B'rith et al., amici curiae, Flast v. Cohen, 392 U.S. 83 (1968), pp. 4–12.

20. Letter, Judge Gus J. Solomon to Sol Rabkin, Oct. 23, 1967, ADL Archives, New York.

21. See Phillip B. Kurland and Dennis J. Hutchinson, "The Business of the Supreme Court, O.T., 1982."

22. See, for example, Caldeira and Wright, "Amici Curiae before the Supreme Court," pp. 784–86; Karen O'Connor and Lee Epstein, "Court Rules and Workload: A Case Study of Rules Governing Amicus Curiae Participation."

23. Flast v. Cohen, 392 U.S. 83 at 92, n. 6 (1968).

24. Ibid., at 102–3.

25. Ibid., at 107–14; Justice Douglas, concurring.

26. Ibid., pp. 117–33; Justice Harlan, dissenting.

27. Board of Education v. Allen, 392 U.S. 236 at 252 (1968); Justice Black, dissenting.

28. Ibid., at 243.

29. Ibid., at 251; Justice Black, dissenting.

30. Cox, *Court and the Constitution,* pp. 179, 182.

31. Pfeffer, "An Autobiographical Sketch," p. 519.

32. Author interview with Marc D. Stern, codirector of the Commission on Law and Social Action of the AJCongress, March 2, 1990.

33. Walker, *In Defense of American Liberties,* p. 223.

34. Memorandum, Joseph B. Robison to Howard M. Squadron, Feb. 2, 1968, Leo Pfeffer papers, box 16.

35. Minutes, Meeting of the Joint Advisory Committee of the NCRAC, June 5, 1969, p. 2, ADL Archives, New York.

36. Minutes, Special Meeting of the Joint Advisory Council of the NCRAC, June 18, 1969, p. 1, ADL Archives, New York. This view was corroborated in an author interview with Charles Wittenstein, June 2, 1988.

37. Walz v. Tax Commission, 397 U.S. 664 at 676 (1970).

38. Ibid., at 703; Justice Douglas, dissenting.

39. Ibid., at 703.

40. Ivers, "Religious Organizations as Constitutional Litigants," pp. 243–44.

41. Walz v. Tax Commission, 397 U.S. 664 at 674 (1970) (my emphasis).

42. Ibid., at 668, 669.

43. Memorandum, Leo Pfeffer to Will Maslow, Sept. 19, 1967, Leo Pfeffer papers, box 24.

44. Tilton v. Richardson, 403 U.S. 672 (1971).

45. "Major Court Test of Federal Aid to Church Colleges," report of the executive director of the American Jewish Congress, Sept. 1968, p. 1, Leo Pfeffer papers, box 1.

46. Litigation docket no. 14, American Jewish Congress, Jan. 15, 1972, p. 12, American Jewish Congress Archives, New York.

47. Report of the Commission on Church-State and Interreligious Relationships, National Jewish Community Relations Advisory Council, New York, April 2, 1968, pp. 10–11, Leo Pfeffer papers, box 17.

48. Minutes, Meeting of the Joint Advisory Council of the NCRAC, May 14, 1970, pp. 4–5, Leo Pfeffer papers, box 17. This is corroborated in Sorauf, *Wall of Separation*, pp. 326–27.

49. Lemon v. Kurtzman, 310 F. Supp. 35 (1969).

50. DiCenso v. Robinson, 316 F. Supp. 112 (1970); Leo Pfeffer, "Testimony in Opposition to the Rhode Island Supplemental Salaries Act, January Session 1969," submitted on behalf of the Rhode Island affiliate of the American Civil Liberties Union, Leo Pfeffer papers, box 12.

51. Leo Pfeffer, "Memorandum on the Constitutionality of H 1462, January Session 1968," submitted on behalf of the Rhode Island affiliate of the American Civil Liberties Union, March 25, 1968, pp. 2–3, 8–10, Leo Pfeffer papers, box 12.

52. Pfeffer, "Testimony in Opposition to the Rhode Island Supplemental Salaries Act," pp. 7, 9–11.

53. Tilton v. Richardson, 312 F. Supp. 1191 (1970).

54. Memorandum, Lester Greenberg to Leo Pfeffer, Sept. 11, 1968, pp. 1–2, Leo Pfeffer papers, box 24.

55. Minutes, Meeting of the Joint Advisory Committee of the NCRAC, May 14, 1970, pp. 1–3, Leo Pfeffer papers, box 17.

56. Minutes, Meeting of the Joint Advisory Committee of the NCRAC, Feb. 2, 1968, pp. 3–4, Leo Pfeffer papers, box 17.

57. Minutes, Meeting of the Joint Advisory Committee of the NCRAC, May 14, 1970, p. 3, Leo Pfeffer papers, box 17.

58. Ivers, "Religious Organizations as Constitutional Litigants," pp. 249–52.

59. "Summary of the Argument of Leo Pfeffer in *Earley v. DiCenso*," provided to the National Catholic News Service, March 10, 1971, pp. 1–2, Leo Pfeffer papers, box 22.

60. Brief of the plaintiffs, Earley v. DiCenso, 403 U.S. 602 (1971), pp. 56, 62–63.

61. Brief of the plaintiffs, Lemon v. Kurtzman, 403 U.S. 602 (1971), pp. 47–57.

62. Minutes, Meeting of the Joint Advisory Committee of the NCRAC, May 14, 1970, p. 2, Leo Pfeffer papers, box 17.

63. Brief of the plaintiffs, Earley v. DiCenso, 403 U.S. 602 (1971), pp. 24–38.

64. Brief of the plaintiffs, Lemon v. Kurtzman, 403 U.S. 602 (1971), pp. 19–23.

65. Brief of the American Jewish Congress, the American Jewish Committee, and the Anti-Defamation League of B'nai B'rith et al., amici curiae, Earley v. DiCenso, Robinson v. DiCenso, and Lemon v. Kurtzman, 403 U.S. 602 (1971), passim.

66. Brief of the American Association of School Administrators, American Vocational Association, Association for Supervision and Curriculum Development, Horace Mann League, National Association of High School Principals, National Education Association, and the Rural Education Association, amici curiae, Lemon v. Kurtzman, 403 U.S. 602 (1971).

67. Lemon v. Kurtzman, 403 U.S. 602 at 603, 613, 614, 619 (1971).

68. Tilton v. Richardson, 403 U.S. 672 at 688, 688–89 (1971).

69. "Summary of the Argument of Leo Pfeffer in *Tilton v. Richardson*," provided to the National Catholic News Service, March 10, 1971, p. 3, Leo Pfeffer papers, box 22.

70. Memorandum, Leo Pfeffer to Will Maslow, Nov. 20, 1968, Leo Pfeffer papers, box 24. Pfeffer would later remark to Maslow that Williams's fee in *Tilton* alone "exceeds the sum of all of the salary I have received from the American Jewish Congress in the entire twenty-five years of my association with it" (memorandum, Leo Pfeffer to Will Maslow, Oct. 29, 1970, Leo Pfeffer papers, box 24).

71. Letter, Edward Bennett Williams to Sol Rabkin, Aug. 12, 1970, ADL Archives, New York.

72. Letter, Joseph B. Robison to Sol Rabkin, Aug. 12, 1970, Leo Pfeffer papers, box 24; Letter, Sol Rabkin to Joseph B. Robison, Aug. 20, 1970, ADL Archives, New York.

73. Data collected by and available from the author.

74. The seven cases in which the decision went against the government were: New York v. Cathedral Academy, 434 U.S. 125 (1977); Wolman v. Walter, 432 U.S. 229 (1977) (striking down, in part, provisions of an Ohio statute that permitted state reimbursement to parochial schools for the purchase of special educational services); Meek v. Pettinger, 421 U.S. 349 (1975); Wheeler v. Barrera, 417 U.S. 402 (1974); Sloan v. Lemon, 413 U.S. 825 (1973); PEARL v. Nyquist, 413 U.S. 756 (1973);

Levitt v. PEARL, 413 U.S. 472 (1973). The government managed to prevail in PEARL v. Regan, 444 U.S. 646 (1980); and Lemon v. Kurtzman II, 411 U.S. 192 (1973).

75. On the movement of parochial aid toward the center of the Court's church-state docket, see, for example, Bernard Schwartz, *The Ascent of Pragmatism: The Burger Court in Action*, pp. 187–214.

76. Pfeffer argued the case as lead counsel in PEARL v. Regan, 444 U.S. 646 (1980); Meek v. Pettinger, 421 U.S. 349 (1975); Wheeler v. Barerra, 417 U.S. 402 (1974); Levitt v. PEARL, 413 U.S. 472 (1973); PEARL v. Nyquist, 413 U.S. 756 (1973); and Sloan v. Lemon, 413 U.S. 825 (1973). He authored the amicus brief filed by PEARL in Wolman v. Walter, 432 U.S. 229 (1977).

77. Report of the executive director of the American Jewish Congress, March 1967, p. 1, Leo Pfeffer papers, box 21. The charter members of PEARL were the American Ethical Union; the American Jewish Committee; the American Jewish Congress; Americans for Democratic Action; Americans for Public Schools; the Association of Reform Rabbis of New York City; B'nai B'rith, including the Anti-Defamation League; the City Club of New York; the National Council of Jewish Women; the National Women's Conference; the New York Civil Liberties Union; the New York Jewish Labor Committee; the New York Metropolitan Council; the New York Metropolitan Region; the New York Society for Ethical Culture; the New York State Council of Churches; the New York State Federation of Reform Synagogues; the Protestant Council of the City of New York; the Public Education Association; the State Congress of Parents and Teachers, New York City District; the Unitarian Universalist Ministers Association of Metropolitan New York; the United Federation of Teachers; the United Parents Association; and the United Synagogues of America.

78. Douglas Robinson, "School Aid Suits Set for Six States," *New York Times*, July 2, 1971.

79. Author interview with Samuel Rabinove, legal director of the AJCommittee, May 20, 1988, New York.

Chapter 6. Defending the Status Quo: Litigation in a Changed Environment

1. See, for example, Clyde Wilcox, *God's Warriors: The Christian Right in Twentieth-Century America;* Moen, *Christian Right and Congress;* Hertzke, *Representing God in Washington;* Reichley, *Religion in American Public Life;* and Weber, "Examining the Religious Lobbies."

2. For further discussion on this point, see David M. O'Brien, "The Reagan Judges: His Most Enduring Legacy?" pp. 60–101. For a longitudinal assessment of the Reagan administration's success in altering the composition of the federal judiciary and the continuation of this effort by his successor, George Bush, see Sheldon Goldman's periodic assessments published in *Judicature* between 1985 and 1993:

"Reaganizing the Judiciary: The First Term Appointments," "Reagan's Judicial Legacy: Completing the Puzzle and Summing Up," "The Bush Imprint on the Judiciary: Carrying on a Tradition," and "Bush's Judicial Legacy: The Final Imprint."

3. For a useful description of the rise of conservative organized interests in litigation generally, see Epstein, *Conservatives in Court.*

4. For an elaboration on this point, see Ivers, "Religious Organizations as Constitutional Litigants," pp. 252–57.

5. Data collected by the author.

6. Samuel Krislov, "Alternatives to Separation of Church and State," pp. 421–22.

7. Author interview with Marc D. Stern, codirector of the CLSA of the AJCongress, May 20, 1988, New York.

8. Ibid.

9. Financial data provided to the author by the American Jewish Congress, New York.

10. Author interviews with Marc D. Stern, May 20, 1988, and March 2, 1990.

11. Author interview with Marc D. Stern, May 20, 1988.

12. Financial data provided to the author by the Anti-Defamation League, New York.

13. Data collected by the author.

14. Author interview with Steven K. Freeman, legal affairs director of the ADL, May 19, 1988.

15. Author interview with Stuart Lewengrub, director of the ADL for the Southeast, June 2, 1988, Atlanta.

16. Financial data provided to the author by the American Jewish Committee, New York.

17. Author interview with Samuel Rabinove, legal director of the AJCommittee, March 1, 1990, New York.

18. Ibid. In Lynch v. Donnelly, 465 U.S. 668 (1984), the Court ruled that a publicly funded nativity scene displayed in a private park did not violate the establishment clause as long as religious symbols were part of a larger secular presentation.

19. Data collected by the author.

20. Author interview with Samuel Rabinove, March 1, 1990, New York. By "equal access," Rabinove is referring to the landmark cases Board of Westside Schools v. Mergens, 110 S.Ct. 2356 (1990), which held that student-initiated religious organizations had the constitutional right to meet in public schools after hours, and Widmar v. Vincent, 454 U.S. 263 (1981), in which the Court ruled that public universities could not exclude student religious organizations from meeting in campus classrooms if such facilities were also made available to other student groups.

21. See Tushnet, *NAACP's Legal Strategy against Segregated Education,* pp. 146–51, for a description of how such concerns influenced the way in which the NAACP designed its litigation campaign to attack school segregation.

22. Ibid., pp. 70–80, 147–56.

23. Author interview with Jill Kahn, assistant legal affairs director of the ADL, Sept. 21, 1989, New York.

24. Richard F. Fenno, Jr., *Home Style: House Members in Their Districts.*

25. Author interview with Marc D. Stern, March 2, 1990.

26. Bob Jones v. U.S., 461 U.S. 574 (1983). The Court, eight-to-one, ruled in favor of the IRS.

27. Author interview with Marc D. Stern, March 2, 1990.

28. Author interview with Marc D. Stern, May 20, 1988. The case in question was Aguilar v. Felton, 473 U.S. 402 (1985).

29. Epstein, *Conservatives in Court,* p. 156. For similar arguments, see Kay L. Schlozman and John T. Tierney, *Organized Interests and American Democracy,* pp. 376–85; Kobylka, "A Court-Created Context for Group Litigation"; and O'Connor and Epstein, "Rise of Conservative Interest Group Litigation." In "Organized Interests and Agenda Setting in the U.S. Supreme Court," Calderia and Wright have made the same argument to explain in part how the Court sets its case agenda at the certiorari stage. I no longer find this argument persuasive, even though I once offered it as a partial explanation for the plurality of interest groups represented on the Court's criminal procedure docket (Gregg Ivers and Karen O'Connor, "Friends as Foes: The Amicus Curiae Participation and Effectiveness of the American Civil Liberties Union and the Americans for Effective Law Enforcement in Criminal Cases, 1969–82").

30. Calderia and Wright, "Amici Curiae before the Supreme Court," pp. 801–2. Their aggregate measure of intergroup competition is quite simple, but effective. It consists of the number of cases attracting opposition amicus curiae briefs as a percentage of all cases decided.

31. On this latter point, see Keynes and Miller, *Court vs. Congress: Prayer, Busing, and Abortion,* pp. 174–205.

32. Ivers, "Religious Organizations as Constitutional Litigants." The data presented in the preceding paragraph can be found on pp. 260–61 of this article.

33. Author interview with Jill Kahn and Steven Freeman, May 19, 1988. Kahn and Freeman are referring to Edwards v. Aguillard, 482 U.S. 578 (1987), in which the Court struck down by a seven-to-two margin the Louisiana Balanced Treatment for Creation-Science and Evolution-Science Act. Its decision was based on the argument that, in wishing to include "creation-science" in the public school curriculum, the state legislature was primarily motivated by a desire to incorporate religious teaching on the origin of the human species. In Epperson v. Arkansas, 393 U.S. 97 (1968), the Warren Court had ruled against the teaching of creationism in the public schools.

34. Author interview with Samuel Rabinove, March 1, 1990.

35. Author interview with Marc D. Stern, March 2, 1990.

36. Data collected by the author.

37. Author interviews with Marc D. Stern, May 20, 1988, and March 2, 1990.

38. Epstein and Kobylka, *Supreme Court and Legal Change,* pp. 299–312.

39. Lee v. Weisman, 112 S.Ct. 2649 (1992). Examples of earlier rulings denying public schools the right to introduce prayer include Jager v. Douglas County School District, 862 F.2d 824 (11th Cir. 1989), cert. denied, 490 U.S. 1090 (1989); Wallace v. Jaffree, 472 U.S. 38 (1985); Karen B. v. Treen 653 F.2d 897 (5th Cir. 1981), aff'd mem., 455 U.S. 913 (1982).

40. See County of Allegheny v. American Civil Liberties Union, 109 S.Ct. 3086, 3134–46 (1989); Justice Kennedy concurring in part and dissenting in part.

41. For examples, see Marcia Coyle, "Not Just a Prayer," *National Law Journal,* Nov. 11, 1991, p. 1; and David G. Savage, "U.S. Seeks to Ease Ban on School Prayer," *Los Angeles Times,* Nov. 7, 1991. I must confess that I agreed with them (*Redefining the First Freedom: The Supreme Court and the Consolidation of State Power,* pp. 1–4.)

42. I summarize these arguments in *Redefining the First Freedom,* pp. 116–22.

43. The most provocative and well-known are the dissents of then–Associate Justice William H. Rehnquist in Wallace v. Jaffree, 472 U.S. 38 at 91–114 (1985), and of Justice Antonin Scalia in Edwards v. Aguillard, 482 U.S. 578 at 636–40 (1987). "There is simply no historical foundation for the proposition that the Framers intended to build the 'wall of separation' that was constitutionalized in *Everson,*" argued Rehnquist. "The *Lemon* test has no more grounding in the history of the First Amendment than does the wall theory upon which it rests. The 'wall of separation between church and State' is a metaphor based on bad history [and] should be frankly and explicitly abandoned" (pp. 113, 106). Two years later, and with reference to the opinion offered by Rehnquist (now chief justice) in *Wallace,* Justice Scalia wrote: "I think the pessimistic evaluation that the Chief Justice made of the totality of *Lemon* is particularly applicable to the 'purpose' prong: it is a 'constitutional theory [that] has no basis in the history of the amendment it seeks to interpret" (p. 636).

44. Lee v. Weisman, 112 S.Ct. 2649, slip opinion at 7–8 (1992). Compare Justice Kennedy's majority opinion with Justice Souter's concurring opinion. Justice Souter's analysis, his first extended treatment of the Court's establishment clause jurisprudence, was far more wide-ranging and discursive than Justice Kennedy's. Rejecting the nonpreferentialist and noncoercion theories offered by Justices Rehnquist, Scalia, and Kennedy, Justice Souter instead argued: "While we may be unable to know for certain what the Framers meant by the Clause, we do know that, around the time of its ratification, a respectable body of opinion supported a considerably broader reading than petitioners urge upon us." In Justice Souter's opinion, that broader reading implied neutrality toward religion. Souter added that "our recent cases have invested it with specific content: the state may not favor or endorse either religion generally over nonreligion or one religion over others. . . . Our aspiration to religious liberty, embodied in the First Amendment, permits no other standard" (ibid., at 18–19; Justice Souter, concurring). Another interesting

note on Justice Souter's opinion is this: in addition to his analysis of the historical sources relevant to First Amendment's creation and the Court's post-*Everson* church-state jurisprudence, he cited throughout his opinion the more recent work and commentary of Douglas Laycock—who is, in my estimation, the most clear and persuasive writer on contemporary church-state issues. Justice Souter makes a total of seven references to three of Laycock's articles. This observation might be of lesser interest had Laycock not also authored the joint amicus curiae brief submitted in *Weisman* by the American Jewish Congress, the Baptist Joint Committee, the American Jewish Committee, the National Council of Churches, the Anti-Defamation League, the Seventh-Day Adventists, People for the American Way, the National Jewish Relations Advisory Council (NCRAC), PEARL, and the Presbyterian Church, U.S.A. In the "Interest of the *Amici*" section of the brief, Laycock states that "these *amici* are concerned principally with rejecting petitioners' proposed coercion rule, and with preserving this Court's settled rule that government must be neutral toward religion. . . . The bulk of this brief is devoted to the choice between the two rules, defending the neutrality rule in terms of constitutional text, history, precedent, and policy" (pp. 1–2). I will not claim that Justice Souter was dependent on a little help from his friends in formulating his position on the Court's proper approach to establishment clause jurisprudence, but I think a credible argument can be made that the similarities between his opinion and the line of argument in Laycock's brief are more than coincidental. Still, such speculation bears a closer relationship to the game of three-card monte that characterized much of the analysis offered by Kremlinologists of Soviet Russia—when influence and power were gauged by physical proximity of Politburo *apparatchiks* to the premier during the May Day parade—than to systematic political science.

45. The data collected as a result of such kind permission is what makes the recent study by H. W. Perry, Jr., on the internal dynamics of how the Court's chooses which cases to include on its agenda, *Deciding to Decide: Agenda Setting in the United States Supreme Court*, such a fine book.

Conclusion

1. Krislov, "Alternatives to Separation of Church and State," p. 422.

2. See, especially, Cord, *Separation of Church and State: Historical Fact and Current Fiction*. But see also Richard John Neuhaus, "Genuine Pluralism and the Pfefferian Inversion"; Dreisbach, *Real Threat and Mere Shadow*.

BIBLIOGRAPHY

Manuscript and Archive Collections

American Jewish Committee Archives, Blaustein Library, Institute for Human Relations, New York
American Jewish Congress Archives, Stephen Wise House, New York Anti-Defamation League Archives of B'nai B'rith, New York
Leo Pfeffer papers, George Arendts Research Library, Syracuse University, Syracuse, N.Y.

Records, Documents, and Reports

American Jewish Committee. *Litigation Docket,* 1973–1992.
American Jewish Congress. "The Case of the Jewish People: Addresses Delivered before the American Jewish Congress by Dr. Stephen Wise," 1925.
———. Draft memorandum, "The Two Commissions and Their Role in the Congress Movement," August 31, 1945.
———. "The Distinctive Name Method of Determining Jewish Enrollment in Medical School," 1947.
———. "Surveys of College Application Blanks in New York State," 1948.
———. "How CLSA Selects Its Projects," December 12, 1955.
———. "Early History of the CLSA," April 4, 1984.
Anti-Defamation League. *ADL Annual Law Report,* 1977–1992.
———. "ADL Proclamation," October 1, 1913.

Personal Interviews

American Jewish Committee: Richard T. Foltin (correspondence), Samuel Rabinove, and three confidential interviews.
American Jewish Congress: Will Maslow, Marc Pelavin, Leo Pfeffer (correspondence), Marc Stern, and Lois Waldman (correspondence).
Anti-Defamation League of B'nai B'rith: Steven Freeman, Jill Kahn, Stuart Lewengrub, Michael Lieberman, Ruti Teitel, Charles Wittenstein.

Newspapers and Magazines

America	*Moment*
Atlanta Constitution	*The Nation*
B'nai B'rith News	*National Jewish Monthly*
Catholic Reporter	*National Jewish Post*
Commentary	*National Review*
Commonweal	*New Republic*
Christian Century	*Newsday*
Churchman	*Newsweek*
Commentary	*New York Times*
Congress Weekly	*New York World-Telegram and Sun*
Congressional Quarterly	*Philadelphia Inquirer*
Jewish Floridian	*Present Tense*
Jewish Ledger	*Reconstructionist*
Jewish Record	*Southern Israelite*
Los Angeles Times	*The Tablet*
Miami Herald	*Time*
Miami News	*Washington Post*

Books and Dissertations

Adams, James L. *The Growing Church Lobby in Washington.* Grand Rapids, Mich., 1970.

Bentley, Arthur. *The Process of Government.* Chicago, 1908.

Berry, Jeffrey. *Lobbying for the People.* Princeton, N.J., 1977.

Blasi, Vincent, ed. *The Burger Court: The Counterrevolution That Wasn't.* New Haven, Conn., 1983.

Borden, Morton. *Jews, Turks, and Infidels.* Chapel Hill, N.C., 1984.

Brigham, John. *Civil Liberties and American Democracy.* Washington, D.C., 1984.

Brinkley, Alan. *Voices of Protest: Huey Long, Father Coughlin, and the Great Depression.* New York, 1982.

Casper, Jonathan D. *Lawyers before the Warren Court.* Champaign, Ill., 1972.

Cohen, Naomi. *The Struggle for Religious Equality: Jews in Christian America.* New York, 1992.

——. *Not Free to Desist: The American Jewish Committee, 1906–1966.* Philadelphia, 1972.

——. *The Public Career of Oscar S. Straus.* Phildelphia, 1969.

Cord, Robert L. *Separation of Church and State: Fact and Fiction.* New York, 1982.

Cortner, Richard C. *The Supreme Court and the Second Bill of Rights.* Madison, Wisc., 1981.

Cox, Archibald. *The Court and the Constitution.* Boston, 1987.

Curry, Thomas J. *The First Freedoms: Church and State in America to the Passage of the First Amendment.* New York, 1986.

Dinnerstein, Leonard. *The Leo Frank Case.* Athens, Ga., 1987.

Dolbeare, Kenneth M., and Philip E. Hammond. *The School Prayer Decisions: From Court Policy to Local Practice.* Chicago, 1971.

Dreisbach, Daniel L. *Real Threat or Mere Shadow: Religious Liberty and the First Amendment.* Westchester, Ill., 1987.

Drinan, Robert F. *Religion, the Courts, and Public Policy.* New York, 1963.

Ebersole, Luke Eugene, *Church Lobbying in the Nation's Capitol.* New York, 1951.

Elazar, Daniel J. *Community and Polity: The Organizational Dynamics of American Jewry.* Philadelphia, 1976.

Epstein, Lee. *Conservatives in Court.* Knoxville, Tenn., 1985.

Epstein, Lee, and Joseph F. Kobylka. *The Supreme Court and Legal Change.* Chapel Hill, N.C., 1992.

Fenno, Richard F., Jr. *Home Style: House Members in Their Districts.* Boston, 1978.

Frommer, Morris. *The American Jewish Congress: A History, 1914–1950.* Ph.D. diss., Ohio State University, Columbus, Ohio, 1978.

Funston, Richard. *A Vital National Seminar: The Supreme Court in American Political Life.* Palo Alto, Calif., 1978.

Gerber, David A., ed. *Anti-Semitism in American History.* Champaign, Ill., 1987.

Goldstein, Judith. *The Politics of Ethnic Pressure: The American Jewish Committee as Lobbyist, 1906–1917.* Ph.D. diss., Columbia University, New York, 1972.

Hamilton, Alexander, James Madison, and John Jay. *The Federalist Papers.* Edited by Clinton Rossiter. New York, 1961.

Herberg, Will. *Protestant, Catholic, and Jew: An Essay in Religious Sociology.* Chicago, 1960.

Hertzberg, Arthur. *The Jews in America: Four Centuries of Uneasy Encounter.* New York, 1989.

Hertzke, Allen D. *Representing God in Washington.* Knoxville, Tenn., 1988.

Hofstadter, Richard. *The Paranoid Style in American Politics.* Chicago, 1965.

Howe, Irving. *World of Our Fathers.* New York, 1976.

Irons, Peter. *The Courage of Their Convictions.* New York, 1988.

Issacs, Stephen D. *Jews and American Politics.* Garden City, N.Y., 1974.

Ivers, Gregg. *Redefining the First Freedom: The Supreme Court and the Consolidation of State Power.* New Brunswick, N.J., 1992.

Johnson, Paul. *A History of the Jews.* New York, 1987.

Johnson, Richard M. *The Dynamics of Compliance: Supreme Court Decision-Making from a New Perspective.* Evanston, Ill., 1967.

Jones, Charles O. *The Reagan Legacy: Promise and Performance.* Chatham, N. J., 1988.

Keynes, Edward, and Randall K. Miller. *The Court vs. Congress: Prayer, Busing, and Abortion.* Durham, N.C., 1989.

Kluger, Richard. *Simple Justice.* New York, 1975.

Lamb, Charles M., and Stephen C. Halpern. *The Burger Court: Political and Judicial Profiles.* Champaign, Ill., 1991.

Lawrence, Susan E. *The Poor in Court: The Legal Services Program and Supreme Court Decision Making.* Princeton, N.J., 1990.

Levy, Leonard. *The Establishment Clause: Religion and the First Amendment.* New York, 1986.

Lindbloom, Charles. *Politics and Markets.* New York, 1976.

Lipset, Seymour Martin, ed. *American Pluralism and the Jewish Community.* New Brunswick, N.J., 1990.

McGuire, Kevin T. *The Supreme Court Bar: Legal Elites in the Washington Community.* Charlottesville, Va., 1993.

Manwaring, David. *Render unto Caesar: The Flag Salute Controversy.* Chicago, 1962.

Marshall, Thomas R. *Public Opinion and the Supreme Court.* Boston, 1989.

Moe, Terry M. *The Organization of Interests.* Chicago, 1980.

Moen, Matthew C. *The Transformation of the Christian Right.* Tuscaloosa, Ala., 1992.

——. *The Christian Right and Congress.* Tuscaloosa, Ala., 1989.

Moore, Deborah Dash. *At Home in America.* New York, 1981.

——. *B'nai B'rith and the Challenge of Ethnic Leadership.* Albany, 1981.

Morgan, Richard E. *The Supreme Court and Religion.* New York, 1972.

——. *The Politics of Religious Conflict.* New York, 1968.

Neuhaus, Richard John. *The Naked Public Square.* Grand Rapids, Mich., 1984.

O'Connor, Karen. *Women's Organizations' Use of the Courts.* Lexington, Mass., 1980.

Olson, Mancur. *The Logic of Collective Action.* Cambridge, Mass., 1965.

Olson, Susan M. *Clients and Lawyers.* Westport, Conn., 1984.

O'Neill, Timothy. *Bakke and the Politics of Inequality.* Middletown, Conn., 1985.

Pacelle, Richard L., Jr. *The Transformation of the Supreme Court's Agenda.* Boulder, Colo., 1991.

Perry, H. W., Jr. *Deciding to Decide: Agenda Setting in the United States Supreme Court.* Cambridge, Mass., 1991.

Perry, Michael J. *Love and Power: The Role of Religion and Morality in American Politics.* New York, 1991.

Pfeffer, Leo. *Religion, State, and the Burger Court.* Buffalo, 1984.

——. *God, Caesar, and the Constitution.* Boston, 1975.

——. *Church, State, and Freedom.* 2d ed. Boston, 1967.

Przeworski, Adam, and Henry Teune. *The Logic of Comparative Inquiry.* New York, 1970.

Puro, Stephen. *The Role of the Amicus Curiae in the United States Supreme Court.* Ph.D. diss., State University of New York—Buffalo, 1971.

Reichley, A. James. *Religion in American Public Life.* Washington, D.C., 1985.

Roche, John P. *The Quest for the Dream: The Development of Civil Rights and Liberties.* New York, 1973.

Rosen, Paul. *The Supreme Court and Social Science.* Champaign, Ill., 1982.

Rosenberg, Gerald N. *The Hollow Hope: Can Courts Bring about Social Change?* Chicago, 1991.

Scheingold, Stuart. *The Politics of Rights.* New Haven, Conn., 1974.

Schlozman, Kay L., and John T. Tierney. *Organized Interests in American Democracy.* New York, 1985.

Schwartz, Bernard. *The Ascent of Pragmatism: The Burger Court in Action.* Reading, Mass., 1990.

———. *Super Chief: Earl Warren and His Supreme Court—A Judicial Biography.* New York, 1983.

Shapiro, Yonathan. *Leadership of the American Zionist Organizations, 1897–1930.* Ph.D. diss., Columbia University, New York, 1964.

Silk, Mark. *Spiritual Politics.* New York, 1988.

Sorauf, Frank J. *The Wall of Separation: The Constitutional Politics of Church and State.* Princeton, N.J., 1976.

Strum, Phillipa. *Brandeis: Portrait of a Progressive* Lawrence, Kans., 1992.

———. *Louis Brandeis: A Justice for the People.* Cambridge, Mass., 1984.

Swanson, Wayne R. *The Christ Child Goes to Court.* Philadelphia, 1990.

Tenofsky, Eliot. *Interest Groups and Litigation: The Commission on Law and Social Action of the American Jewish Congress.* Ph.D. diss., Brandeis University, Waltham, Mass., 1979.

Tocqueville, Alexis de. *Democracy in America.* Edited by J. P. Mayer. Garden City, N. Y., 1969.

Truman, David. *The Governmental Process.* New York, 1951.

Tushnet, Mark V. *The NAACP's Legal Strategy against Segregated Education, 1925–1950.* Chapel Hill, N.C., 1987.

Vose, Clement. *Constitutional Change.* Lexington, Mass., 1972.

———. *Caucasians Only.* Berkeley, Calif., 1959.

Walker, Samuel. *In Defense of American Liberties.* New York, 1990.

Wasby, Stephen L. *The Supreme Court in the Federal Judicial System.* 3d ed. Chicago, 1988.

Weisbrod, Burton, Joel Handler, and Neil Komesar. *Public Interest Law: An Economic and Institutional Analysis.* Berkeley, Calif., 1978.

Wilcox, Clyde. *God's Warriors: The Christian Right in Twentieth-Century America.* Baltimore, 1993.

Wilson, James Q. *Political Organizations*. New York, 1973.

Wood, James E., Jr. *Ecumenical Perspectives on Church and State: Protestant, Catholic, and Jewish*. Waco, Tex., 1988.

———, ed. *Religion and State: Essays in Honor of Leo Pfeffer*. Waco, Tex., 1985.

Wuthnow, Robert. *The Restructuring of American Religion*. Princeton, N.J., 1988.

Articles

Barker, Lucius. "Third Parties in Litigation: A Systematic View of the Judicial Function." *Journal of Politics* 29 (1967): 41–69.

Beckwith, Edmund, and Rudolph Soberheim. "Amicus Curiae—Minister of Justice." *Fordham Law Review* 17 (1948): 38–62.

Birkby, Robert H., and Walter Murphy. "Interest Group Conflict in the Judicial Arena." *Texas Law Review* 42 (1964): 1018–48.

"Book Note." *Harvard Law Review* 106 (1993): 2009–14.

Calderia, Gregory A., and John R. Wright. "Amici Curiae before the Supreme Court: Who Participates, When, and How Much?" *Journal of Politics* 52 (1990): 782–806.

———. "Organized Interests and Agenda Setting in the U.S. Supreme Court." *American Political Science Review* 82 (1988): 1109–27.

Casper, Jonathan D. "The Supreme Court and National Policy-Making." *American Political Science Review* 70 (1976): 50–63.

Cortner, Richard C. "Strategies and Tactics of Litigants in Constitutional Cases." *Journal of Public Law* 17 (1968): 287–307.

Cowan, Ruth B. "Women's Rights through Litigation: An Examination of the American Civil Liberties Union Women's Rights Project, 1971–76." *Columbia Human Rights Law Review* 8 (1976): 373–412.

Dahl, Robert A. "Decision-Making in a Democracy: The Role of the Supreme Court as a National Policy-Maker." *Journal of Public Law* 6 (1957): 279–95.

Ennis, Bruce J. "Effective Amicus Briefs." *Catholic University Law Review* 33 (1984): 603–9.

Epstein, Lee, and C. K. Rowland. "Debunking the Myth of Interest Group Invincibility in the Courts." *American Political Science Review* 85 (1991): 205–17.

Frankel, Marvin E. "Religion in Public Life—Reasons for Minimal Access." *George Washington University Law Review* 60 (1992): 633–44.

Galanter, Marc. "Why the 'Haves' Come Out Ahead: Speculation on the Limits of Legal Change." *Law and Society Review* 9 (1974): 95–160.

Goldman, Sheldon. "Bush's Judicial Legacy: The Final Imprint." *Judicature* 76 (1993): 282–94.

———. "The Bush Imprint on the Judiciary: Carrying on a Tradition." *Judicature* 74 (1991): 284–305.

———. "Reagan's Judicial Legacy: Completing the Puzzle and Summing Up." *Judicature* 72 (1989): 318–30.

———. "Reaganizing the Judiciary: The First Term Appointments." *Judicature* 68 (1985): 313–29.

Greenberg, Jack. "Litigation for Social Change: Methods, Limits, and Role in Democracy." *Records of New York City Bar Association* 29 (1974): 9–63.

Hakman, Nathan. "Lobbying the Supreme Court: An Appraisal of Political Science Folklore." *Fordham Law Review* 35 (1966): 15–50.

Harper, Fowler V., and Edwin Etherington. "Lobbyists before the Court." *University of Pennsylvania Law Review* 101 (1952): 1172–77.

Heck, Edward V., and Joseph M. Stewart. "Ensuring Equal Access to Justice: The Role of Interest Group Lawyers in the 1960s Campaign for Civil Rights." *Judicature* 66 (1982): 84–95.

Howard, A. E. Dick. "The Wall of Separation: The Supreme Court as Uncertain Stonemason." In *Religion and the State: Essays in Honor of Leo Pfeffer*, edited by James E. Wood, Jr., pp. 85–118. Waco, Tex., 1985.

Ivers, Gregg. "Religious Organizations as Constitutional Litigants." *Polity* 25 (1992): 243–66.

———. "Organized Religion and the Supreme Court." *Journal of Church and State* 32 (1990): 775–93.

Ivers, Gregg, and Karen O'Connor. "Friends as Foes: The Amicus Curiae Participation and Effectiveness of the American Civil Liberties Union and Americans for Effective Law Enforcement in Criminal Cases, 1969–82." *Law and Policy* 9 (1987): 161–78.

Jeansonne, Glen. "Combating Anti-Semitism: The Case of Gerald K. Smith." In *Anti-Semitism in American History*, edited by David A. Gerber, pp. 152–66. Champaign, Ill., 1987.

Jelen, Ted G. "The Political Consequences of Religious Group Attitudes." *Journal of Politics* 55 (1993): 178–90.

Kobylka, Joseph F. "A Court-Created Context for Group Litigation." *Journal of Politics* 49 (1987): 1061–78.

Krislov, Samuel. "Alternatives to Separation of Church and State in Countries Outside the United States." In *Religion and State: Essays in Honors of Leo Pfeffer*, edited by James E. Wood, Jr., pp. 421–40. Waco, Tex., 1985.

———. "The Amicus Curiae Brief: From Friendship to Advocacy." *Yale Law Journal* 72 (1963): 694–721.

Kurland, Phillip B., and Dennis J. Hutchinson. "The Business of the Supreme Court, O.T., 1982." *University of Chicago Law Review* 50 (1983): 628–51.

Laycock, Douglas. "Summary and Synthesis: The Crisis in Religious Liberty." *George Washington Law Review* 60 (1992): 841–56.

———. "Formal, Substantive, and Disaggregated Neutrality toward Religion." *De Paul Law Review* 39 (1990): 993–1018.

——. "'Nonpreferential Aid to Religion': A False Claim about Original Intent." *William and Mary Law Review* 27 (1986): 875–85.

McIntosh, Wayne V. "Litigating Scientific Creationism, or Scopes I, II, III . . ." *Law and Policy* 7 (1985): 375–94.

Mann, Theodore. "The Courts." *Present Tense*, January–February 1985, pp. 25–28.

Marshall, Thomas R. "The Supreme Court as an Opinion Leader: Court Decisions and the Mass Public." *American Politics Quarterly* 15 (1987): 148–60.

Maslow, Will. "The Use of Law in the Struggle for Equality." *Social Research* 22 (1955): 297–314.

Mauro, Tony. "Court Gets a Tad Less Friendly to Amici." *Legal Times*, February 19, 1990.

Moe, Terry M. "Towards a Broader View of Interest Groups." *Journal of Politics* 43 (1981): 531–43.

Neuhaus, Richard John. "Genuine Pluralism and the Pfefferian Inversion." *This World* 25 (1989): 69–98.

O'Brien, David M. "The Reagan Judges: His Most Enduring Legacy?" In *The Reagan Legacy: Promise and Performance*, edited by Charles O. Jones, pp. 66–101. Chatham, N.J., 1988.

O'Connor, Karen, and Lee Epstein. "Rebalancing the Scales of Justice: An Assessment of Public Interest Law." *Harvard Journal of Law and Public Policy* 7 (1984): 483–506.

——. "Beyond Legislative Lobbying: Women's Rights Groups and the Supreme Court." *Judicature* 67 (1983): 134–43.

——. "Court Rules and Workload: A Case Study of Rules Governing Amicus Curiae Participation." *Justice System Journal* 8 (1983): 35–45.

——. "The Rise of Conservative Interest Group Litigation." *Journal of Politics* 45 (1983): 479–89.

——. "Amicus Curiae Participation in U.S. Supreme Court Litigation: An Appraisal of Hakman's 'Folklore.'" *Law and Society Review* 16 (1981–82): 701–11.

Pfeffer, Leo. "An Autobiographical Sketch." In *Religion and the State: Essays in Honor of Leo Pfeffer*, edited by James E. Wood, Jr., pp. 487–533. Waco, Tex., 1985.

——. "Amici in Church-State Litigation." *Law and Contemporary Problems* 44 (1981): 83–110.

Pickus, Noah. "Before I Built a Wall—Jews, Religion, and American Public Life." *This World* 15 (1986): 28–43.

Salisbury, Robert H. "An Exchange Theory of Interest Groups." *Midwest Journal of Political Science* 13 (1969): 1–32.

Singer, David. "One Nation Completely under God? The American Jewish Congress and the Catholic Church in the United States, 1947–1984." *Journal of Church and State* 26 (1984): 473–85.

Songer, Donald R., and Reginald S. Sheehan. "Interest Group Success in the Court: Amicus Participation in the Supreme Court." *Political Research Quarterly* 46 (1993): 339–52.

Stewart, Joseph M., and James F. Sheffield. "Does Interest Group Litigation Matter? The Case of Black Political Mobilization in Mississippi." *Journal of Politics* 49 (1987): 780–98.

Van Der Slik, Jack R. "Mixing Religion and Politics in the American Republic." *Polity* 21 (1988): 201–13.

Vose, Clement. "Litigation as a Form of Pressure Group Activity." *Annals of the American Academy of Political Science* 319 (1958): 20–31.

——. "National Consumer's League and the Brandeis Brief." *Midwest Journal of Political Science* 1 (1957): 178–90.

——. "NAACP Strategy in Restrictive Convenant Cases." *Western Reserve Law Review* 6 (1955): 101–45.

Walker, Jack L. "Origin and Maintenance of Interest Groups in America." *American Political Science Review* 77 (1983): 390–406.

Wasby, Stephen L. "The Multi-Faceted Elephant: Litigator Perspectives on Planned Litigation for Social Change." *Capital University Law Review* 15 (1986): 143–89.

——. "How Planned is 'Planned Litigation'?" *American Bar Association Research Journal* 1 (1984): 83–138.

Way, Frank H. "The Death of a Christian Nation: The Judiciary and Church-State Relations." *Journal of Church and State* 29 (1987): 509–29.

——. "Religious Marginality and the Free Exercise Clause." *American Political Science Review* 77 (1983): 652–65.

Weber, Paul J. "Examining the Religious Lobbies." *This World* 1 (1982): 97–107.

Wood, James E., Jr. "Church Lobbying and Public Policy." *Journal of Church and State* 28 (1986): 183–92.

Yale Comment. "Private Attorneys-General in the Fight for Civil Liberties." *Yale Law Journal* 58 (1949): 574–98.

Abington v. Schempp, 102, 105, 113–15,
120, 127, 135, 142–44, 156, 163–64,
191
   facts, 129–30
   development of case, 130–34, 136
   decision by Supreme Court, 137–38
   ramifications, 138–41
   see also "Purpose and effect" test
Abram, Morris (attorney), 132
Aguilar v. Felton, 206
Allegheny v. ACLU, 202, 216
America, 83, 102–3
   criticism of AJCongress, 102–3
   response to school prayer decisions,
138–42
   and *Pierce v. Society of Sisters*, 141
American Civil Liberties Union
(ACLU), 17, 102, 105, 127, 148
   early litigation strategy, 12, 15–16, 51
   relationship with Jehovah's Witnesses, 15
   in flag salute cases, 15–16
   "test case" approach, 44, 55
   alliance with AJCongress, 53
   and released time, 72, 86–87, 115, 118
   role in school prayer litigation, 120–
21, 124–26
   role in parochial school aid litigation,
19, 152–53, 159, 172, 173–75, 178,
185
   opposition to ESEA of 1965, 152
American Communist Party, 107
American Jewish Committee (AJCommittee)
   opposition to funds for parochial
schools, 19–20
   absence from *Everson v. Board of Education*, 20–22
   founding, 2, 36

and Louis Marshall, 36–42, 45
and John Slawson, 36–42, 45
relationship with NAACP, 45
relationship with Christian groups,
45
financial resources of, 46, 48, 200–202
composition of, 36–37, 46, 123, 225
in *McCollum v. Board of Education*, 70,
74–75, 82–83
in *Zorach v. Clausen*, 87–90, 115
in *Torcaso v. Watkins*, 109–10
in *Engel v. Vitale*, 114
in *Abington v. Schempp*, 114, 131–32,
156
absence from *Doremus v. Board of Education*, 115–16, 118–20
opposition to school prayer, 120, 125
debate following school prayer decisions, 138, 140–41
conflict with AJCongress, 27–28, 64–
65, 73, 76, 77–80, 110, 111, 115–
16, 134–36
rejoining NCRAC, 156
in *Flast v. Cohen*, 157–58
after *Board of Education v. Allen*,
170–71
as amicus in *Lemon v. Kurtzman, Di-
Censo v. Robinson*, 175–76, 177, 179
amicus difficulties in *Tilton v. Richardson*, 181–82
leadership-membership concerns,
203–7
relationship with ADL, 45, 53, 55,
64–65, 73–74, 75, 77, 79–80, 85,
94–95, 97–99, 100–101, 104–5,
121, 122–23, 133–35, 167–68
American Jewish Congress (AJCongress)
   founding, 2, 42, 46

American Jewish Congress (*cont.*)
    early litigation efforts, 3–5, 10, 28
    opposition to funds for parochial
        schools, 19–20
    "test case" approach generally, 83
    goals and methods, 46, 48–55
    composition, 46–47, 123
    developmental difficulties, 48–49
    relationship with Christian organiza-
        tions, 50
    alliance with ACLU and NAACP, 52,
        55
    in *McCollum v. Board of Education*, 70–
        74, 75, 76, 77–80, 82–83
    on released time, 71–72, 83–90, 102–
        4, 115, 120
    opposition to school prayer, 121–27
    considerations in *Carden v. Board of
        Education*, 127–29
    hesitance in *Abington v. Schempp*,
        130–31
    in *Chamberlin v. Dade County*, 136–37
    debate following school prayer deci-
        sions, 138
    in *Flast v. Cohen*, 155, 157–58, 169–70
    religious tax exemptions and, 165–67
    departure of Leo Pfeffer from, 192–
        97, 224–25
    changes in staff and resources,
        194–97
    leadership-membership concerns,
        202–7
    external influences on, 207–13,
        224–25
Americans United, 26, 193
    after *Everson v. Board of Education*, 26
    opposition to parochial school aid,
        155, 161, 182
    see also Protestants and Other Ameri-
        cans United
Amicus briefs
    organized interests' use of, 2, 5, 194–
        95, 197, 198, 200–201, 209,
        212–13
    in Supreme Court, 195, 208, 209, 211,
        213

    influence of, 194–95, 213
    as litigation strategy, 2, 5, 194–95,
        200–201
Anti-Defamation League (ADL)
    founding, 2, 56, 57–58
    early litigation efforts, 4, 5, 10
    opposition to funding of parochial
        schools, 19–20
    goals and methods, 56–63
    resources, 62–63
    participation in *McCollum v. Board of
        Education*, 70, 75–80
    conflict with AJCongress, 27–28, 64–
        65, 73, 76, 77–80, 110, 111, 115–
        16, 134–36
    cooperation with AJCommittee, 45,
        53, 55, 64–65, 73–74, 75, 77, 79–80,
        85, 94–95, 97–99, 100–101, 104–5,
        121, 122–23, 133–35, 167–68
    opposition to school prayer, 120–21,
        125, 126
    composition, 123, 225
    debate following school prayer cases,
        138, 140–41
    rejoining NCRAC, 156
    participation as amicus curiae, 175–
        76, 177, 179, 181–82, 186–87
    influence of staff, 197–200
    leadership-membership concerns,
        202–7, 225
    external influences, 207–19, 224–25
Anti-Semitism, 31–32, 35, 40–41, 43,
        49–50, 51, 56–57
    in *Leo Frank* case, 41–42, 57
    Jewish organizations' fear of, 2, 21,
        32, 85, 114, 134, 159
    of Father Coughlin, 43, 50, 60
    in *America*, 51, 57–58, 71, 73
    "Atlantic City agreement," 85, 87

Babigan, John, 124, 125
Baptist Joint Committee on Public Af-
        fairs, 118, 141, 202
    and *Everson v. Board of Education*, 19
    and ESEA of 1965, 152
Baum, Phil (attorney), 95

Becker, Frank (congressman), 151
Becker Amendment, 143, 151–52
Black, Hugo (Supreme Court justice)
  and parochial school aid, 23–25, 66–
    68, 81–82, 91, 111, 163–64
  and released time, 81–82, 91
  and dismissed time, 91–92
  and religious oaths, 111–12
  and school prayer, 137
B'nai B'rith
  founding and purpose, 56–57
  see also ADL
Board of Education v. Allen, 154–55,
  163–64
Bolz, Sandy, 109–10
Borden, Morton, 149
Brandeis, Louis
  relationship with AJCongress, 46–47,
    57
Brown v. Board of Education, 107, 113,
  144
Bryson, Joseph R. (congressman), 26
Burger, Warren Earl (Supreme Court
    justice)
  judicial appointment of, 165
  opinions of, 168–69, 179–80, 183
  "Burger Court," 147, 183–84, 211, 225
Burton, Harold (Supreme Court jus-
    tice), 25

Carden, Philip M. (plaintiff), 127
Carlson, C. Emmanuel, 141
Catholic Church, 43, 66–67, 82–84, 96,
  101
  educational objectives, 23, 27–28, 66
  support for parochial aid, 25–27, 66–
    67, 100–102
  conflict with Jewish organizations,
    102–5, 106, 117
  anger following school prayer deci-
    sion, 137–40, 141–42
  strategy after *Board of Education v.
    Allen*, 171, 173
  "child benefit" theory, 19, 154, 163,
    173
Christian Century, 139

Christian Legal Society, 202
Citizens for Educational Freedom, 152
Commentary, 103
Commission on Economic Discrimina-
    tion, 50, 220. *See also* CLSA
Commission on Law and Legislation,
    50, 220. *See also* CLSA
Commission on Law and Public Affairs
    (COLPA), 176
Commission on Law and Social Action
    (CLSA), 51, 95–97, 199, 205, 220
  involvement in *Everson v. Board of Ed-
    ucation*, 21–22
  legal strategies of, 51–56
  alliance with NAACP, ACLU, 52–53
  on released time, 71
  see also AJCongress
Committee for Public Education and
    Religious Liberty. *See* PEARL
Connecticut Civil Liberties Union
    (CCLU), 169, 174, 182
Connecticut Council of Churches, 182
Connecticut Jewish Community Rela-
    tions Council (CJCRC), 169, 174,
    182
Cortner, Richard C., 11–15, 17
Coughlin, Father Charles E.
  anti-Semitism of, 43, 50, 60
Cox, Archibald, 148, 165
Creationism, 147

Department of Justice, U.S., 54, 61, 107
Department of State, U.S., 61
"Dismissed time," 84–93
Douglas, William O. (Supreme Court
    justice)
  opinion in *Zorach v. Clausen*, 90–91,
    93
  concurrence in *Flast v. Cohen*, 162
  dissent in *Walz*, 168
Drinan, Father Robert, 32, 82

Elementary and Secondary Education
    Act of 1965 (ESEA of 1965), 151–
    55, 157, 165, 170–71, 183

Engel v. Vitale, 102, 105, 113–15, 123,
    125–27, 132–34, 135, 136–38
  development, 133–34, 136
  opinion of the court, 137
Epstein, Benjamin, 62, 110
Epstein, Lee, 214–15, 217
Equal protection clause
  importance of, 108, 172
Establishment clause, 17, 18, 24–25, 68–
    69, 116, 122, 127, 130, 132, 162
  made applicable to the states, 10, 18,
    23, 25, 108
  in *Everson v. Board of Education,* 17–28,
    66–70, 81, 92, 168
  absolutist position of AJCongress,
    95, 97, 102, 103, 106
  under Warren Court, 146–47
  in *Flast v. Cohen,* 162
  Lemon test, changing interpretations
    of, 172, 190–91
Everson, Arch P. (plaintiff), 18, 19, 152
Everson v. Board of Education, 81–83, 91,
    92, 94, 111, 114, 116, 120, 147, 152,
    154, 163
  as a test case, 18–19
  development, 17–28
  controversy, 66–70
"Excessive entanglement," 164, 168–69,
    174, 177–81

Fenno, Richard F., Jr., 205
Financial resources
  as determinant of litigation strategy,
    194, 195–98, 200–202
Flag Salute Cases, 13–16, 18
Flast v. Cohen, 150, 153–65, 169–70, 185
Frankfurter, Felix M. (Supreme Court
    justice), 25, 81–82, 92
Free exercise clause, 10–17
  made applicable to states, 10, 16
  contributions of Jehovah's Witnesses,
    13–17
Freeman, Steven (attorney), 198, 210
Fundamentalists
  organizational representation of, 188,
    189

  involvement in litigation, 188, 189–
    92, 209
  views of Jewish organizations on,
    210

Gitlow v. New York, 11–12
Greenwalt, Kenneth (attorney), 87,
    89–90
Gutstadt, Richard, 75–76

Harlan, John (Supreme Court justice),
    162–63
"Hate crimes" law, 199
Hebrew Union College, 59
Herberg, Will, 64, 103
Higher Education Facility Act of 1963
    (HEFA), 169–70, 174, 180–81
Hines, C. Vernon (attorney), 127–29
Howard, A. E. Dick, 24

"Incorporation doctrine," 11–12
  and religion clauses, 10–26

Jackson, Robert H. (Supreme Court jus-
    tice), 23, 25, 68, 81, 92
Jehovah's Witnesses
  litigation efforts of, 13–16
Jewish Floridian, 134, 135
Johnson, Lyndon B., 151, 152
Joint Baptist Conference Committee on
    Public Relations. *See* Baptist Joint
    Committee on Public Affairs
Junior Order of United American Me-
    chanics (JOUAM)
  involvement in *Everson v. Board of Ed-
    ucation,* 17–25

Kahn, Jill L. (attorney), 204, 210
Kelley, Dean M., 141
Kennedy, Anthony M. (Supreme Court
    justice), 216–18
Klavan, Israel, 176–77
Kluger, Richard, 30
Kobylka, Joseph F., 214–15, 217
Kraus, Adolph, 57–58
Krislov, Samuel, 192, 222

Legal doctrine
 as determinant of litigation strategy,
  193–94, 198–201, 207, 212–15
Lemon v. Kurtzman
 background, 171–72
 development, 175–79
 opinion of court, 179–80
 significance of decision, 183–89
Leo Frank case, 41–42, 57–58
 AJCommittee involvement in, 41–42
 reaction of ADL to, 42, 57–58
Leskes, Theodore, 110–11
Litigation campaign
 role of amicus briefs in, 2, 5, 194–95,
  198–201, 209, 212–13
 planned vs. ad hoc nature of, 14–17,
  30–31, 215–16, 224
 "test case" approach to, 2, 15–16, 44,
  55, 83, 203
 utility of, 2–6, 8–10, 209–14
 objections to, 2–3, 30–31, 40–42, 44–
  45, 49, 55–56, 59, 102, 139–40
Litigation process
 organized interests and, 29–33, 202–
  4, 207–10, 218–19, 221–22
 political nature of, 7–10, 12–13, 29–
  31, 189–90, 207–8, 221
 utility of, 3–4, 8–10, 12–13, 15–16,
  207–14
 social dimension of, 29–30, 202–8,
  224–25
Livingston, Samuel, 57–60
Long, Huey, 60
Lord's Prayer, 136, 138, 145
 target of litigation campaign, 106,
  125–26, 129–31, 136–37
 opposition of Jewish organizations
  to, 22, 126, 145
 in public schools, 22, 106, 116, 126,
  129, 136, 138, 145
Lukas, Edwin J. (attorney), 97, 118–19,
  132, 200
Lutheran Council USA, 202

McCollum v. Board of Education, 5, 70,
 116, 119

significance of, 5, 82–83, 99, 107, 115,
 117
NCRAC amicus strategy, 71–83
 opinion of the Supreme Court, 81–
  82, 90, 139
 as basis for *Zorach v. Clausen*, 86–93
McCollum, Vashti (plaintiff), 76, 79,
 86–87
Mann, Theodore (attorney), 131
Manwaring, David, 13–15
Marshall, Louis (attorney), 36–45, 58–
 60, 74
 litigation strategy, 36–42, 45, 58–59
 cooperation with NAACP, 40
 approach to anti-Semitism, 40–42
Marshall, Thurgood (Supreme Court
 justice), 144, 221–23
Maslow, Will (attorney), 21, 52–55, 96,
 110, 117, 181
 on released time, 71, 73
 as legal strategist, 52–53
Morgenstern, Julius, 59

National Association for the Advancement of Colored People (NAACP)
 contrast with litigation strategy of
  Jewish organizations, 4, 223
 Legal Defense Fund (LDF), 8, 12, 30,
  214
 Shelley v. Kraemer, 9, 45, 62
 in *Brown v. Board of Education*, 30
 litigation strategies, 12–13, 14–15, 30,
  40, 51, 143
 Louis Marshall involvement with, 40
 test case approach, 44
 cooperation with AJCongress, 52
 involvement in religious cases, 182
 relations with membership, 203–4
 parallels with Jewish organizations,
  221–22
National Catholic Welfare Conference,
 66
 support for parochial school aid, 152
 as amicus curiae, 101
 see also United States Catholic Conference

National Community Relations Advisory Council (NCRAC)
organizational difficulties of, 20–21, 27–28, 72–73, 76, 77–80
favoring AJCongress, 65
in *Zorach v. Clausen,* 84–85, 90
split with AJCommittee and ADL, 101, 111, 115
position on ESEA of 1965, 153
in *Flast v. Cohen,* 157–58
readmission of AJCommittee and ADL, 156
as amicus curiae, 175–77
National Council of Churches (NCC), 201, 202
opposition to Becker Amendment, 152
opposition to ESEA of 1965, 152
ally of Jewish organizations, 155, 161
National Council of Jewish Women, 177
National Review, 138
Neuborne, Burt (attorney), 206
New Republic, 138
New York Civil Liberties Union, 153
New York State Commission Against Discrimination, 53–54

Ochs, Adolf, 41
Orthodox Judaism, 48
organizational representation of, 176–77
support for ESEA of 1965, 152
opposition to NCRAC brief in *Lemon v. Kurtzman,* 176–78
Orthodox Rabbinical Council of America, 176–77

Palko v. Connecticut, 11
Parochial school aid, 146–50, 159, 163–65, 176–80, 183–85, 224
transportation subsidies, 17–26, 66–69, 116, 120
target of litigation campaign, 147,

150, 153–55, 163, 169–71, 174–82, 184–85
general legislative efforts to secure, 149, 152, 154, 171, 173–74, 183
in ESEA of 1965, 151–52, 165, 169
PEARL (Committee for Public Education and Religious Liberty), 184–86, 193, 206
Pekelis, Alexander (attorney), 51–55, 71, 73
Pennsylvania Civil Liberties Union, 172
Pennsylvania Jewish Community Relations Council, 172
Pennsylvania Non-Public Elementary and Secondary Education Act, 171–72
Pennsylvania State Education Association, 172
Petegorsky, David, 28, 73
Pfeffer, Leo (attorney), 51, 55, 96, 98, 99, 102, 105
recommendations in *Everson v. Board of Education,* 21–22, 26–28
"absolutist" doctrine advocated by, 28, 95, 97–98, 149, 154
personal differences with AJCommittee and ADL, 95, 98–99
strategy after *Zorach v. Clausen,* 101–2, 105
in *Engel v. Vitale,* 102, 132, 138–39
in *Abington v. Schempp,* 102, 130, 138–39
in *Torcaso v. Watkins,* 107–8, 110, 112
in *Doremus v. Board of Education,* 116–19
role in school prayer litigation, 121–27
in *Chamberlin v. Dade County,* 133–36
on standing to sue, 150, 151, 153, 169–70
involvement with ESEA of 1965, 151, 153–54
opposition to Becker Amendment, 151
in *Flast v. Cohen,* 153–55, 159, 161–62

(*cont.*)
in *Board of Education v. Allen*, 153–55
stature, 155–56, 167, 176, 185–88, 222–24
with ACLU in *Walz v. Tax Commission*, 165–67
in *Lemon v. Kurtzman*, 172, 173, 178–79
as counsel in *Tilton v. Richardson*, 174, 180–81
in *DiCenso v. Robinson*, 175, 177–79
split with AJCongress, 184, 186
association with PEARL, 184–86
Phagan, Mary, 41
Polier, Shad (attorney), 51–52, 55, 73, 85, 97, 108, 131
Powell, Lewis F., Jr. (Supreme Court justice), 183
"Private attorneys general," 20, 160, 199
Proskauer, Joseph K., 21, 44, 74
Protestants and Other Americans United for the Separation of Church and State (POAU), 26, 82, 118. *See also* Americans United
Protestant State Council of Churches, 172
Protocols of the Elders of Zion, 43
Public Education Association, 86, 117
Public education organizations
support for *Everson v. Board of Education*, 152
with ESEA of 1965, 152–53
in *Flast*, 154–55, 161
as amicus in *Lemon v. Kurtzman*, 179
"Purpose and effect" test, 164, 168–69, 172, 174, 177, 179–80

Rabinove, Samuel (attorney), 200–202, 211, 212
Rabkin, Sol (attorney), 159, 176, 181–82
Reagan, Ronald
judicial appointments of, 190
doctrinal evolution of Reagan Court, 211–12, 225
Reform Central Committee of American Rabbis, 177
Reform Judaism, 38, 48, 61

Regents' prayer, 121–22, 125–26, 127, 133, 136, 137
as target of litigation campaign, 121, 125–26, 137
Rehnquist, William H. (Supreme Court justice), 183
Reichley, A. James, 38
"Released time," 70, 84, 116
and "dismissed time," 88–93
Religion and the Public Schools, 71, 72, 77, 78
Religious tax exemptions, 165–69
Rhode Island ACLU, 173–74
Rhode Island Salary Supplement Act, 173–74
Robison, Joseph B. (attorney), 182
Roosevelt, Franklin D., 36, 189
Rosenbaum, Arthur, 27
Rutledge, Wiley (Supreme Court justice), 23–24, 25, 68–69, 81
in *McCollum v. Board of Education*, 81

Sawyer, Henry (attorney), 130, 172, 175, 178
Schempp, Ellory (plaintiff), 129–30
School prayer, 22, 105–6, 113, 116, 120–22, 125–27, 129–33, 136–38, 141–42, 145, 149
as target of litigation campaign, 105, 106, 114–15, 120–21, 125–26, 129–31, 136–37
opposition of Jewish organizations to, 22, 105, 113–14, 126, 145
in public schools, 22, 106, 113, 116, 126, 129, 136, 138, 145
see also Lord's Prayer, Regents' Prayer
Senate Internal Security Subcommittee, 107
Seventh-Day Adventists, 19, 118
Sickles, Joseph (attorney), 108–9
Slawson, John (attorney), 43–45, 74
Solomon, Gus J. (Federal district judge), 159–60
Southern Baptists
reaction to school prayer cases, 141–42

Southern Baptists (*cont.*)
   see also Baptist Joint Committee on
      Public Affairs
Standing to sue, 150–51, 153, 156–57,
   160, 162, 224
   impact on legal process, 151, 156–57,
      162
Stern, Marc D. (attorney), 193–97, 205–
   6, 211–13
Stewart, Potter (Supreme Court justice), 137, 183
Straus, Oscar, 37–39
Synagogue Council of America (SCA),
   77, 90

Tannenbaum, Rabbi Marc, 202
Tax exemptions. *See* Religious tax ex-
   emptions
Tilton v. Richardson, 170, 174–75, 180–83
   opinion of court, 180–81
Torcaso v. Watkins, 105, 107–12, 125
   facts, 107–8
   opinion of court, 110–11
   significance of, 146, 149
Trager, Frank N., 27, 76
Truman, David, 29
Truman, Harry S., 45, 62
Tushnet, Mark V., 29–30, 203–4, 207,
   221

Union of American Hebrew Congrega-
   tions (UAHC), 177
Unitarian Church, 110, 130
United Americans for Public Schools,
   155
United Federation of Teachers, 153
United Parents Association, 86, 117

   opposition to Becker Amendment,
      151
   in *Flast v. Cohen*, 153
United States Catholic Conference, 66,
   101
   as amicus curiae, 101
   support for parochial aid, 152

Vose, Clement E., 8–9, 29

"Wall of separation" metaphor, 67, 68,
   114, 137
Walz v. Tax Commission, 1, 165–69
   opinion of Court, 168
   "excessive entanglement" test, 168–
      69, 177–80
Warren, Earl (Supreme Court justice),
   107, 113, 146–47, 161–62
   retirement, 165
   leadership of, 107, 113, 146–49, 162,
      184, 211, 225
Wasby, Stephen L., 221
White, Byron R. (Supreme Court justice), 163, 183
Williams, Edward Bennett (attorney),
   181–82
Wise, Rabbi Stephen, 46, 48–49, 51
   role in founding AJCongress, 48–49
Wittenstein, Charles (attorney), 134–35

Zimmel, Heyman, 116–17
Zorach, Tessim (plaintiff), 86–87
Zorach v. Clausen, 70, 83, 94, 97–98, 105–
   6, 112, 115, 118–21, 138
   in lower courts, 88–89
   significance of, 91–95, 97–98, 111–12,
      121